Warman's PATTERN GLASS

Edited by
ELLEN TISCHBEIN SCHROY

krause
publications

Copyright © 1993 by Rinker Enterprises, Inc.

Published by Krause Publications, Iola, Wisconsin

Manufactured in the United States of America

Library of Congress Cataloging-in-Publication Data
Warman's pattern glass / edited by Ellen Tischbein Schroy.
    p.   cm.—(Encyclopedia of antiques and collectibles)
  ISBN 0-87069-673-4
  1. Pattern glass—Collectors and collecting—United States—
Catalogs. I. Schroy, Ellen Tischbein. II. Series.
NK5439.P36W37   1993
748.2'075—dc20   92-56761
                                            CIP

8 9 0   2 1 0 9 8

Warman's PATTERN GLASS

CONTENTS

INTRODUCTION

Pattern glass is clear or colored glass pressed into a pattern. There are hundreds of patterns. Each pattern contains a variety of useful tableware pieces and occasionally some specialized serving pieces. Many patterns are found only in clear, while others are found with additional adornment, such as colored staining, gilt trim, and enameled decoration.

Warman's Pattern Glass is designed to help the collector and dealer decipher the current pattern glass market. The intent is to provide as accurate information as possible for a broad sampling of the pattern glass market. Hopefully you will find our effort successful.

Warman's Pattern Glass is a handy reference, one that you can take comfortably to the antiques shows and flea markets, shops, malls, or wherever pattern glass is sold. Use it as a reference point for pattern identification, price values, and reproduction alerts. If you want to learn more, you will find an extensive listing of the major pattern glass reference books. Refer to those when searching for additional history and complete production runs of a particular pattern.

The following criteria were used to select patterns represented in *Warman's Pattern Glass*: (1) they are major patterns being collected today, (2) they represent the finest work of a particular company, and (3) they are patterns which can be used as comparables for less popular patterns among collectors. It is impossible to list every item in every pattern in this book. This is a price guide, designed to "guide" you through the exciting world of pattern glass collecting.

What can you hope to learn by using *Warman's Pattern Glass*? If you are willing to take the time and follow up on the information in this book, you will be able to: (1) locate particular patterns through the alphabetical listings, (2) identify a pattern through the use of line drawings, (3) learn the manufacturer(s) of the pattern, (4) determine the value of a specific piece, (5) be aware of known reproductions, (6) and use the detailed cross index to locate a pattern that you may know by an obscure name.

Names: One of the most confusing issues in collecting pattern glass is the name of the pattern. The period (original) manufacturer named each pattern. Sometimes the name reflected a design element found in the pattern, i.e., Daisy and Button. Other times it utilized the company's manufacturing name or number, i.e., Duncan & Miller #42.

The glass industry was one of the leading American industries during the late 1880s and into the early 1900s. Competition was fierce. Unfortunately when companies went out of business, the molds were often sold to a new manufacturer, who promptly renamed the pattern. Through the years, researchers added to the confusion by renaming patterns and assigning names where they did not exist historically. These well-meant efforts often proved disastrous.

The listings in *Warman's Pattern Glass* use the name by which the pattern is commonly sold or collected. Further, we have attempted to include, in parenthesis, many additional names by which a pattern is known.

Drawings: A detailed drawing is included with every pattern. These drawings give you enough detail to adequately identify the major design components of each pattern. The pattern may differ slightly from the example shown as the design elements were incorporated into different forms. A tall slender celery vase allows more space to incorporate a design element than does an individual open salt.

Warman's has always used drawings to help identify patterns. Most of the patterns covered in this edition of *Warman's Pattern Glass* are clear and simplistic in their approach. It is very difficult to photograph clear glass patterns without having the background show through the pattern. It is our belief that the use of drawings enables you to understand the design element more clearly.

Manufacturers: Each pattern listing identifies the principal manufacturers, their principal factory location, and date. Pattern glass manufacturers designed tableware lines that expanded throughout the period of production. Initial production may have been limited, e.g., a table service consisting of a covered butter dish, creamer, spooner, and covered sugar. If the pattern was a success, the manufacturer added more pieces in the pattern, such as a water service or serving pieces. The circa date usually indicates the date when a pattern first appeared in a manufacturer's catalog. Production often spanned several years or decades for a specific pattern.

Values: The price values are only a guide for what you should expect to pay if you purchase the piece from a reputable pattern glass dealer. In other words, these are retail prices.

The listings are extensive, but do not include every form produced. If the particular form you are researching is not listed, there are enough examples to make a value judgement based on comparable prices. Just remember to be conservative.

Many of the pattern headings have information regarding how other colors and rarer items are priced. We have given specific prices and/or ranges to allow you more flexibility in determining the value of your pattern or object.

Reproductions: We have tried to identify the known reproductions for each pattern with an asterisk next to the object. In several cases the manufacturer of these reproductions is noted. Unfortunately, many reproductions are unmarked and the manufacturers are unknown. This is an area where active research is continuing. A few years ago we were only able to identify, with certainty, a limited number of reproductions. Today, you will see that the number of asterisked items has increased dramatically. We are constantly on the alert for additions to the reproduction list. Especially recommended is Bill Jenks, Jerry Luna, and Darryl Reilly's, *Identifying Pattern Glass Reproductions*, Wallace–Homestead Book Co., 1993. **Index:** Because of the multiplicity of names given to pattern glass, we have provided a detailed cross–name index. Each pattern name is listed with the appropriate page number.

HISTORY

Glass production in America began with the settlement of Jamestown, Virginia, shortly after the English arrived. Detailed accounts of furnaces and other glass manufacturing tools document this early glassware production. This glassware was largely free blown. Some was pressed using crude molds. This method of glass production predominated until the early 1820s. Press molded handles, pillar molded items, etc., did occur, but the process was time consuming and difficult. Glassblowers completed one piece at a time. As America expanded, consumers wanted more and more glassware.

During the early years of the 19th century, the country enjoyed a period of prosperity and industrial growth. The demand for inexpensive utilitarian items, such as bottles, windows, and tableware created many jobs as new companies sprang up. Small scale operations of blown glass which was pressed into molds by hand grew up in the Northeast and Pittsburgh areas. These operations were still laborious and could not match the demand.

In the early 1820s J. P. Bakewell of Bakewell and Company, Pittsburgh, PA, obtained a patent for the manufacture of pressed glass furniture knobs. Additional patents were issued for refinements in pressing techniques. These patents lead to the production of lacy type pressed glass. Lacy glass was still largely hand made and consisted primarily of small items. Early patterns were often ornate in design, giving the appearance of lace, hence the term *lacy*.

While patents were being developed and advances made in the mechanical aspects of glass production, the formulas to make glass also had to be refined. The lacy patterns, although pressed, are not part of the traditional collector interpretation of pattern glass. As the technology developed, flint glass patterns were designed that were entirely machine made. These early pressing machines worked best with newer formulas, ones requiring more expensive materials and a higher concentration of lead.

Several key companies were responsible for early advancements in the industry. One of the most important centers around Deming Jarves of the Boston and Sandwich Glass Company, who invented the first successful pressing machine in 1828. Jarves patented several processes related to mechanical glass production. His importance manifested itself as he became involved in the establishment of other glass companies, including the Mount Washington Glass Company and later the Cape Cod Glass Company.

By the 1860s glass pressing machinery had been improved. Mass production of good quality matched tableware sets began in earnest. The idea of a matched glassware table service, comprising goblets, tumblers, creamers, sugars, compotes, cruets, etc., quickly found favor across America. Numerous accessory pieces, e.g., banana stands, molasses cans, water bottles, etc., joined the more common pieces.

Americans were delighted with the variety of patterns, colors, and shapes offered for sale by numerous companies. Early patterns were designed to compete with the hand blown patterns previously known. Design elements were simple, incorporating thumbprints, bull's eyes, and points. As the years progressed, patterns became more intricate and included ribbing, florals, and swirls. As the Brilliant Period of cut glass evolved, pattern glass designers worked hard to develop intricate patterns which imitated the expensive cut glass pieces.

The flint glass formula helped initiate the production of pattern glass. The development of a non–flint formula provided the key for economical mass production and the true popularization of pattern glass. The non–flint formula was discovered around the time of the Civil War, which saw lead reserved for military purposes, not the glassware industry. A non–flint formula that used no lead allowed production to continue.

William Leighton, Sr., of Hobbs, Brockunier of Wheeling, West Virginia, developed a formula that utilized soda lime instead of lead. This glass mixture could be pressed quicker and thinner. More detailed patterns were possible. Some patterns continued to be produced only in flint. Other flint patterns were now produced utilizing the lighter non–flint formula.

By the 1880s, the American pattern glass industry reached maturity. The geographic center of the industry shifted to the Pittsburgh and Ohio Valleys, rich in natural resources and having good transportation centers. A tremendous expansion occurred.

Patterns became more detailed. The production of non–flint glass in colors followed rapidly. Among the rainbow of colors available were amber, blue, green, purple, and vaseline. The first patterns produced in milk glass were made in the 1880s.

New colors and decorative techniques allowed table settings to become quite complex. This matched similar Victorian trends in silverplate and ceramics. The glass industry showed few restraints in respect to form, color, staining, and a myriad of other types of ornamentation.

In 1891 a giant glass manufacturing combine was formed. The United States Glass Company combined fifteen well-established glass companies in a single unit. National Glass Company, the second large combine, included nineteen glass companies and was organized in 1899. The impact of these combines on the marketplace was tremendous. They increased production along with sales staff. They retooled some molds. In many cases they reissued existing patterns in new colors and with new names. One example is United States Glass Company's states series. It was an instant hit with the American public. Today, dealers and collectors often return to the original pattern name as the popularity of the states series has waned, i.e. Beaded Grape (California) and Beaded Loop (Oregon #1).

Carnival and custard glass patterns imitated expensive art glass. Simpler designs came into vogue during the early part of the 20th century as companies such as Cambridge, Fostoria, and Heisey began production. These new patterns mirrored the sleeker style of the Art Nouveau and Art Deco periods.

Pattern glass was always an important American industry. The Depression years saw a decline in the production of fine pattern glass. Factories closed. When the Depression ended and the World War II began, the demand for pattern glass was waning. The production of elegant etched patterns was an attempt to appeal to war brides. Many pattern glass manufacturers closed. Those that gained a post–war following, e.g., Heisey and Fostoria, survived.

MANUFACTURERS

The hundreds of companies which produced pattern glass have complex histories that include formation, expansions, personnel issues, material and supply requirements, fires, and mergers. Detailed histories have been written for some of these companies. Much more research remains to be done.

Collecting by company is an excellent alternative to collecting by pattern or type of object. Because of the regionalism of the glass industry, many new collectors are broadening their collecting perspective and focusing on a geographic area. The first significant glass manufacturing center in America was in New England. Leading companies include Boston & Sandwich Glass Company, Cape Cod Glass Company, New England Glass Company, Portland Glass Company, and others.

The most prolific glass manufacturing state was Pennsylvania. Philadelphia was home to early companies such as Gillander. However, it was the Pittsburgh area that developed as the state's leading glass manufacturing center in the late 19th century and early 20th century. Leading manufacturers were Adams & Company; Bakewell, Pears & Company; Bryce Brothers; George Duncan & Sons; King Glass Company; McKee & Brothers; O'Hara Glass Company; Pioneer Glass Company; Richards & Hartley Glass Company; and United States (U. S.) Glass Company.

Ohio manufacturers include A. J. Beatty & Sons of Steubenville and Tiffin, Bellaire Goblet Company in Findlay, Cambridge Glass Company in Cambridge, A. H. Heisey & Company in Newark, and Model Flint Glass Company in Findlay.

West Virginia featured companies such as Central Glass Company, Fostoria, and Hobbs, Bruckunier & Company, all of Wheeling, New Martinsville Glass Company in New Martinsville, and Union Stopper Company in Morgantown.

Cambridge Glass Company, Fostoria Glass Company, A. H. Heisey, and Imperial Glass Company are among the manufacturers who dominated the pressed glass market in the 20th century. Their enormous variety and long term production have created a collecting interest than transcends their patterned pieces.

The United States Glass Company (1891) and the National Glass Company (1899) united small companies in Pennsylvania, Ohio, Indiana, West Virginia, and Maryland to keep the production of glass a vital American industry. These combines pooled talents, resources, and patterns. As a result, the same pattern was made by more than one company. United States Glass Company has been credited with the production of over three hundred different patterns.

There are several excellent reference books on specific companies. We highly recommend that you learn more about the companies that interest you. Remember that research into pattern glass and its makers is an on–going process. New discoveries and attributions about a specific pattern are made every year. As company archives, old catalogs, advertisements, and periodicals become available to scholars, expect even more revisions to our present approach.

An exciting research area in the 1990s is the excavation of former glass manufacturing centers, such as Boston and Sandwich Glass Company in Sandwich, Massachusetts, and the Burlington Glass Works in Hamilton, Ontario, Canada. Both sites have yielded a vast number of shards. By carefully studying these shards (handles, stems, and other bits of objects), researchers can identify patterns, colors, and production dates. This work continues. As the results are published, it also will affect how we look at pattern glass manufacturers, especially those in the early period of production.

REPRODUCTIONS

Reproductions Abound: Pattern glass has been widely reproduced. When collecting, it is critical to identify period (initial period of production) forms and colors. Know if the pattern was made in flint or non–flint and, in some cases, when flint changed to non–flint. Reproductions and reissues tend to be non–flint.

Careful attention to details is the first clue to determining if a piece is a reissue or reproduction. The stag on Westward Ho! period pieces should be well-formed, fur details evident, and the frosting strong. Early glass manufacturers were proud of their wares—they had no need to sell seconds. Frosting, staining, and other types of decoration will be found between well-defined lines, not trailing off or shaded in coloration. This same attention to detail is found in most period pieces.

Glass manufacturers recycled their mistakes and damaged pieces during the 19th century. The high standards expected by the American consumers of that period were reflected in the high quality produced.

Pattern glass was produced using molds. Period pieces featured sharp, relief details. Carefully examine a piece of Beaded Loop, the beads are sharp little points. Check a reproduction. A reproduction Beaded Loop object will be much smoother. The details of the original mold were lost in the reproduction process. The small pyramid–shaped points on the period piece have become small raised dots on the reproductions. Early examples of Daisy and Button will feel sharp to the touch. Later examples often will be less distinct and the buttons may actually be hazy.

The key is feel. Feel the detail. Feel the weight. Reproductions are often much heavier. Look at the thickness of the stem. The thicker the stem, the more likely it is a reproduction.

Manufacturers: Surprisingly, some of the earliest reproductions were made by glass manufacturers producing new patterns. Some utilized the period models (reissue). In other cases, new molds were made from using period pieces as the prototype. Look for slight variations in size. These reissues and reproductions are collectible. A dangerous market trend is to assign them the same value as the period piece. Premium prices should never be paid for the later objects, no matter what anyone says to the contrary.

Companies like Westmoreland, Summit Glass, Imperial, and Fenton have and still produce vast numbers of reproductions. These companies never intended to deceive the public, merely to supplement table services with additional pieces. Alas, novices are still fooled by them because of the lack of an identifiable mark.

Several prestigious museums, including the Metropolitan in New York City, and the Henry Ford Museum in Dearborn, Michigan, have commissioned reproductions. These are marked in the mold and should pose no problems to collectors.

L. G. Wright of New Martinsville, West Virginia, and A. A. Importing of St. Louis, Missouri, sell pieces whose identification can be easily removed. Their catalogs include a wide variety of material, including reproductions (often in a different color), new patterns in a wide variety of forms, and exact copies of period pieces.

Collectors know that Emerald Green Herringbone, also known as Florida, was made initially in clear and green. The manufacture of Emerald Green Herringbone in blue is troublesome for novice collectors when the pattern name is sold as Florida.

Because of the reproduction issue, buyers are urged to get a sales receipt that contains the seller's name, address, and telephone number.

SOME ADDITIONAL HINTS

Another clue to help identify reproductions is a variation in size. Sometimes the changes are slight, other times more noticeable. Use a tape measure to record the sizes of objects. The listings include sizes to help you in your attempt at authentication.

It would be nice if only the most popular patterns were plagued by the reproduction problem. However, since a pattern's popularity may have changed through the years, the likelihood that it was reproduced must be considered. The Swan pattern was rather elusive for years. It was produced initially in a small number of pieces. Careful study would lead one to think that the retooling of its molds would be prohibitive. Not so. Reproductions were made in the early part of the 20th century and are excellent. The creamer, sugar, and now sauces are among the forms known to have been reproduced. The new pieces are heavier and lack detail. Unlike Paneled Thistle, these reproductions do not seem to affect the price of Swan pattern. Paneled Thistle has been made by so many different manufacturers over an extended period of time that prices for period pieces have remained low.

REFERENCE BOOKS AND PERIODICALS

Pattern Glass, like other areas of the antiques and collectibles market, is the subject of a large number of reference books and periodicals. In the Warman tradition, these books and periodicals appear below. Unlike other Warman's books, we also list out–of–print sources. Pattern glass is a field where classic studies count.

Pattern glass has been blessed with a number of pioneering and contemporary researchers. Among the pioneers and their efforts are George P. and Helen McKearin, *American Glass*, Crown Publishers, 1941; E. M. Belnap, *Milk Glass*, Crown Publishers, Inc., 1949; Ruth Webb Lee, *Early American Pressed Glass*, Lee Publications, 1966, 36th edition; Ruth Webb Lee, *Victorian Glass*, Lee Publications, 1944, 13th edition; Alice Hulett Metz, *Early American Pattern Glass*, published by author, 1958; Alice Hulett Metz, *Much More Early American Pattern Glass*, published by author, 1965; S. T. Millard, *Goblets II*, privately printed, 1940, reprinted by Wallace–Homestead, 1975.

Regis F. and Mary F. Ferson, William Heacock, and Minnie Kamm continued in the footsteps of these pioneers. Contemporary research continues with books such as those by: Bill Jenks and Jerry Luna, *Early American Pattern Glass–1850 to 1910: Major Collectible Table Settings with Prices*, Wallace–Homestead Book Co., 1990; Bill Jenks, Jerry Luna, and Darryl Reilly, *Identifying Pattern Glass Reproductions*, Wallace–Homestead Book Co., 1993; and Kyle Husfloen, *Collector's Guide To American Pressed Glass, 1825–1915*, Wallace–Homestead Book Co., 1992. Specialized glass books dealing with one particular company or type of glass are also important reference books for glass collectors.

Reference Books: The standard reference books relating to pattern glass include: E. M. Belnap, *Milk Glass*, Crown Publishers, Inc., 1949; Bill Edwards, *The Standard Opalescent Glass Price Guide*, Collector Books, 1992; Elaine Ezell and George Newhouse, *Cruets, Cruets, Cruets, Volume I*, Antique Publications, 1991; Regis F. and Mary F. Ferson, *Yesterday's Milk Glass Today*, published by author, 1981; William Heacock, *Toothpick Holders from A to Z, Book 1, Encyclopedia of Victorian Colored Pattern Glass*, Antique Publications, 1981; William Heacock, *Opalescent Glass from A to Z, Book 2*, Antique Publications, 1981; William Heacock, *Syrups, Sugar Shakers & Cruets, Book 3*, Antique Publications, 1981; William Heacock, *Custard Glass From A to Z, Book 4*, Antique Publications, 1980; William Heacock, *U. S. Glass From A to Z, Book 5*, Antique Publications, Inc. 1980; William Heacock, *Oil Cruets From A to Z, Book 6*, Antique Publications, 1981; William Heacock, *Ruby Stained Glass From A To Z, Book 7*, Antique Publications, Inc., 1986; William Heacock, *More Ruby Stained Glass, Book 8*, Antique Publications, 1987; William Heacock and William Gamble, *Cranberry Opalescent From A to Z, Book 9*, Antique Publications, 1987; William Heacock, *Old Pattern Glass*, Antique Publications, 1981; William Heacock, *1000 Toothpick Holders: A Collector's Guide*, Antique Publications, 1977; William Heacock, *Rare and Unlisted Toothpick Holders*, Antique Publications, 1984; William Heacock, James Measell and Berry Wiggins, *Harry Northwood: The Early Years, 1881–1900*, Antique Publications, 1990; William Heacock, James Measell and Berry Wiggins, *Harry Northwood: The Wheeling Years, 1901–1925*, Antique Publications, 1991; Joyce A. Hicks, *Just Jenkins*, published by author, 1988.

Minnie Watson Kamm, *Pattern Glass Pitchers, Books 1 through 8*, published by author, 1970, 4th printing; Lorraine Kovar, *Westmoreland Glass: 1950–1984*, Antique

Publications, 1991; Lorraine Kovar, *Westmoreland Glass: 1950–1984, Volume II,* Antique Publications, 1991; Thelma Ladd and Laurence Ladd, *Portland Glass: Legacy Of A Glass House Down East,* Collector Books, 1992; Ruth Webb Lee, *Early American Pressed Glass,* Lee Publications, 1966, 36th edition; Ruth Webb Lee, *Victorian Glass,* Lee Publications, 1944, 13th edition; Bessie M. Lindsey, *American Historical Glass,* Charles E. Tuttle Co., 1967; Robert Irwin Lucas, *Tarentum Pattern Glass,* privately printed, 1981; Mollie H. McCain, *Pattern Glass Primer,* Lamplighter Books, 1979; Mollie H. McCain, *The Collector's Encyclopedia of Pattern Glass,* Collector Books, 1982, value update 1990; George P. and Helen McKearin, *American Glass,* Crown Publishers, 1941; James Measell, *Greentown Glass,* Grand Rapids Public Museum Association, 1979; James Measell and Don E. Smith, *Findlay Glass: The Glass Tableware Manufacturers, 1886–1902,* Antique Publications, Inc., 1986.

Dori Miles and Robert W. Miller, *Wallace–Homestead Price Guide To Pattern Glass, 11th Edition,* Wallace–Homestead, 1986; S. T. Millard, *Goblets I,* privately printed, 1938, reprinted by Wallace–Homestead, 1975; Arthur G. Peterson, *Glass Salt Shakers: 1,000 Patterns,* Wallace–Homestead, 1970; Jane Shadel Spillman, *American and European Pressed Glass in the Corning Museum of Glass,* Corning Museum of Glass, 1981; Jane Shadel Spillman, *The Knopf Collectors Guides to American Antiques, Glass Volumes 1 and 2,* Alfred A. Knopf, Inc., 1982, 1983; Doris and Peter Unitt, *American and Canadian Goblets,* Clock House, 1970; Doris and Peter Unitt, *Treasury of Canadian Glass,* Clock House, 1969, 2nd edition; Peter Unitt and Anne Worrall, *Canadian Handbook, Pressed Glass Tableware,* Clock House Productions, 1983.

Periodicals: *Antique Glass Quarterly,* Rudi Publishing, P. O. Box 1364, Iowa City, IA 52244; *Glass Collector's Digest,* Richardson Printing Corp., P. O. Box 663, Marietta, OH 45750; *Glass Shards,* National Early American Glass Club, P. O. Box 8489, Silver Spring, MD 20907.

BOARD OF ADVISORS

To produce *Warman's Pattern Glass,* we requested and received the assistance of several pattern glass collectors, dealers, and experts to review the manuscript. The time and talents of these people have greatly enhanced the quality of this book.

Each individual brought a specialized area of expertise and geographic divergence. The advisor team carefully reviewed the patterns previously listed in *Warman's Antiques And Their Prices,* and suggested several new patterns. Primary pattern names were considered and sometimes changed to reflect changing attitudes among today's collectors. Pattern histories were carefully evaluated. Current research was included. The price listings were carefully studied.

The Board of Advisors serving for this first edition of *Warman's Pattern Glass* include: Mike Anderton, Marysville, Washington, a noted pattern glass dealer and collector as well as a writer and columnist; Kyle Husfloen, Dubuque, Iowa, author of *Collector's Guide To American Pressed Glass, 1825–1915,* and known for his thorough knowledge in the world of glass collecting; and, pattern glass dealers John and Alice Ahlfeld, Lancaster, Pennsylvania. Several collectors also have contributed information about a specific pattern. We thank them for sharing their knowledge with us.

COMMENTS WELCOMED

Readers' comments are important to us. Like *Warman's Antiques and Their Prices,* a leading price guide in the antiques and collectibles field, *Warman's Pattern Glass* is designed to be user friendly.

This is the first edition of *Warman's Pattern Glass.* It will not be the last. As such, we invite our users to share information with us. Tell us about your collections, including reproductions. When appropriate, we will incorporate this information in our next edition.

We do want to hear from you. Send your comments and observations to: *Warman's Pattern Glass* Editors, Rinker Enterprises, Inc., 5093 Vera Cruz Road, Emmaus, PA 18049.

STATE OF THE MARKET

The pattern glass market has remained stable during the economic hard times of the early 1990s. This traditional segment of the antiques marketplace appears able to attract a core of new buyers. Prices across the country show a modest upward advance, although in most cases only keeping up with inflation.

Patterns continue to rise and fall in popularity. As a result, price variation is encountered throughout the market. One interesting trend is the emphasis on non–flint over flint patterns, partially due to the high flint prices of the 1960s and 1970s.

Pattern glass dealers and collectors know their patterns and pricing structures. It is rare to find rapid price jumps in a pattern or color. Collectors continue to be very focused. Many buy primarily at specialized glass shows where top prices, even for common material, prevail. One collector mentioned that he would like to buy at prices listed in price guides, which reflect field more than specialized dealer prices, if he could only find them. He can if he is willing to invest his time to hunt.

Rarity in pattern glass usually leads to higher prices. Scarcity of the older patterns is a more critical element in price. Expect to pay a premium for an early Boston and Sandwich flint pattern, such as Bellflower. The Indiana Glass Company's Bird and Strawberry pattern in non–flint is pretty and desirable, but much less expensive.

Pattern glass prices are not generally geographically driven. A States pattern is often more popular in the named state, but the constant movement of the American populace has transplanted many pieces of the Pennsylvania pattern across the nation. Geographic areas known for overall higher prices in the antiques market are also higher in the pattern glass market.

It pays to comparison shop, especially at a large glass show. The price on a piece may vary as much as fifty to one hundred percent. When encountering this phenomenon beware of hidden flaws or reproductions. Bargains can be found, but you have to hunt.

The pattern glass marketplace has suffered tremendously through the past years by the introduction of large numbers of reproductions. When a "bargain" price is found, be on guard for a reproduction. All too often the piece is a reproduction or fantasy, a piece that never existed during the initial period of production.

Strangely enough there are collectors for reissues, reproductions, and copycat pieces. Some use them instead of their historic counterparts. Some forms that have never been produced historically, such as the Eyewinker goblet, or Wisconsin toothpick, fill in gaps in collections. Just make certain that reissues, reproductions, and copycats are clearly identified as such in your collection.

ABBREVIATIONS

The following are standard abbreviations which we have used throughout **Warman's Pattern Glass**.

ah	= applied handle	ls	= low standard
C	= century	mkd	= marked
c	= circa	MOP	= mother of pearl
circ	= circular	NE	= New England
cov	= cover	No.	= number
d	= diameter or depth	opal	= opalescent
dec	= decorated	orig	= original
DQ	= Diamond Quilted	os	= orig stopper
emb	= embossed	pat	= patent
ext.	= exterior	pcs	= pieces
ftd	= footed	pr	= pair
ground	= background	rect	= rectangular
h	= height	sgd	= signed
hp	= hand painted	sngl	= single
hs	= high standard	SP	= silver plated
imp	= impressed	SS	= Sterling silver
int.	= interior	sq	= square
irid	= iridescent	w	= width
IVT	= inverted thumbprint	#	= numbered
l	= length		

Alphabetical Listing
of Patterns

ABERDEEN

Non-flint, maker unknown, c1870.

	Clear		Clear
Butter, cov	45.00	Goblet	25.00
Compote		Pitcher, water, ah	60.00
Cov.	42.50	Sauce, flat	8.00
Open	25.00	Sugar	
Creamer	35.00	Cov.	40.00
Egg Cup	20.00	Open	20.00

ACORN VARIANTS (Acorn, Acorn Band, Acorn Band with Loops, Paneled Acorn Band, and Beaded Acorn)

Flint and non-flint, c1860s–70s. The Acorn goblet is reported to be reproduced in blue. Originally it was only made in clear. There are additional Acorn patterns, but they were not made in sets.

	Flint	Non-Flint		Flint	Non-Flint
Bowl			Egg Cup	25.00	15.00
Cov.	—	50.00	* Goblet	40.00	25.00
Open	—	35.00	Pitcher, water	150.00	75.00
Butter, cov	65.00	—	Sauce, flat	—	7.50
Celery	50.00	—	Spooner	40.00	30.00
Compote			Sugar		
Cov.	185.00	75.00	Cov.	75.00	50.00
Open	75.00	60.00	Open, buttermilk		
Creamer	45.00	35.00	type	35.00	20.00

ACTRESS

Made by Adams & Company, Pittsburgh, PA, c1880. All clear 20% less. Some items have been reproduced in clear and color by Imperial Glass Co., including amethyst pickle dish.

	Clear and Frosted		Clear and Frosted
Bowl		Dresser Tray	60.00
6", ftd	45.00	Goblet, Kate Claxton (2	
7", ftd	50.00	portraits)	85.00
9½", ftd	85.00	Marmalade Jar, cov	125.00
8", Miss Neilson	85.00	Mug, HMS Pinafore	50.00
Bread Plate		* Pickle Dish, Love's Request	
7 x 12", HMS Pinafore	90.00	is Pickles	45.00
9 x 13", Miss Neilson	72.00	Pickle Relish, different ac-	
Butter, cov	90.00	tresses	
Cake Stand, 10"	150.00	4½ x 7"	35.00
Candlesticks, pr	250.00	5 x 8"	35.00
Celery Vase		5½ x 9"	35.00
Actress Head	130.00	Pitcher	
HMS Pinafore, pedestal	145.00	Milk, 6½", HMS Pinafore	275.00
Cheese Dish, cov, The Lone		Water, 9", Romeo & Juliet	250.00
Fisherman on cov, Two		Salt, master	70.00
Dromios on base	250.00	Salt Shaker, orig pewter top	42.50
Compote		Sauce	
Cov, hs, 12" d	300.00	Flat	15.00
Open, hs, 10" d	90.00	Footed	20.00
Open, hs, 12" d	120.00	Spooner	60.00
Open, ls, 5" d	45.00	Sugar, cov	100.00
Creamer	75.00		

ADONIS (Pleat and Tuck, Washboard)

Pattern made by McKee & Bros. Glass Co., Pittsburgh, PA, in 1897.

	Canary	Clear	Deep Blue
Bowl, 5", berry	15.00	10.00	20.00
Butter, cov	70.00	48.00	80.00
Cake Plate, 11". . . .	25.00	20.00	32.00
Cake Stand, 10½". .	45.00	30.00	50.00
Celery Vase	35.00	25.00	40.00
Compote			
Cov, hs	65.00	40.00	75.00
Open, hs, 8"	45.00	30.00	50.00
Open, jelly, 4½" . .	28.00	18.00	32.00
Creamer.	28.00	22.50	32.00
Pitcher, water	55.00	35.00	60.00
Plate, 10"	25.00	18.00	32.00
Relish.	18.00	15.00	20.00
Salt & Pepper, pr. . .	40.00	35.00	45.00
Sauce, flat, 4"	10.00	8.00	12.00
Spooner	35.00	20.00	40.00
Sugar, cov	40.00	35.00	45.00
Syrup	150.00	50.00	150.00
Tumbler	20.00	16.00	20.00

AEGIS (Bead and Bar Medallion, Swiss)

Non-flint pattern made by McKee & Bros. Glass Co., Pittsburgh, PA, in the 1880s. Shards have also been found at the site of Burlington Glass Works, Hamilton, Ontario, Canada.

	Clear		Clear
Bowl, oval.	15.00	Pickle, 5 x 7"	15.00
Butter, cov	35.00	Pitcher, water	55.00
Compote		Salt	15.00
Cov, hs	50.00	Sauce	
Open, hs.	25.00	Flat.	7.50
Creamer.	25.00	Footed	10.00
Egg Cup.	25.00	Spooner	20.00
Goblet	30.00	Sugar, cov	35.00

ALABAMA (Beaded Bull's Eye and Drape)

Made by U. S. Glass Co. c1898 as one of the States patterns. Also found in green (rare). Castor set ($275.00).

	Clear	Ruby Stained		Clear	Ruby Stained
Bowl, berry, master .	30.00	—	Dish, rect	20.00	—
Butter, cov	50.00	150.00	Honey Dish, cov . . .	60.00	—
Cake Stand	65.00	—	Pitcher, water	72.00	—
Castor Set, 4 bottles,			Relish.	24.00	35.00
glass frame.	125.00	—	Salt & Pepper.	65.00	—
Celery Vase	35.00	110.00	Sauce	18.00	—
Compote, cov			Spooner	30.00	—
7"	100.00	—	Sugar, cov	48.00	—
8"	125.00	—	Syrup	125.00	250.00
Compote, open, 5",			Toothpick	60.00	150.00
jelly.	35.00	—	Tray, water, 10½" . .	50.00	—
Creamer.	45.00	60.00	Tumbler	45.00	—
Cruet, os	65.00	—			

ALASKA (Lion's Leg)

Non-flint opalescent made by Northwood Glass Co. 1897–1910. Forms are square except for cruet, tumblers, and salt and pepper shakers. Some pieces are found with enamel decoration. Sauces can be found in clear ($30.00); the creamer ($110.00) and spooner ($95.00) are known in clear blue.

	Clear Emerald Green	Blue Opal	Vaseline Opal	White Opal
Banana Boat.	85.00	250.00	250.00	125.00
Bowl, berry, ftd	65.00	100.00	95.00	45.00
Butter, cov	150.00	280.00	275.00	150.00
Celery Tray.	45.00	125.00	120.00	85.00
Creamer.	40.00	75.00	65.00	40.00
Cruet	225.00	250.00	265.00	135.00
Pitcher, water	75.00	385.00	375.00	175.00
Salt Shaker, dec . . .	—	60.00	55.00	45.00
Sauce	30.00	45.00	45.00	25.00
Spooner.	55.00	65.00	55.00	50.00
Sugar, cov	65.00	150.00	130.00	100.00
Tumbler	45.00	75.00	65.00	55.00

ALL-OVER DIAMOND (Diamond Splendor, Diamond Block #3)

Made by George Duncan and Sons, Pittsburgh, PA, c1891 and continued by U. S. Glass Co. It was occasionally trimmed with gold, and had at least sixty-five pieces in the pattern. Biscuit jars are found in three sizes; bowls are both crimped and non-crimped; and nappies are also found crimped and non-crimped in fifteen sizes. Also made in ruby stained.

	Clear		Clear
Biscuit Jar, cov	60.00	Lamp, Banquet, tall stem . . .	150.00
Bitters Bottle.	30.00	Nappy	
Bowl		4"	10.00
7"	20.00	9"	25.00
11"	35.00	Plate	
Cake Stand	35.00	6"	15.00
Candelabrum, very ornate, 4		7"	15.00
arm with lusters	175.00	Pickle Dish, long	15.00
Celery Tray, crimped or		Pitcher, water, bulbous, 6	
straight	20.00	sizes.	45–60.00
Claret Jug.	50.00	Punch Bowl	50.00
Compote, cov	60.00	Punch Cup	8.00
Condensed Milk Jar, cov . . .	25.00	Salt Shaker.	15.00
Cordial.	35.00	Spooner	20.00
Creamer.	20.00	Sugar	
Cruet, patterned stopper		Cov.	35.00
1 oz	50.00	Open	18.00
2 oz	45.00	Syrup.	55.00
4 oz	45.00	Tray	
6 oz	25.00	Ice Cream	30.00
Decanter		Water	30.00
Pint.	45.00	Wine.	30.00
Quart	45.00	Tumbler	15.00
Egg Cup.	20.00	Water Bottle	35.00
Goblet	25.00	Wine	15.00
Ice Tub, handles	35.00		

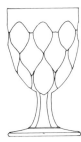

ALMOND THUMBPRINT (Pointed Thumbprint, Finger Print)

An early flint glass pattern with variants in flint and non-flint. Pattern has been attributed to Bryce, Bakewell, and U. S. Glass Co. Sometimes found in milk glass.

	Flint	Non-Flint		Flint	Non-Flint
Bowl, 4½" d, ftd . . .	—	20.00	Cov, ls, 7"	45.00	25.00
Butter, cov	80.00	40.00	Open, hs, 10½" . .	65.00	—
Celery Vase	50.00	25.00	Cordial	40.00	30.00
Champagne	60.00	35.00	Creamer.	60.00	40.00
Compote			Cruet, ftd, os.	55.00	—
Cov, hs, 4¾", jelly	60.00	40.00	Decanter	70.00	—
Cov, hs, 10".	100.00	45.00	Egg Cup.	45.00	25.00
Cov, ls, 4¾".	55.00	30.00	Goblet	30.00	12.00

	Flint	Non-Flint		Flint	Non-Flint
Punch Bowl	—	75.00	Spooner	20.00	15.00
Salt			Sugar, cov	60.00	40.00
Flat, large	25.00	15.00	Sweetmeat Jar, cov.	65.00	45.00
Ftd, cov.	45.00	25.00	Tumbler	60.00	20.00
Ftd, open	25.00	10.00	Wine	28.00	12.00

AMAZON (Sawtooth Band)

Non-flint made by Bryce Bros., Pittsburgh, PA, c1890 and by U. S. Glass Co. Mostly found in clear, either etched or plain. Heacock notes pieces in amber, blue, vaseline, and ruby stained. Over sixty-five pieces made in this pattern, including a toy set. Add 200% for color, e.g., pedestalled amber cruet with maltese cross stopper ($165.00) and pedestalled blue cruet with hand and bar stopper ($200.00). An amethyst cruet with a hand and bar stopper ($275.00) also is known.

	Etched	Plain		Etched	Plain
Banana Stand	95.00	65.00	Cordial	40.00	25.00
Bowl			Creamer	30.00	28.00
4", scalloped	—	10.00	Cruet, os	50.00	45.00
4½", scalloped	—	10.00	Egg Cup	—	14.00
5", scalloped	—	15.00	Goblet		
6", scalloped	—	25.00	4½"	30.00	—
6½", cov, oval	—	50.00	5"	25.00	—
7", scalloped	—	20.00	6"	30.00	—
8", scalloped	—	25.00	Pitcher, water	60.00	55.00
9", cov	30.00	25.00	Relish	28.00	25.00
Butter, cov	65.00	50.00	Salt & Pepper, pr.	50.00	40.00
Cake Stand			Salt		
Large	—	50.00	Individual	—	15.00
Small	—	40.00	Master	—	18.00
Celery Vase	35.00	30.00	Sauce, ftd	10.00	10.00
Champagne	—	35.00	Spooner	25.00	20.00
Claret	35.00	30.00	Sugar, cov	55.00	45.00
Compote			Syrup	50.00	42.50
Cov, hs 7"	—	66.00	Tumbler	25.00	20.00
Open, 4½", jelly	45.00	35.00	Vase	30.00	25.00
Open, hs, 9½",			Wine	25.00	20.00
sawtooth edge	—	45.00			

AMBERETTE (Daisy and Button-Paneled-Single Scallop, Daisy and Button-Single Panel, Paneled Daisy, Paneled Daisy and Button)

Non-flint pattern made by George Duncan & Sons, Pittsburgh, PA, 1885. It was reissued by U. S. Glass Co., Pittsburgh, PA, c1892. Found in clear with amber or ruby stained ribs, solid canary and blue.

	Clear with Amber Stain		Clear with Amber Stain
Bowl		Compote, open, hs, 8" d,	
5" l, oval, flat	60.00	scalloped	125.00
6" w, square, flat,		Creamer, ah	70.00
scalloped	65.00	Goblet	65.00
7" d, round, collared base,		Pickle Dish	35.00
cov	110.00	Pitcher, ah	225.00
8" d, round, collared base	85.00	Plate, dinner	45.00
9" d, round, flared rim	95.00	Sauce, 4½" w, sq, flat	25.00
Butter Dish, cov, scalloped	125.00	Spooner	65.00
Cake Stand, hs	150.00	Sugar, cov	125.00
Celery Vase	85.00		

ANTHEMION (Albany)

Non-flint made by Model Flint Glass Co., Findlay, OH, c1890–1900 and by Albany Glass Co. Also found in amber and blue.

	Clear		Clear
Bowl, 7", sq, turned-in edge	20.00	Pitcher, water	50.00
Butter, cov	65.00	Plate, 10"	20.00
Cake Plate, 9½"	35.00	Sauce	8.00
Cake Stand	40.00	Spooner	25.00
Celery Vase	35.00	Sugar, cov	35.00
Creamer	30.00	Tumbler	25.00
Marmalade Jar, cov	45.00		

APOLLO (Canadian Horseshoe, Shield Band)

Non-flint first made by Adams & Co., Pittsburgh, PA, c1890, and later by U. S. Glass Co. Frosted increases price 20%. Also found in ruby stained and engraved.

	Clear		Clear
Bowl		Egg Cup	30.00
4"	10.00	Goblet	35.00
5"	10.00	Lamp, 10"	125.00
6"	12.00	Pickle Dish	15.00
7"	15.00	Pitcher, water	65.00
8"	22.50	Plate, 9½", sq	28.00
Butter, cov	55.00	Salt	20.00
Cake Stand		Salt Shaker	25.00
8"	35.00	Sauce	
9"	40.00	Flat	10.00
10"	50.00	Ftd, 5"	12.00
Celery Tray, rect	22.50	Spooner	28.50
Celery Vase	35.00	Sugar, cov	45.00
Compote		Sugar Shaker	45.00
Cov, hs	65.00	Syrup	110.00
Open, hs	35.00	Tray, water	45.00
Open, ls, 7"	25.00	Tumbler	30.00
Creamer	35.00	Wine	35.00
Cruet	60.00		

ARABESQUE

Non-flint produced by Bakewell, Pears and Co., Pittsburgh, PA, c1870.

	Clear		Clear
Butter, cov	50.00	Goblet	35.00
Celery	40.00	Pitcher, water, ah	75.00
Compote, cov		Spooner	25.00
hs, 8"	60.00	Sugar	
ls, 8"	50.00	Cov	45.00
Creamer, ah	55.00	Open, buttermilk	25.00

ARCHED FLEUR-DE-LIS (Late Fleur-De-Lis)

Made by Bryce, Higbee and Co. 1897–98. Also gilded.

	Clear	Ruby Stained		Clear	Ruby Stained
Banana Stand	35.00	150.00	Mug, 3¼"	20.00	40.00
Bowl, 9", oval	18.00	—	Olive, handled	15.00	—
Butter, cov	40.00	135.00	Pitcher, water	125.00	300.00
Cake Stand	35.00	—	Plate, 7", sq	12.00	45.00
Compote, jelly	20.00	—	Relish, 8"	15.00	—
Creamer	30.00	60.00	Salt Shaker	16.00	45.00
Dish, shallow, 7"	12.50	25.00	Sauce	8.00	20.00

	Clear	Ruby Stained		Clear	Ruby Stained
Spooner, double handled	20.00	65.00	Toothpick	30.00	100.00
			Tumbler	15.00	45.00
Sugar, cov, double handled	35.00	100.00	Vase, 10"	35.00	75.00
			Wine	25.00	65.00

ARCHED GRAPE

Flint and non-flint made by Boston and Sandwich Glass Co., Sandwich, MA, c1880.

	Non-Flint		Non-Flint
Butter, cov	45.00	Pitcher, water, ah	60.00
Celery Vase	35.00	Sauce, flat	8.00
Champagne	35.00	Spooner	30.00
Compote, cov, hs	50.00	Sugar, cov	45.00
Creamer	40.00	Wine	25.00
Goblet	25.00		

ARCHED OVALS (Concaved Almond)

Made by U. S. Glass Co., Pittsburgh, PA, c1908. Found in gilt, ruby stained, green, and rarely in cobalt blue. Popular pattern for souvenir wares, which are worth less than the prices below in the pattern glass market. A few pieces have been found in cobalt blue. They include: celery vase ($40.00), mug ($30.00), toothpick ($60.00), and a tumbler ($25.00).

	Clear	Cobalt	Green	Ruby Stained
Bowl, berry	12.50	—	18.00	—
Bowl, cov, 7"	40.00	—	—	—
Butter, cov	45.00	—	50.00	80.00
Cake Stand	35.00	—	—	—
Celery Vase	15.00	40.00	20.00	—
Compote				
Cov, hs, 8", belled	42.00	—	—	—
Open, hs, 8"	30.00	—	—	—
Open, hs, 9"	35.00	—	—	—
Creamer				
Individual	20.00	—	—	—
Regular	30.00	—	—	25.00
Cruet	35.00	—	45.00	—
Goblet	20.00	—	30.00	35.00
Mug	18.00	30.00	20.00	25.00
Pitcher, water	30.00	—	40.00	—
Plate, 9"	20.00	—	25.00	—
Punch Cup	8.00	—	—	—
Relish, oval, 9"	20.00	—	—	—
Salt & Pepper, pr.	45.00	—	50.00	—
Sauce	7.50	—	—	—
Syrup	35.00	—	—	—
Spooner	20.00	—	25.00	35.00
Sugar, cov	35.00	—	40.00	—
Toothpick	18.00	50.00	25.00	35.00
Tumbler	12.00	25.00	18.00	30.00
Wine	15.00	—	20.00	30.00

ARGONAUT SHELL (Nautilus)

Made by Northwood Glass Co. c1897. Also made in carnival glass. Heavily reproduced in blue and custard.

	Blue Opal	Custard	Vaseline Opal
Bonbon	60.00	—	—
Bowls			
Berry, large	150.00	125.00	125.00
Small	45.00	50.00	45.00
Butter, cov	250.00	280.00	225.00
Compote, jelly.	150.00	135.00	250.00
Creamer.	200.00	125.00	175.00
Cruet, os	250.00	350.00	175.00
Pitcher, water	300.00	350.00	375.00
Salt & Pepper Shakers, pr.	100.00	350.00	100.00
Spooner	75.00	100.00	95.00
Sugar, cov	250.00	225.00	225.00
Toothpick	—	295.00	—
Tray.	60.00	—	45.00
Tumbler	185.00	75.00	175.00

ARGUS

Flint thumbprint type pattern made by Bakewell, Pears and Co. Pittsburgh, PA, in the early 1860s. Copiously reproduced, some by Fostoria Glass Co. with raised "H.F.M." trademark for Henry Ford Museum, Dearborn, MI. Reproduction colors include clear, red, green and cobalt blue.

	Clear		Clear
Ale Glass	75.00	* Goblet	40.00
Bitters Bottle.	60.00	Lamp, ftd	100.00
Bowl, 5½".	30.00	Mug, ah	65.00
* Butter, cov	85.00	Pitcher, water, ah	225.00
Celery Vase	90.00	Salt, master, open.	30.00
Champagne	65.00	* Spooner	45.00
Compote, open, 6" d, 4½" h	50.00	* Sugar, cov	65.00
* Creamer, applied handle . . .	100.00	Tumbler, bar.	65.00
Decanter, qt	70.00	Whiskey, ah	75.00
Egg Cup.	30.00	* Wine	35.00

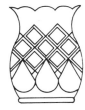

ART (Jacob's Tears, Job's Tears, Teardrop and Diamond Block)

Non-flint produced by Adams & Co., Pittsburgh, PA, in the 1880s. Reissued by U. S. Glass Co. in the early 1890s. A milk glass covered compote is known.

	Clear	Ruby Stained		Clear	Ruby Stained
Banana Stand.	95.00	175.00	Creamer		
Biscuit Jar	135.00	175.00	Hotel, large, round shape	45.00	90.00
Bowl			Regular.	55.00	100.00
6" d, 3¼" h, ftd . .	30.00	—	Cruet, os	125.00	250.00
7", low, collar base	35.00	—	Goblet	58.00	—
8", berry, one end pointed	50.00	85.00	Pitcher		
			Milk.	115.00	175.00
Butter, cov	60.00	125.00	Water, 2½ qt	100.00	—
Cake Stand			Plate, 10"	40.00	—
9".	55.00	—	Relish.	20.00	65.00
10¼".	65.00	—	Sauce		
Celery Vase	40.00	100.00	Flat, round, 4" . . .	15.00	—
* Compote			Pointed end.	18.50	—
Cov, hs, 7".	100.00	185.00	Spooner	25.00	85.00
Open, hs, 9"	50.00	—	Sugar, cov	45.00	125.00
Open, hs, 9½" d	60.00	—	Tumbler	45.00	—
Open, hs, 10" . . .	65.00	—	Vinegar Jug, 3 pt. . .	75.00	—

ARTICHOKE (Frosted Artichoke, Valencia)

Non-flint made by Fostoria Glass Co, Moundsville, WV, January, 1891. Made in clear and frosted (add 50%). Limited production in opalescent and satin glass. Reportedly no goblet was originally produced, but reproductions do exist.

	Clear		Clear
Bobeche	35.00	Miniature Lamp	250.00
Bowl, 8"	30.00	Pitcher, water	90.00
Butter, cov	50.00	Rose Bowl	35.00
Cake Stand	42.50	Sauce, flat	8.00
Celery Vase	35.00	Spooner	25.00
Compote, cov, hs	90.00	Sugar, cov	55.00
Creamer	35.00	Tray, water	45.00
Finger Bowl, underplate	40.00	Tumbler	35.00

ASHBURTON

A popular pattern produced by Boston and Sandwich Glass Co. and by McKee & Bros. Glass Co. from the 1850s to the late 1870s with many variations. Originally made in flint by New England Glass Co. and others and later in non-flint. Prices are for flint. Non-flint values 65% less. Also reported is an amber handled whiskey mug, flint canary celery vase ($750.00), and a scarce emerald green wine glass ($200.00). Some items known in fiery opalescent.

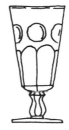

	Clear		Clear
Ale Glass, 5"	90.00	Honey Dish	15.00
Bar Bottle		* Jug, qt	90.00
Pint	55.00	Lamp	75.00
Quart	75.00	* Lemonade Glass	55.00
Bitters Bottle	55.00	Mug, 7"	100.00
* Bowl, 6½"	76.00	* Pitcher, water	450.00
Carafe	175.00	Plate, 6⅝"	75.00
Celery Vase, scalloped top	125.00	Sauce	10.00
Champagne, cut	75.00	* Sugar, cov	90.00
* Claret, 5¼" h	50.00	Toddy Jar, cov	375.00
* Compote, open, ls, 7½"	65.00	* Tumbler	
Cordial, 4¼" h	75.00	Bar	75.00
* Creamer, ah	210.00	Water	75.00
Decanter, qt, cut and		Whiskey	60.00
pressed, os	250.00	Whiskey, ah	125.00
Egg Cup		Water Bottle tumble up	95.00
Double	95.00	* Wine	
Single	25.00	Cut	65.00
Flip Glass, handled	140.00	Pressed	40.00
* Goblet	40.00		

ASHMAN

Non-flint, c1880. Pieces are square in shape. Also made in amber and blue.

	Clear		Clear
Bread Tray, motto	55.00	Creamer	35.00
Bowl	20.00	Goblet	35.00
Butter, cov		Pitcher, water	65.00
Conventional final	38.00	Relish	15.00
Large ball-type finial,		Spooner	40.00
sometimes with flowers		Sugar, cov	45.00
within the ball	50.00	Tray, water	40.00
Cake Stand, 9"	40.00	Tumbler	25.00
Compote		Wine	25.00
Cov, hs, 12"	95.00		
Open hs	37.50		

ATLANTA (Clear Lion Head, Frosted Atlanta, Square Lion)

Produced by Fostoria Glass Co., Moundsville, WV, c1895. Pieces are usually square in shape. Also found in milk glass, ruby, and amber stain.

Bowl	Clear	Frosted		Clear	Frosted
7", scallop rim . . .	60.00	75.00	* Goblet	50.00	60.00
8", low collar			Marmalade Jar	75.00	85.00
base	55.00	85.00	Pitcher, water	125.00	175.00
Butter, cov	85.00	125.00	Relish, oval.	35.00	40.00
Cake Stand, 10" . . .	95.00	110.00	Salt & Pepper, pr. . .	100.00	125.00
Celery Vase	45.00	75.00	Salt		
Compote			Individual.	30.00	40.00
Cov, hs, 7".	90.00	125.00	Master	50.00	70.00
Cov, hs, 8" d,			Sauce, 4"	22.00	25.00
9½" h.	110.00	150.00	Spooner	50.00	60.00
Open, hs, 5", jelly	55.00	65.00	Sugar, cov	85.00	100.00
Creamer.	50.00	65.00	Toothpick	55.00	60.00
Cruet	125.00	150.00	Tumbler	45.00	55.00
Egg cup	25.00	30.00	Wine	40.00	65.00

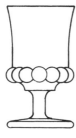

ATLAS (Bullet, Cannon Ball, Crystal Ball)

Non-flint, occasionally ruby stained and etched, made by Adams & Co.; U. S. Glass Co. in 1891; and Bryce Bros., Mt. Pleasant, PA, in 1889.

	Clear	Ruby Stained		Clear	Ruby Stained
Bowl, 9"	20.00	—	Pitcher, water	65.00	—
Butter, cov, regular	45.00	75.00	Salt		
Cake Stand			Master	20.00	—
8"	35.00	—	Individual.	15.00	—
9"	40.00	95.00	Salt & Pepper, pr. . .	20.00	—
Celery Vase	28.00	—	Sauce		
Champagne, 5½" h	35.00	55.00	Flat.	10.00	—
Compote			Footed	15.00	25.00
Cov, hs, 8".	65.00	—	Spooner	30.00	45.00
Cov, hs, 5", jelly . .	50.00	80.00	Sugar, cov	40.00	65.00
Open, ls, 7".	40.00	—	Syrup, molasses		
Cordial	35.00	—	can.	65.00	—
Creamer			Toothpick	20.00	50.00
Table, ah.	30.00	55.00	Tray, water	75.00	—
Tankard	25.00	—	Tumbler	28.00	—
Goblet	45.00	65.00	Whiskey	20.00	45.00
Marmalade Jar	45.00	—	Wine	25.00	—

AURORA (Diamond Horseshoe)

Made in 1888 by the Brilliant Glass Works, which only existed for a short time. Taken over by the Greensburg Glass Co. who continued the pattern. Also found etched.

	Clear	Ruby Stained		Clear	Ruby Stained
Bread Plate, 10",			Relish Scoop,		
round, large star in			handle.	10.00	25.00
center	30.00	60.00	Salt & Pepper, pr. . .	45.00	80.00
Butter, cov	45.00	90.00	Sauce, flat	8.00	15.00
Cake Stand	35.00	85.00	Spooner	25.00	48.00
Celery Vase	35.00	60.00	Sugar, cov	45.00	65.00
Compote, cov, hs . .	65.00	110.00	Tray, water	45.00	60.00
Creamer.	35.00	50.00	Tray, wine.	35.00	60.00
Goblet	30.00	60.00	Tumbler	25.00	45.00
Mug, handle	50.00	65.00	Waste Bowl.	30.00	45.00
Olive, oval	20.00	35.00	Wine	25.00	50.00
Pitcher, water	40.00	100.00	Wine Decanter, os. .	75.00	150.00

AUSTRIAN (Finecut Medallion)

Made by Indiana Tumbler and Goblet Co., Greentown, IN, 1897. Experimental pieces were made in cobalt blue, Nile green, and opaque colors.

	Amber	Canary	Clear	Emerald Green
Bowl				
8", round	—	150.00	55.00	—
8¼", rect	—	145.00	50.00	—
Butter, cov	185.00	300.00	90.00	—
Children's table set .	—	550.00	325.00	—
Compote, open, ls. .	—	150.00	75.00	—
Cordial	145.00	150.00	50.00	150.00
Creamer	120.00	125.00	40.00	120.00
Goblet	—	150.00	40.00	—
Mug, child's	—	—	45.00	—
Nappy, cov	—	135.00	55.00	—
Pitcher, water	—	350.00	100.00	—
Plate, 10"	—	—	40.00	—
Punch Cup	150.00	150.00	18.00	125.00
Rose Bowl	—	150.00	50.00	—
Sauce, 4⅝" d	—	50.00	20.00	—
Spooner	—	100.00	40.00	—
Sugar, cov	—	175.00	45.00	—
Tumbler	175.00	85.00	25.00	—
Wine	175.00	150.00	30.00	150.00

AZTEC (New Mexico)

Made by McKee & Bros. Glass Co. 1900–10. Late imitation cut pattern, often marked "PRES-CUT" in circle in base; about seventy-five items in pattern.

Clear		Clear
Bonbon, ftd, 7"	15.00	
Bowl, berry	15.00	
Butter, cov	40.00	
Cake Plate, trilobed	20.00	
Cake Stand	30.00	
Carafe, water	40.00	
Celery Tray	15.00	
Celery Vase	18.00	
Champagne	25.00	
Compote, open	30.00	
Condensed Milk Jar	20.00	
Cordial	20.00	
Cracker Jar, cov	50.00	
Creamer		
Individual	15.00	
Regular	25.00	
Cruet	35.00	
Crushed Fruit Bowl, cov,		
8½"	75.00	
Cup	8.00	
Decanter, cut stopper	32.50	
Finger Bowl, underplate	20.00	

	Clear
Goblet	25.00
Pitcher, ah, ½ gal	35.00
Plate	20.00
* Punch Bowl, stand, and 12	
handled cups	125.00
Punch Cup	5.00
Relish	15.00
Salt & Pepper, pr.	35.00
Sauce	5.00
Soda Fountain Accessories	
Crushed Fruit Jar	55.00
Straw Holder, glass lid . . .	65.00
Spooner	15.00
Sugar, cov	25.00
Syrup	50.00
Toothpick	24.00
Tumbler	
Iced Tea	22.00
Water	20.00
Whiskey	12.00
Wine	15.00

BABY FACE (Cupid)

Non-flint made by McKee & Bros. Glass Co., Pittsburgh, PA, in the late 1870s.

	Clear
Butter, cov	250.00
Celery Vase	75.00
Champagne	100.00
Compote	
Cov, hs, 5¼"	165.00
Cov, hs, 7"	225.00
Cov, hs, 8"	250.00
Open, ls, 7"	95.00
Open, ls, 8"	100.00

	Clear
Creamer	110.00
* Goblet	100.00
Pitcher, water	300.00
Salt	50.00
Spooner	95.00
Sugar, cov	195.00
* Wine	160.00

BALL AND SWIRL (Swirl and Ball)

Made by McKee Glass Co, Jeanette, PA, 1894.

	Clear		Clear
Butter, cov	35.00	Pitcher, water	40.00
Cake Stand	35.00	Sauce, ftd	10.00
Compote, open, hs	30.00	Spooner	20.00
Creamer	20.00	Sugar, cov	25.00
* Goblet	20.00	Syrup	40.00
Mug		Tumbler	15.00
Large	15.00	* Wine	20.00
Small	10.00		

BALTIMORE PEAR (Double Pear, Fig, Gipsy, Maryland Pear, Twin Pear)

Non-flint originally made by Adams & Company, Pittsburgh, PA, in 1874. Also made by U. S. Glass Company in the 1890s. There are eighteen different size compotes. Given as premiums by different manufacturers and organizations. Heavily reproduced. Reproduced in clear and cobalt blue.

	Clear		Clear
Bowl		Pickle	20.00
6"	30.00	* Pitcher	
9"	35.00	Milk	80.00
Bread Plate, 12½"	70.00	Water	95.00
* Butter, cov	75.00	* Plate	
* Cake Stand, 9"	65.00	8½"	30.00
* Celery Vase	50.00	10"	40.00
Compote		Relish	25.00
Cov, hs, 7"	80.00	* Sauce	
Cov, ls, 8½"	45.00	Flat	8.00
Open, hs	30.00	Footed	15.00
Open, jelly	25.00	Spooner	40.00
* Creamer	30.00	* Sugar, cov	50.00
* Goblet	35.00	Tray, 10½"	35.00

BAMBOO EDGE (Bamboo)

Made by LaBelle Glass Co., Bridgeport, OH, c1883.

	Clear	Ruby Stained		Clear	Ruby Stained
Butter, cov	85.00	160.00	Relish, 8"	20.00	45.00
Celery Vase	30.00	65.00	Salt & Pepper, pr	36.00	75.00
Compote, oval,			Sauce, flat	12.00	—
etched	45.00	—	Spooner	30.00	65.00
Creamer	35.00	75.00	Sugar, cov	45.00	90.00
Pitcher, water	75.00	150.00	Tumbler	35.00	70.00

BANDED BUCKLE (Union)

Non-flint pattern made by King, Son and Co., Pittsburgh, PA, c1875.

	Clear		Clear
Bowl	25.00	Goblet	50.00
Butter Dish, cov	85.00	Salt, master, ftd	25.00
Compote, cov, ls, 6" d	45.00	Spooner	35.00
Creamer, ftd, ah	85.00	Sugar, cov	50.00
Egg Cup	40.00	Tumbler	50.00

BANDED PORTLAND (Virginia #1, Maiden's Blush)

States pattern, originally named Virginia, by Portland Glass Co., Portland, ME. Painted and fired green, yellow, blue, and possibly pink; ruby stained, and rose-flashed (which Lee notes is Maiden's Blush, referring to the color rather than the pattern, as Metz lists it). Double-flashed refers to color above and below the band, single-flashed refers to color above or below the band only.

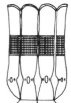

	Clear	Color-Flashed	Maiden's Blush Pink
Bowl			
4″ d, open	10.00	—	20.00
6″ d, cov	40.00	—	55.00
7½″ d, shallow. . .	30.00	—	55.00
8″ d, cov	50.00	—	75.00
Butter, cov	50.00	165.00	85.00
Cake Stand	55.00	—	90.00
Candlesticks, pr . . .	80.00	—	125.00
Carafe	80.00	—	90.00
Celery Tray.	25.00	—	40.00
Celery Vase	35.00	—	45.00
Cologne Bottle	50.00	65.00	85.00
Compote			
Cov, hs, 7″.	65.00	—	125.00
Cov, hs, 8″.	75.00	—	115.00
Cov, jelly, 6″.	40.00	65.00	90.00
Creamer			
Individual, oval. . .	25.00	35.00	38.00
Regular, 6 oz.	35.00	45.00	50.00
Cruet, os	60.00	90.00	125.00
Decanter, handled. .	50.00	—	100.00
Dresser Tray.	50.00	—	65.00
Goblet	40.00	55.00	65.00
Lamp			
Flat.	45.00	—	—
Tall	50.00	—	—
Nappy, sq	15.00	55.00	65.00
Olive	18.00	—	35.00
Pin Tray	16.00	—	25.00
Pitcher, tankard. . . .	75.00	95.00	240.00
Pomade Jar, cov . . .	35.00	45.00	65.00
Punch Bowl, hs. . . .	110.00	—	300.00
Punch Cup	20.00	—	30.00
Relish			
6½″.	25.00	30.00	20.00
8¼″.	20.00	35.00	40.00
Ring Holder	75.00	—	125.00
Salt & Pepper, pr. . .	45.00	75.00	75.00
Sardine Box	55.00	—	90.00
Sauce, round, flat,			
4 or 4½″	10.00	—	20.00
Spooner	28.00	—	46.00
Sugar, cov	48.00	75.00	75.00
Sugar Shaker, orig			
top	45.00	—	85.00
Syrup	50.00	—	135.00
Toothpick	40.00	45.00	45.00
Tumbler	25.00	35.00	45.00
Vase			
6″	20.00	—	38.00
9″	35.00	—	50.00
Wine	35.00	—	75.00

BARBERRY (Berry, Olive, Pepper Berry)

Non-flint made by McKee & Bros. Glass Co. in the 1860s. The 6″ plates are found in amber, canary, pale green, and pale blue; they are considered scarce. Pattern comes in "9 berry bunch" and "12 berry bunch" varieties.

	Clear		Clear
Bowl		7″, oval	25.00
6″, oval	20.00	8″, oval	28.00

	Clear		Clear
8″, round, flat	30.00	Egg Cup	18.00
9″, oval	32.00	Goblet	25.00
Butter		Pickle	10.00
Cov	50.00	Pitcher, water, ah	100.00
Cov, flange, pattern on		Plate, 6″	20.00
edge	80.00	Salt, master, ftd	25.00
Cake Stand	90.00	Sauce	
Celery Vase	40.00	Flat	10.00
Compote		Footed	15.00
Cov, hs, 8″, shell finial	85.00	Spooner, ftd	30.00
Cov, ls, 8″, shell finial	75.00	Sugar, cov	45.00
Open, hs, 8″	35.00	Syrup	150.00
Creamer	30.00	Tumbler, ftd	25.00
Cup Plate	15.00	Wine	25.00

BARLEY (Sprig)

Non-flint originally made by Campbell, Jones and Co. c1882 in clear; possibly by others in varied quality. Add 100% for color, which is hard to find.

	Clear		Clear
Bowl		Honey Dish, ftd, 3½″	8.00
8″, berry	15.00	Marmalade Jar	65.00
10″, oval	15.00	Pickle Castor, SP frame	85.00
Bread Tray	30.00	Pitcher, water	
Butter, cov	45.00	Applied handle	100.00
Cake Stand		Pressed handle	45.00
8″	30.00	Plate, 6″	35.00
10″	35.00	Platter, 13″ l, 8″ w	30.00
Celery Vase	25.00	Sauce	
Compote		Flat	8.00
Cov, hs, 6″	45.00	Footed	10.00
Cov, hs, 8½″	60.00	Spooner	20.00
Open, hs, 8½″	35.00	Sugar, cov	35.00
Cordial	50.00	Vegetable Dish, oval	15.00
Creamer	30.00	Wine	30.00
Goblet	35.00		

BARRED FORGET-ME-NOT

Made by Canton Glass Co., Canton, OH, c1883. There are two goblet styles; the larger has a coarser pattern.

	Amber	Apple Green	Blue	Clear	Milk or Vaseline
Butter, cov	50.00	60.00	60.00	40.00	60.00
Cake Stand	55.00	65.00	65.00	45.00	65.00
Celery Vase	50.00	60.00	60.00	30.00	60.00
Compote					
Cov, hs	70.00	80.00	80.00	55.00	80.00
Open, ls	45.00	50.00	50.00	35.00	50.00
Creamer	40.00	50.00	50.00	30.00	50.00
Goblet	45.00	60.00	60.00	30.00	60.00
Pitcher					
Milk	55.00	60.00	60.00	40.00	60.00
Water	65.00	80.00	80.00	45.00	80.00
Plate, 9″, handles	45.00	50.00	50.00	30.00	50.00
Relish	25.00	30.00	30.00	15.00	30.00
Sauce, flat	15.00	20.00	20.00	8.00	20.00
Spooner	30.00	40.00	40.00	20.00	40.00
Sugar, cov	45.00	60.00	60.00	35.00	60.00
Wine	40.00	45.00	45.00	30.00	45.00

BARRED OVALS (Banded Portland, Banded Portland-Frosted, Buckle, Frosted Banded Portland, Purple Block, Oval and Crossbar)

Non-flint pattern made by George Duncan & Sons, Pittsburgh, PA, c1892. Reissued by U. S. Glass Co., Pittsburgh, PA, Factory D, 1891. Made in clear with frosting or ruby stain. Found plain or with copper wheel engraving. Prices listed below are for plain pieces.

	Clear	Ruby Stained		Clear	Ruby Stained
Bowl, 8" d.	20.00	35.00	Creamer	50.00	75.00
Butter Dish, cov . . .	50.00	125.00	Goblet	45.00	75.00
Cake Stand, hs, 10"			Sauce, flat, 4" d . . .	10.00	20.00
d.	45.00	100.00	Spooner	40.00	65.00
Celery Tray	35.00	70.00	Sugar, cov	70.00	100.00

BASKETWEAVE

Non-flint, c1880. Some covered pieces have a stippled cat's head finial.

	Amber or Canary	Apple Green	Blue	Clear	Vaseline
Bowl	22.00	—	25.00	18.00	—
Bread Plate, 11" . . .	35.00	—	35.00	10.00	—
Butter, cov	35.00	60.00	40.00	30.00	40.00
Compote, cov, 7" . . .	—	—	—	40.00	—
Cordial	25.00	40.00	28.00	20.00	30.00
Creamer	30.00	50.00	35.00	28.00	36.00
Cup and Saucer . . .	35.00	60.00	35.00	30.00	38.00
Dish, oval	12.00	20.00	15.00	10.00	16.00
Egg Cup	18.00	30.00	20.00	15.00	25.00
* Goblet	28.00	50.00	35.00	20.00	30.00
Mug	25.00	40.00	25.00	15.00	30.00
Pickle	18.00	30.00	20.00	15.00	22.00
Pitcher					
Milk	40.00	60.00	45.00	35.00	50.00
* Water	60.00	75.00	80.00	45.00	85.00
Plate, 11", handled	25.00	38.00	25.00	20.00	30.00
Sauce	10.00	10.00	12.00	8.00	12.00
Spooner	30.00	36.00	30.00	20.00	30.00
Sugar, cov	35.00	60.00	35.00	30.00	40.00
Syrup	50.00	75.00	50.00	45.00	55.00
* Tray, water, scenic					
center	35.00	45.00	40.00	30.00	55.00
* Tumbler, ftd	18.00	30.00	20.00	15.00	20.00
Waste Bowl	20.00	36.00	25.00	18.00	25.00
Wine	30.00	50.00	30.00	20.00	30.00

BEADED ACORN MEDALLION (Beaded Acorn)

Made by Boston Silver Glass Co., East Cambridge, MA, c1869.

	Clear		Clear
Butter, cov, acorn finial	65.00	Plate, 6"	30.00
Champagne	65.00	Relish	15.00
Compote, cov, hs	60.00	Salt, master	30.00
Creamer	40.00	Sauce, flat	12.00
Egg Cup	25.00	Spooner	25.00
Goblet	30.00	Sugar, cov	45.00
Pitcher, water	125.00	Wine	45.00

BEADED BAND (Thousand Eye Band)

Attributed to Burlington Glass Co., Hamilton, Ontario, Canada, c1884 as well as by an American midwestern factory. May have been made in light amber and other colors.

	Clear		Clear
Butter, cov	35.00	Relish	
Cake Stand, 7⅝"	25.00	Double	30.00
Compote, cov		Single	15.00
hs, 7"	50.00	Sauce, ftd	10.00
hs, 8"	55.00	Spooner	25.00
ls, 9"	80.00	Sugar, cov	40.00
Creamer	30.00	Syrup	95.00
Goblet	30.00	Wine	30.00
Pickle, cov	45.00		
Pitcher, water, applied strap handle	75.00		

BEADED GRAPE (Beaded Grape and Vine, California, Grape and Vine)

Non-flint made by U. S. Glass Co., Pittsburgh, PA, c1890. Also attributed to Burlington Glass Works, Hamilton, Ontario, and Sydenham Glass Co., Wallaceburg, Ontario, Canada, c1910. Made in clear and emerald green, sometimes with gilt trim. Reproduced in a variety of clear, milk glass, and several colors by many, including Westmoreland Glass Co.

	Clear	Emerald Green		Clear	Emerald Green
Bowl			Cruet, os	65.00	125.00
5½", sq	17.50	20.00	* Goblet	35.00	50.00
5½ x 8"	25.00	30.00	Olive, handle	20.00	35.00
6" sq	20.00	25.00	Pickle	20.00	30.00
7½", sq	25.00	35.00	Pitcher		
8", round	28.00	35.00	Milk	75.00	90.00
Bread Plate	25.00	45.00	Water	85.00	120.00
Butter, cov	65.00	85.00	* Plate, 8¼", sq	28.00	40.00
Cake Stand, 9"	65.00	85.00	Salt & Pepper	45.00	65.00
Celery Tray	30.00	45.00	* Sauce, 4"	15.00	20.00
Celery Vase	40.00	60.00	Spooner	35.00	45.00
* Compote			Sugar, cov		
Cov, hs, 7"	75.00	85.00	Large, ftd, Australian	60.00	75.00
Cov, hs, 8"	80.00	90.00	Table	45.00	55.00
Cov, hs, 9"	100.00	110.00	Sugar Shaker	75.00	85.00
Open, hs, 5", sq	55.00	75.00	Toothpick	40.00	65.00
Open, hs, 7"	45.00	65.00	* Tumbler	25.00	40.00
Open, hs, 8"	55.00	70.00	Vase, 6" h	25.00	40.00
Open, hs, 9"	65.00	75.00	* Wine	35.00	65.00
Open, hs, jelly	55.00	65.00			
Creamer	40.00	50.00			

BEADED GRAPE MEDALLION

Non-flint possibly made by Boston Silver Glass Co., East Cambridge, MA, c1868. Shards have been found at Boston and Sandwich Glass Co., Sandwich, MA. Several variations are known. When bands are found on this heavily stippled pattern, it is known as Beaded Grape Medallion Banded. Also found in flint (add 40%).

	Clear		Clear
Bowl, 7"	25.00	Relish	
Butter, cov, acorn finial	75.00	Cov	140.00
Cake Stand, 11"	100.00	Open, mkd "Mould Pat'd	
Celery Vase	75.00	May 11, 1868"	40.00
Castor Set, 4 bottles	110.00	Salt	
Champagne	85.00	Individual, flat	20.00
Compote		Master, ftd	25.00
Cov, collared base	150.00	Spooner	35.00
Cov, hs	100.00	Sugar	
Cordial	55.00	Cov	60.00
Creamer, ah	50.00	Open	30.00
Egg Cup	30.00	Sweetmeat, cov	115.00
Goblet	30.00	Syrup	150.00
Honey Dish, 3½"	10.00	Tumbler, ftd	45.00
Pitcher, water, ah	115.00	Vegetable, cov, ftd	75.00
Plate, 6"	30.00	Wine	55.00

BEADED LOOP (Oregon #1)

Non-flint made by U. S. Glass Co., Pittsburgh, PA, as Pattern Line No. 15,073. Reissued after the 1891 merger as one of the States series. Reproduced in clear and color by Imperial.

	Clear		Clear
Berry Set, master, 6 sauces	72.00	Creamer	
Bowl		Flat	30.00
3½"	10.00	Footed	35.00
4"	10.00	Cruet	50.00
6"	12.00	* Goblet	35.00
7"	15.00	Honey Dish	10.00
8"	15.00	Mug	35.00
9", berry, cov	25.00	Pickle Dish, boat shape	15.00
Bread Plate	35.00	Pitcher	
Butter, cov		Milk	40.00
English	65.00	Water	60.00
Flanged	50.00	Relish	15.00
Flat	40.00	Salt, master	20.00
Cake Stand		Salt & Pepper Shakers, pr	40.00
8"	40.00	Sauce	
9"	45.00	Flat, 3½ to 4"	5.00
10"	55.00	Footed, 3½"	10.00
Carafe, water	35.00	Spooner	
Celery Vase	30.00	Flat	24.00
Compote		Footed	26.00
Cov, hs, 5", jelly	45.00	Sugar, cov	
Cov, hs, 6"	50.00	Flat	25.00
Cov, hs, 7"	60.00	Footed	30.00
Cov, hs, 8"	65.00	Syrup	55.00
Open, hs, 5"	25.00	Toothpick	55.00
Open, hs, 6"	30.00	Tumbler	25.00
Open, hs, 7"	35.00	Wine	50.00
Open, hs, 8"	40.00		

BEADED MIRROR (Beaded Medallion)

Flint made by Boston Silver Glass Co., East Cambridge, MA, and patented May 11, 1869. Shards have been found at Boston and Sandwich Glass Co., Sandwich, MA. Like its contemporary, Beaded Grape Medallion, both have heavy stippling as a design element. Finials are acorn shaped. Also found in non-flint (25% less).

	Clear		Clear
Butter, cov	40.00	Goblet	25.00
Castor Bottle		Pitcher, water	85.00
Mustard	18.00	Plate, 6"	20.00
Oil	25.00	Relish	15.00
Set, 5 pcs, metal frame	100.00	Salt, ftd	15.00
Celery	35.00	Sauce, flat	8.00
Compote, cov, hs	50.00	Spooner	25.00
Creamer	40.00	Sugar, cov	45.00
Egg Cup	20.00		

BEADED OVAL WINDOW (Argyle, Oval Medallion)

Non-flint made by U. S. Glass Co., Pittsburgh, PA, in 1891. Shards have been found at the site of Burlington Glass Works, Hamilton, Ontario, Canada. Made in clear, amber (add 50%), amethyst (add 200%), blue, and vaseline (add 100%).

	Clear		Clear
Bowl, oval	20.00	Creamer	30.00
Bread Plate, GUTDODB	25.00	Goblet	30.00
Butter, cov	40.00	Sauce, ftd	12.00
Compote, cov	60.00	Wine	30.00

BEADED SWAG (Bead Yoke)

Made by Heisey Glass Co. c1900. Made in emerald green, ruby stained, custard glass, and milk glass (called "opal" by Heisey). Prices listed are for clear glass; ruby stained, custard, and milk (25% more), emerald green (40% more).

	Clear		Clear
Bonbon	25.00	Custard Cup, handled	15.00
Bowl		Finger Bowl	25.00
4"	20.00	Finger Bowl Underplate	20.00
4½"	20.00	Goblet	25.00
5"	20.00	Molasses Jar, metal lid	75.00
7"	25.00	Mug, souvenir type	30.00
8"	35.00	Pickle Tray, rect, deep	30.00
9"	45.00	Pitcher, water, half gallon	
10"	50.00	Bulbous	75.00
Butter, cov	45.00	Tankard	85.00
Cake Stand		Salt Shaker	20.00
9"	65.00	Sauce	10.00
10"	65.00	Spooner	30.00
Celery Vase	45.00	Sugar, cov	35.00
Compote, open	50.00	* Toothpick	38.00
Creamer	35.00	Tumbler	25.00
Cruet	48.00		

BEADED SWIRL (Swirled Column)

Made by George Duncan and Sons, c1890. The dual names are for the two forms of the pattern. Beaded Swirl stands on flat bases and is solid in shape. Swirled Column stands on scrolled (sometimes gilded) feet, and the shape tapered toward the base. Some pieces trimmed in gold and also in milk white.

	Clear	Emerald Green		Clear	Emerald Green
Bowl			Goblet	30.00	25.00
Berry, 7"	10.00	20.00	Mug	10.00	12.00
Flat	15.00	25.00	Pitcher, water	40.00	65.00
Footed, oval	18.00	24.00	Sauce		
Footed, round	18.00	24.00	Flat	8.00	12.00
Butter, cov	35.00	45.00	Footed	10.00	14.00
Cake Stand	35.00	45.00	Spooner		
Celery Vase	30.00	55.00	Flat	25.00	40.00
Compote			Footed	30.00	45.00
Cov, hs	40.00	50.00	Sugar, cov		
Open, hs	35.00	45.00	Flat	35.00	45.00
Creamer			Footed	35.00	45.00
Flat	25.00	35.00	Sugar Shaker	35.00	60.00
Footed	30.00	40.00	Syrup	48.00	100.00
Dish	10.00	15.00	Tumbler	20.00	30.00
Egg Cup	14.00	15.00	Wine	25.00	35.00

BEADED TULIP (Andes, Tulip)

Non-flint made by McKee & Bros. Glass Co., Pittsburgh, PA, c1894.

	Clear	Emerald Green		Clear	Emerald Green
Bowl, 9½", oval	20.00	—	Relish	20.00	—
Butter, cov	50.00	125.00	Sauce		
Cake Stand	50.00	—	Flat, leaf shape		
Compote, cov, hs	55.00	—	edges	10.00	
Creamer	35.00	75.00	Footed	12.00	—
Goblet	35.00	—	Spooner	30.00	—
Marmalade Jar	40.00		Sugar, cov	45.00	80.00
Pickle, oval	18.00	—	Tray		
Pitcher			Water	50.00	—
Milk	45.00	65.00	Wine	50.00	—
Water	65.00	—	Wine	30.00	—
Plate, 6"	25.00	—			

BEATTY HONEYCOMB (Beatty Waffle)

Non-flint made by Beatty and Sons Glass Co., Tiffin, OH, c1888. Reproduced by Fenton Glass in green opalescent (basket, rose bowl, and vases) and milk glass.

	Blue Opal	White Opal		Blue Opal	White Opal
Bowl, berry	100.00	50.00	Pitcher, water	300.00	200.00
Butter, cov	120.00	100.00	Salt & Pepper, pr.	65.00	45.00
Celery Vase	85.00	45.00	Sauce	20.00	20.00
Creamer			Spooner	40.00	30.00
Individual	35.00	20.00	Sugar, cov		
Regular	30.00	25.00	Individual	65.00	55.00
Cruet, os	235.00	175.00	Regular	70.00	65.00
Mug	35.00	25.00	Toothpick	50.00	45.00
Mustard	60.00	45.00	Tumbler	65.00	40.00

BEATTY RIB (Ribbed Opal)

Non-flint made by Beatty and Sons Glass Co., Tiffin, OH, c1000. May have been made in vaseline opalescent.

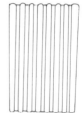

	Blue Opal	Clear Opal		Blue Opal	Clear Opal
Bowl, berry			Relish	25.00	15.00
Rect	60.00	55.00	Salt, individual	30.00	25.00
Round	65.00	50.00	Salt & Pepper, pr.	150.00	100.00
Butter, cov	100.00	75.00	Sauce		
Celery Vase	65.00	50.00	Rect	30.00	15.00
Cracker Jar, cov	300.00	150.00	Round	30.00	15.00
Creamer			Spooner	45.00	35.00
Individual	30.00	25.00	Sugar		
Table	60.00	35.00	Individual	30.00	25.00
Dish, oblong, 4⅛ x			Regular, cov	60.00	40.00
⅝"	25.00	15.00	Toothpick		
Finger Bowl	45.00	30.00	2" h	40.00	30.00
Match Holder, 1¹⁵⁄₁₆"	50.00	45.00	2½" h	50.00	40.00
Pitcher, water	150.00	120.00	Tumbler	45.00	35.00

BEATTY SWIRLED OPALESCENT (Swirled Opal)

Made by Beatty and Sons Glass Co., Tiffin, OH, c1889.

	Blue Opal	Vaseline Opal	White Opal
Bowl, berry	80.00	85.00	70.00
Butter, cov	125.00	150.00	100.00
Celery Vase	50.00	55.00	45.00
Creamer	40.00	50.00	30.00
Cruet, os	120.00	—	—
Mug	35.00	40.00	30.00
Pitcher, water	150.00	165.00	125.00
Sauce	35.00	35.00	30.00
Spooner	50.00	55.00	40.00
Sugar, cov	55.00	100.00	50.00
Syrup	125.00	150.00	115.00
Toothpick	50.00	—	45.00
Tray, water	120.00	125.00	110.00
Tumbler	50.00	55.00	45.00

BEAUTIFUL LADY

Made by Bryce, Higbee and Co. in 1905.

	Clear		Clear
Banana Stand, hs	30.00	Goblet	35.00
Bowl		Pitcher, water	40.00
8", low collared base	15.00	Plate	
9", flat	18.00	7", sq	15.00
Bread Plate	15.00	8"	18.00
Cake Plate, 9"	25.00	9"	25.00
Cake Stand, hs	35.00	11"	27.50
Compote		Salt & Pepper, pr	60.00
Cov, hs	35.00	Spooner	15.00
Open, hs	25.00	Sugar, cov	25.00
Open, jelly	15.00	Tumbler	15.00
Creamer	25.00	Vase, 6½"	15.00
Cruet	30.00	Wine	20.00

BELLFLOWER (Ribbed Bellflower, Ribbed Leaf)

A fine flint glass pattern first made in the 1850s and attributed to Boston and Sandwich Glass Co. Later produced in non-flint by McKee & Bros. Glass Co. and other firms for many years. There are many variations of this pattern—single vine and double vine, fine and coarse rib, knob and plain stems, and rayed and plain bases. Type and quality must be considered when evaluating. Very rare in color. Prices are for high quality flint. Reproductions have been made by the Metropolitan Museum of Art and by Imperial Glass Co. Bellaire, OH. Made in lead crystal, each has a molded "M.M.A." monogram. Abbreviations: DV - double vine; SV - single vine; FR - fine rib; CR - coarse rib.

	Clear		Clear
Bowl		* SV-FR, plain stem, rayed	
6" d, 1¾" h, SV	75.00	base, barrel shape	30.00
8", all types	75.00	Hat, SV-FR, made from tum-	
Butter, cov, SV-FR	175.00	bler mold, rare	350.00
Castor Set, 5 bottle, pewter		Honey Dish, SV-FR, 3"	35.00
stand	225.00	Lamp, whale oil, SV-FR,	
Celery Vase, SV-FR	250.00	brass stem, marble base	175.00
Champagne		Mug, SV-FR	250.00
DV-FR, cut bellflowers	225.00	Paperweight Whimsey	75.00
SV-FR, knob stem, rayed		Pitcher	
base, barrel shape	125.00	Milk, DV-FR	600.00
Compote		Milk, DV, pint	600.00
Cov, hs, 8" d, SV-FR	575.00	* Milk, SV-CR, quart	600.00
Cov, ls, 7" d, SV	200.00	Water, DV-CR	350.00
Cov, ls, 8" d, SV	225.00	* Water, SV-FR	250.00
Cov, ls, 8" d, SV-FR	375.00	Plate, 6", SV-FR	95.00
Open, hs, 8", SV	225.00	Salt, master	
Open, ls, 7", DV-FR	90.00	SV-FR, ftd	60.00
Open, ls, 7", SV	100.00	DV-FR	35.00
Open, ls, 8", SV	100.00	Sauce, flat, SV-FR	15.00
Open, ls, 9", SV-CR	125.00	Spooner	
Cordial, SV-FR, knob stem,		DV	45.00
rayed base, barrel shape	115.00	SV-FR	35.00
Creamer, DV-FR	135.00	Sugar	
Creamer, SV-FR	135.00	Cov, DV	100.00
Decanter		Cov, SV-CR	95.00
Pint, DV-FR, bar top	225.00	Sweetmeat, cov, hs, 6", SV	300.00
Quart		Syrup, ah	
DV-FR, orig patterned		Ftd, 10 sides	750.00
stopper	475.00	SV-FR	550.00
SV-FR, bar top	185.00	Tumbler	
Dish, SV-FR, 8", round, flat,		DV-CR	95.00
scalloped top	65.00	SV-FR, ftd	90.00
Egg Cup		* SV-FR, cut bellflowers	250.00
CR	35.00	Whiskey, 3½", SV-FR	150.00
SV-FR	40.00	Wine	
Goblet		DV-FR, cut bellflowers,	
DV-FR, cut bellflowers	230.00	barrel shape	250.00
SV-CR, barrel shape	45.00	SV-FR, knob stem, rayed	
SV-CR, straight sides	40.00	base, barrel shape	125.00
SV-FR, knob stem, barrel		SV-FR, plain stem, rayed	
shape	55.00	base, straight sides	100.00

BETHLEHEM STAR (Star Burst, Bright Star)

Made by Indiana Glass Co., Dunkirk, IN, c1907.

	Clear		Clear
Butter, cov	35.00	Goblet	30.00
Celery Vase	25.00	Pitcher, water	55.00
Compote, cov, hs		Relish	15.00
4½"	50.00	Sauce, flat	10.00
8"	60.00	Spooner	25.00
Creamer	30.00	Sugar, cov	40.00
Cruet, os	35.00	Wine	25.00

BEVELED DIAMOND AND STAR (Diamond Prism, Princeton)

Non-flint pattern made by Tarentum Glass Co., Tarentum, PA, c1894. Made in clear and clear with ruby stain.

	Clear	Ruby Stained		Clear	Ruby Stained
Bowl, 7" d	15.00	30.00	Sauce, ftd	10.00	20.00
Butter Dish, cov	45.00	90.00	Spooner	25.00	65.00
Cake Stand, hs, 9"			Sugar, cov	40.00	85.00
h	40.00	90.00	Sugar Shaker, orig		
Celery Vase	30.00	75.00	top	40.00	95.00
Cracker Jar, cov	50.00	175.00	Toothpick	25.00	70.00
Creamer, 5½" h	35.00	70.00	Tumbler, 3¾" h	15.00	30.00
Goblet	40.00	70.00	Wine, 4" h	20.00	45.00

BIGLER

Flint made by Boston and Sandwich Glass Co., Sandwich, MA, and by other early factories. A scarce pattern in which goblets are most common and vary in height, shape and flare. Rare in color. The goblet has been reproduced as a commemorative item for Biglerville, PA.

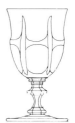

	Clear		Clear
Ale Glass	65.00	Goblet	
Bar Bottle, qt	80.00	Regular	48.00
Bowl, 10" d	40.00	Short Stem	50.00
Butter, cov	125.00	Lamp, whale oil, monument	
Celery Vase	100.00	base	155.00
Champagne	95.00	Mug, ah	60.00
Compote, open, 7" d	40.00	Plate, 6" d	32.00
Cordial	65.00	Salt, master	20.00
Creamer	75.00	Tumbler, water	65.00
Cup Plate	30.00	Whiskey, handled	100.00
Egg Cup, double	50.00	Wine	65.00

BIRD AND STRAWBERRY (Bluebird, Flying Bird and Strawberry, Strawberry and Bird)

Non-flint, c1914. Made by Indiana Glass Co., Dunkirk, IN. Pieces occasionally highlighted by the coloring of birds blue, strawberries pink, and leaves green, plus the addition of gilding.

	Clear	Colors		Clear	Colors
Bowl			Compote		
5"	25.00	45.00	* Cov, hs	125.00	200.00
9½", ftd	50.00	85.00	Open, ls, ruffled	65.00	125.00
10½"	55.00	95.00	Jelly, cov, hs	150.00	225.00
Butter, cov	100.00	175.00	Creamer	55.00	135.00
Cake Stand	65.00	125.00	Cup	25.00	35.00
* Celery Vase	45.00	85.00	Goblet	200.00	300.00

	Clear	Colors		Clear	Colors
Nappy	40.00	65.00	Spooner	50.00	120.00
Pitcher, water	235.00	350.00	Sugar, cov	65.00	125.00
Plate, 12"	125.00	175.00	Tumbler	45.00	75.00
Punch Cup	25.00	35.00	Wine	70.00	100.00
Relish	20.00	45.00			

BLACKBERRY

Clear or milk glass non-flint made by Hobbs, Brockunier & Co. in 1870 and by Phoenix Glass in the 1930s. Reproduced in milk glass after the 1930s. Old milk glass valued at 25% more.

	Clear		Clear
* Butter, cov	60.00	Honey Dish	10.00
* Celery Vase	55.00	* Pitcher, water	175.00
Champagne	45.00	Salt, ftd	25.00
Compote		Sauce, flat	12.00
Cov, hs, 8"	75.00	Spooner	30.00
Open, hs, 8"	25.00	* Sugar, cov	55.00
* Creamer	65.00	Syrup	150.00
* Egg Cup, double	40.50	Tumbler	35.00
* Goblet	35.00	Wine	25.00

BLAZE

Flint pattern made by New England Glass Co., East Cambridge, MA, c1869.

	Clear		Clear
Bowl, 8" d, cov	90.00	Creamer	55.00
Butter Dish, cov	75.00	Goblet	45.00
Celery Vase	80.00	Honey Dish, 3½" d	15.00
Champagne	85.00	Sauce, 4" d	10.00
Cheese Dish, cov	65.00	Spooner	40.00
Compote		Sugar, cov	85.00
Cov, hs, 6" d, deep bowl	80.00	Tumbler, ftd	55.00
Open, ls, 8" d, shallow		Wine	65.00
bowl	45.00		

BLEEDING HEART

Non-flint originally made by King Son & Co., Pittsburgh, PA, c1875, and by U. S. Glass Co. c1898. Also found in milk glass. Goblets are found in six variations. Note: A goblet with a tin lid, containing a condiment (mustard, jelly, or baking powder) was made. It is of inferior quality compared to the original goblet.

	Clear		Clear
Bowl		Dish, cov, 7"	55.00
7¼", oval	30.00	Egg Cup	45.00
8"	35.00	Egg Rack, cov, 3 eggs	350.00
9¼", oval, cov	65.00	Goblet, knob stem	35.00
Butter, cov	75.00	Honey Dish	15.00
Cake Stand		Mug, 3¼"	40.00
9"	60.00	Pickle, 8¾" l, 5" w	30.00
10"	85.00	Pitcher, water, ah	150.00
11"	90.00	Plate	75.00
Dessert slots	125.00	Platter, oval	65.00
Compote		Relish, oval, 5½ x 3⅝"	35.00
Cov, hs, 8"	75.00	Salt, master, ftd	60.00
Cov, hs, 9"	95.00	Salt, oval, flat	20.00
Cov, ls, 7"	60.00	Sauce, flat	15.00
Cov, ls, 7½"	60.00	Spooner	25.00
Cov, ls, 8"	75.00	Sugar, cov	60.00
Open, ls, 8½"	30.00	Tumbler, ftd	80.00
Creamer		Wine	
Applied Handle	60.00	Hexagonal stem	165.00
Molded Handle	30.00	Knob stem	175.00

BLOCK AND FAN (Red Block and Fan, Romeo)

Non-flint made by Richard and Hartley Glass Co., Tarentum, PA, in the late 1880s. Continued by U. S. Glass Co. after 1891.

	Clear	Ruby Stained		Clear	Ruby Stained
Biscuit Jar, cov	65.00	150.00	Ice Tub.	45.00	50.00
Bowl, 4", flat	15.00	—	Orange Bowl.	50.00	—
Butter, cov	50.00	85.00	Pickle Dish	20.00	—
Cake Stand			Pitcher		
9"	35.00	—	Milk.	35.00	—
10"	42.00	—	Water	48.00	125.00
Carafe	50.00	95.00	Plate		
Celery Tray.	30.00	—	6"	15.00	—
Celery Vase	35.00	75.00	10"	18.00	—
Compote, Open, hs,			Relish, rect	25.00	—
8"	40.00	165.00	Rose Bowl	25.00	—
Condiment Set, salt,			Salt & Pepper	30.00	—
pepper & cruet on			Sauce		
tray	75.00	—	Flat, 5"	8.00	—
Creamer			Ftd, 3¾"	12.00	25.00
Individual.	—	35.00	Spooner	25.00	—
Regular.	25.00	45.00	Sugar, cov	50.00	—
Large	30.00	100.00	Sugar Shaker	40.00	—
Small	35.00	75.00	Syrup	75.00	95.00
Cruet, os	35.00	—	Tray, ice cream, rect	75.00	—
Dish, large, rect. . . .	25.00		Tumbler	00.00	40.00
Finger Bowl	55.00	—	Waste Bowl.	30.00	—
Goblet	48.00	120.00	Wine	45.00	80.00

BLOCKED ARCHES (Berkeley)

Made by U. S. Glass Co., Pittsburgh, PA, in 1893. Also found in ruby stained.

	Clear	Frosted		Clear	Frosted
Biscuit Jar, cov	55.00	60.00	Goblet	35.00	38.00
Bowl, berry	20.00	25.00	Pitcher, water	75.00	85.00
Butter, cov	45.00	60.00	Plate, 6"	10.00	20.00
Cake Stand	50.00	55.00	Sugar, cov	35.00	40.00
Creamer.	30.00	35.00	Syrup	40.00	45.00
Cruet, os	60.00	70.00	Tumbler	30.00	35.00
Cup and Saucer . . .	50.00	60.00	Wine	38.00	42.00
Finger Bowl	25.00	30.00			

BOSWORTH (Star Band)

Non-flint made by Indiana Glass Co., Dunkirk, IN, c1907.

	Clear		Clear
Bowl, berry.	12.00	Pitcher, water	30.00
Butter, cov	25.00	Relish.	12.00
Celery Vase, handles.	18.00	Spooner	15.00
Compote, jelly.	15.00	Sugar, cov	30.00
Creamer.	20.00	Tumbler	15.00
Goblet	25.00	Wine	20.00

BOUQUET (Narcissus Spray)

Made by Indiana Glass Co., Dunkirk, IN, c1918. Flowers and leaves are found with cranberry or amethyst flashing. Prices are for clear; flashed pieces would be approximately 20% higher.

	Clear		Clear
Bowl, berry		Butter, cov	40.00
6", individual	12.00	Cake Plate	25.00
8", master	18.00	Creamer.	25.00

	Clear		Clear
Goblet	25.00	Spooner	20.00
Nappy	15.00	Sugar, cov	35.00
Pitcher, water	40.00	Tumbler	15.00
Sauce	5.00	Water Tray	25.00

BOW TIE (American Bow Tie)

Non-flint made by Thompson Glass Co., Uniontown, PA, c1889.

	Clear		Clear
Bowl		Pitcher	
8"	35.00	Milk	85.00
10¼" d, 5" h	65.00	Water	75.00
Butter, cov	65.00	Punch Bowl	100.00
Butter Pat	25.00	Relish, rect	25.00
Cake Stand, large, 9" d	60.00	Salt	
Compote, open		Individual	20.00
hs, 5½"	60.00	Master	45.00
hs, 9¼"	65.00	Salt Shaker	40.00
ls, 6½"	45.00	Sauce, flat	18.00
ls, 8"	55.00	Spooner	35.00
Creamer	45.00	Sugar	
Goblet	65.00	Cov	55.00
Honey Dish, cov	55.00	Open	40.00
Marmalade Jar	65.00	Tumbler	45.00
Orange Bowl, ftd, hs, 10"	75.00		

BRIDAL ROSETTE (Checkerboard)

Made by Westmoreland Glass Co. in the early 1900s. Add 150% for ruby stained values. Reproduced since the 1950s in milk glass and in recent years with pink stain. The Cambridge "Ribbon" pattern, usually marked "Nearcut," is similar.

	Clear		Clear
Bowl, 9", shallow	20.00	Plate	
Butter, cov	40.00	7"	15.00
Celery Tray	20.00	10"	20.00
Celery Vase	30.00	Punch Cup	5.00
Compote, open, ls, 8"	25.00	Salt & Pepper	40.00
Creamer	25.00	Sauce, flat	5.00
Cruet, os	40.00	Spooner	20.00
Cup	8.00	Sugar, cov	35.00
Goblet	28.00	Tumbler	
Honey Dish, cov, sq,		Iced Tea	15.00
pedestal	45.00	Water	18.00
Pitcher		Wine	18.00
Milk	40.00		
Water	35.00		

BRILLIANT, RIVERSIDE'S (Petaled Medallion, Miami)

Non-flint pattern made by Riverside Glass Works, Wellsburg, WV, c1895. Made in clear, ruby stained, and amber stained, and sometimes found with copper wheel engraving. Occasionally found with souvenir engraving.

	Clear	Ruby Stained		Clear	Ruby Stained
Bowl, berry, master	30.00	45.00	Sauce	15.00	25.00
Butter Dish, cov	40.00	100.00	Spooner	25.00	40.00
Celery Vase	35.00	90.00	Sugar, cov	40.00	65.00
Compote, cov, hs	90.00	225.00	Tumbler	20.00	40.00
Creamer	35.00	65.00	Wine	35.00	45.00
Goblet	35.00	65.00			

BRITTANIC

Non-flint made by McKee & Bros. Glass Co. c1902 and by McKee-Jeanette Glass Works c1903. Also made in emerald green in a finger or waste bowl. Also made in amber stain, valued at 80% of ruby stained prices.

	Clear	Ruby Stained		Clear	Ruby Stained
Banana Stand.....	75.00	100.00	Mug, 3¾"........	15.00	25.00
Bowl, berry.......	20.00	30.00	Pitcher, water.....	50.00	100.00
Butter, cov......	40.00	90.00	Rose Bowl.......	20.00	75.00
Cake Stand......	45.00	—	Salt & Pepper....	45.00	85.00
Castor Set, 4 bottles	65.00	175.00	Spooner.........	25.00	45.00
Compote, cov.....	55.00	75.00	Sugar, cov.......	40.00	85.00
Creamer.........	30.00	50.00	Toothpick........	25.00	150.00
Custard Cup......	15.00	—	Tumbler.........	20.00	45.00
Cruet, os........	35.00	150.00	Wine...........	22.00	48.00
Goblet..........	30.00	55.00			
Honey Dish, cov, sq	50.00	—			
Lamp					
7½"..........	65.00	—			
8½"..........	75.00	—			

BROKEN COLUMN (Bamboo Irish Column, Notched Rib, Rattan, Ribbed Fingerprint)

Made in Findlay, OH, c1891, by Columbia Glass Co. c1892; and later by U. S. Glass Co. Notches may be ruby stained. A cobalt blue cup is known. The square covered compote has been reproduced. Some items have been reproduced for the Metropolitan Museum of Art. Some items are reproduced by the Smithsonian Institution with a raised "S I" trademark.

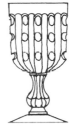

	Clear	Ruby Stained		Clear	Ruby Stained
Banana Stand.....	110.00	—	Open, ls, 5" d, 6"		
Basket, applied han-			h, flared......	65.00	135.00
dle, 12" h, 15" l..	125.00	—	* Creamer........	42.50	125.00
Biscuit Jar.......	85.00	165.00	Cruet, os........	85.00	150.00
Bowl			Decanter........	85.00	—
4", berry.......	15.00	20.00	Finger Bowl......	30.00	—
6", berry.......	20.00	45.00	* Goblet..........	50.00	100.00
* 8"............	35.00	—	Marmalade Jar....	85.00	—
9"............	40.00	—	Pickle Castor, sp		
Bread Plate......	60.00	125.00	frame.........	150.00	450.00
Butter, cov......	85.00	175.00	* Pitcher, water.....	90.00	230.00
Cake Stand			Plate		
9"............	70.00	225.00	4"............	25.00	40.00
10"..........	80.00	245.00	5"............	35.00	—
Carafe, water.....	75.00	150.00	* 7½"..........	40.00	95.00
Celery Tray, oval...	35.00	85.00	Punch Cup.......	15.00	—
Celery Vase......	50.00	135.00	Relish..........	25.00	—
Champagne......	100.00	—	Salt Shaker.......	45.00	65.00
Claret..........	75.00	—	* Sauce, flat.......	15.00	20.00
Compote			* Spooner.........	35.00	85.00
Cov, hs, 5¼" d,			* Sugar, cov.......	70.00	135.00
10¼" h......	90.00	200.00	Sugar Shaker.....	85.00	200.00
Cov, hs, 7" d,			Syrup..........	130.00	400.00
12" h........	85.00	—	Toothpick........	150.00	—
Cov, hs, 10".....	110.00	350.00	Tumbler.........	40.00	50.00
Open, hs, 7" d...	—	150.00	Vegetable, cov....	90.00	—
Open, hs, 8" d...	75.00	175.00	* Wine...........	80.00	125.00

BUCKLE (Early Buckle)

Flint and non-flint pattern. The original maker is unknown. Shards have been found at the sites of the following glass houses: Boston and Sandwich Glass Co., Sandwich, MA; Union Glass Co., Somerville, MA; and Burlington Glass Works, Hamilton, Ontario, Canada. The non-flint production was made by Gillinder and Sons, Philadelphia, PA, in the late 1870s.

	Flint	Non-Flint		Flint	Non-Flint
Bowl			Goblet	40.00	25.00
8"	60.00	50.00	Pickle	40.00	15.00
10"	65.00	50.00	Pitcher, water, ah	500.00	85.00
Butter, cov	65.00	60.00	Salt		
Cake Stand, 9¾"	—	30.00	flat, oval	30.00	15.00
Champagne	60.00	—	footed	20.00	18.00
Compote			Sauce, flat	10.00	8.00
Cov, hs, 6" d	95.00	40.00	Spooner	35.00	27.50
Open, hs, 8½"	40.00	35.00	Sugar, cov	75.00	55.00
Open, ls	40.00	35.00	Tumbler	55.00	30.00
Creamer, ah	110.00	40.00	Wine	75.00	32.00
Egg Cup	38.00	28.00			

BUCKLE WITH STAR (Late Buckle and Star, Orient)

Non-flint made by Bryce, Walker and Co. in 1875 and by U. S. Glass Co. in 1891. Finials are shaped like Maltese crosses.

	Clear		Clear
Bowl		Relish	15.00
6", cov	25.00	Salt, master, ftd	20.00
7", oval	15.00	Sauce	
8", oval	15.00	Flat	8.00
9", oval	15.00	Footed	10.00
10", oval	18.00	Spill holder	55.00
Butter, cov	40.00	Spooner	25.00
Cake Stand, 9"	35.00	Sugar	
Celery Vase	30.00	Cov	45.00
Compote		Open	25.00
Cov, hs, 7"	60.00	Syrup	
Open, hs, 9½"	30.00	Applied handle, pewter or	
Creamer	35.00	Brittania top, man's head	
Cruet	45.00	finial	80.00
Goblet	30.00	Molded handle, plain tin	
Mug	60.00	top	60.00
Mustard, cov	75.00	Tumbler	55.00
Pickle	15.00	Wine	35.00
Pitcher, water, applied			
handle	70.00		

BUDDED IVY

Non-flint, c1870. Contemporary of Stippled Ivy. Pieces have applied handles and ivy leaf finials.

	Clear		Clear
Butter, cov	45.00	Pitcher, water	50.00
Compote		Relish	15.00
Cov, hs	60.00	Salt, ftd	25.00
Cov, ls	45.00	Sauce, ftd	7.50
Open, hs	25.00	Spooner	24.00
Creamer	30.00	Sugar, cov	45.00
Egg Cup	25.00	Syrup	85.00
Goblet	30.00	Wine	35.00

BULLET EMBLEM (Shield in Red, White and Blue)

Made by U. S. Glass Co. c1898 to commemorate the Spanish-American War.

	Clear		Clear
Butter, cov	265.00	Spooner	125.00
Creamer	150.00	Sugar, cov	250.00
Goblet	125.00		

BULL'S EYE

Flint made by the New England Glass Co. in the 1850s. Also found in colors and milk glass, which more than doubles the price.

	Clear		Clear
Bitters Bottle.............	80.00	Lamp.................	100.00
Butter, cov..............	150.00	Mug, 3½", ah...........	110.00
Carafe.................	45.00	Pitcher, water...........	285.00
Castor Bottle............	35.00	Relish, oval............	25.00
Celery Vase............	85.00	Salt	
Champagne............	95.00	Individual.............	40.00
Cologne Bottle..........	85.00	Master, ftd............	100.00
Cordial................	75.00	Spill holder............	85.00
Creamer, ah............	125.00	Spooner..............	40.00
Cruet, os..............	125.00	Sugar, cov............	125.00
Decanter, qt, bar lip.......	120.00	Tumbler..............	85.00
Egg Cup		Water Bottle, tumble up....	125.00
Cov.................	165.00	Whiskey..............	70.00
Open..............	48.00	Wine................	50.00
* Goblet...............	65.00		

BULL'S EYE AND DAISY (Knobby Bull's Eye)

Made by U. S. Glass Co. in 1909. Also made with amethyst, blue, green, and pink stain in eyes.

	Clear	Emerald Green	Ruby Stained
Bowl...........	12.00	16.00	30.00
Butter, cov......	25.00	28.00	90.00
Celery Vase......	20.00	25.00	40.00
Creamer.........	25.00	28.00	50.00
Decanter........	—	110.00	—
Goblet..........	25.00	28.00	50.00
Pitcher, water.....	35.00	40.00	95.00
Salt Shaker.......	20.00	20.00	35.00
Sauce..........	7.50	10.00	20.00
Spooner........	20.00	25.00	40.00
Sugar...........	22.00	30.00	45.00
Tumbler.........	15.00	18.00	35.00
Wine..........	20.00	25.00	40.00

BULL'S EYE WITH DIAMOND POINT (Owl, Union)

Flint made by New England Glass Co. c1869.

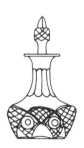

	Clear		Clear
Butter, cov.............	250.00	Salt, master, cov.........	100.00
Celery Vase............	150.00	Sauce...............	20.00
Champagne............	145.00	Spill................	75.00
Cologne Bottle, os.......	90.00	Spooner..............	125.00
Creamer...............	200.00	Sugar, cov............	175.00
Cruet, os..............	225.00	Syrup...............	175.00
Decanter, qt, os..........	200.00	Tumbler..............	145.00
Egg Cup..............	90.00	Tumble-Up............	165.00
Goblet...............	120.00	Whiskey..............	150.00
Honey Dish, flat.........	25.00	Wine................	135.00
Lamp, finger, ah........	165.00		
Pitcher, water, 10¼", tankard.............	275.00		

BULL'S EYE WITH FLEUR-DE-LIS (Bull's Eye and Princess Feather, Bull's Eye with Fleur-de-Lis, Bull's Eye with Princess Feather, Prince's Feather, Princess Feather)

Flint attributed to Union Glass Co., Somerville, MA, c1850. Shards have been found at Boston and Sandwich Glass Co., Sandwich, MA.

	Clear		Clear
Ale Glass	250.00	Goblet	85.00
Bar Bottle, qt	110.00	Honey Dish	20.00
Bowl, fruit	85.00	Lamp, marble base	175.00
Butter, cov	175.00	Lemonade Glass	110.00
Carafe	85.00	Mug, ah	100.00
Celery Vase	95.00	Pitcher, water, ah	400.00
Compote, open		Salt, master	55.00
hs	150.00	Sauce, flat	20.00
ls	125.00	Spooner	50.00
Creamer	250.00	Sugar, cov	115.00
Egg Cup	50.00	Tumbler	100.00
Decanter, bar lip		Whiskey	95.00
1 pint	110.00	Wine	75.00
1 quart	110.00		

BUTTERFLY AND FAN (Bird in Ring, Fan, Grace, Japanese)

Non-flint made by George Duncan & Sons, Pittsburgh, PA, c1880 and by Richards and Hartley Glass Co., Pittsburgh, PA, c1888.

	Clear		Clear
Bowl	30.00	Creamer, ftd	45.00
Bread Plate	50.00	Goblet	50.00
Butter, cov		Marmalade Jar	75.00
Flat	100.00	Pickle Jar, SP frame and	
Footed	75.00	cov	80.00
Celery Vase	75.00	Pitcher, water	115.00
Compote		Sauce, ftd	15.00
Cov, hs, 8" d	95.00	Spooner	30.00
Cov, hs, 7" d	95.00	Sugar cov, ftd	50.00
Open, hs	30.00		

BUTTON ARCHES (Scalloped Diamond, Scalloped Daisy-Red Top)

Non-flint made by Duncan and Miller Glass Co. c1898. Some pieces have frosted band. Some pieces, known as "Koral," usually souvenir type, are also seen in clambroth, trimmed in gold. The toothpick holder comes in both a smooth scallop and beaded scallop variety. They have the same value. In the early 1970s souvenir ruby stained pieces, including a goblet and table set, were reproduced by Westlake Ruby Glass Works, Columbus, OH. A few items documented in amethyst, including small mug. Scarce in other colors.

	Clambroth	Clear	Ruby Stained
Bowl, 8"	—	20.00	50.00
* Butter, cov	—	50.00	100.00
Cake Stand, 9"	—	35.00	180.00
Celery Vase	—	30.00	75.00
Compote, jelly	—	48.00	50.00
* Creamer	25.00	20.00	45.00
Cruet, os	—	55.00	175.00
Custard Cup	—	15.00	25.00
* Goblet	40.00	25.00	40.00
Mug	30.00	25.00	30.00
Mustard, cov, underplate	—	—	100.00
Pitcher			
Milk	—	35.00	100.00
Water, tankard	—	75.00	125.00
Plate, 7"	—	10.00	25.00
Punch Cup	—	15.00	25.00
Salt, individual	—	15.00	—
Salt Shaker	—	15.00	30.00
Sauce, flat	—	8.00	22.00
* Spooner	—	25.00	40.00
* Sugar, cov	—	35.00	75.00

	Clambroth	Clear	Ruby Stained
Syrup	—	65.00	175.00
* Toothpick	30.00	20.00	35.00
Tumbler	20.00	25.00	35.00
Wine	25.00	15.00	35.00

BUTTON BAND (Umbilicated Hobnail, Wyandotte)

Non-flint made by Ripley and Co. in the 1880s and by U. S. Glass Co. in the 1890s. Can often be found engraved, priced the same.

	Clear		Clear
Bowl, 10"	30.00	Goblet	40.00
Butter, cov	45.00	Pitcher	
Cake Stand, 10"	70.00	Milk.	40.00
Castor Set, 5 bottles in glass		Water, tankard	50.00
stand	135.00	Spooner	28.00
Compote		Sugar, cov	35.00
Cov, hs, 9"	120.00	Tray, water	40.00
Open, ls	65.00	Tumbler	25.00
Cordial.	35.00	Wine	35.00
Creamer.	30.00		

BUTTRESSED SUNBURST

Non-flint made by Tarentum Glass Co., Tarentum, PA, 1909–11.

	Clear		Clear
Bowl.	20.00	Pitcher, water	50.00
Butter, cov	40.00	Plate, 9" d	25.00
Celery	25.00	Sauce, flat	8.00
Creamer.	25.00	Spooner	20.00
Cruet	35.00	Sugar, cov	35.00
Goblet	25.00	Wine	20.00

CABBAGE ROSE

Non-flint made by Central Glass Co., Wheeling, WV, c1870. Reproduced in clear and colors by Mosser Glass Co., Cambridge, OH, during the early 1960s.

	Clear		Clear
Basket, handled, 12"	125.00	Cov, ls, 7½"	100.00
Bitters Bottle, 6½" h	125.00	Cov, ls, 8½"	110.00
Bowl, oval		Open, hs, 7½"	75.00
7½"	32.50	Open, hs, 9½"	100.00
8½"	38.00	Creamer, 5½", ah	55.00
9½"	40.00	Egg Cup.	45.00
Bowl, round		* Goblet	42.50
6"	25.00	Mug	60.00
7½", cov	65.00	Pickle Dish	35.00
7½", open	35.00	Pitcher	
Butter, cov	60.00	Milk.	150.00
Cake Stand		Water	125.00
11"	40.00	Relish, 8½" l, 5" w, rose-filled	
12½"	50.00	horn of plenty center	38.00
Celery Vase	48.00	Salt, master, ftd.	25.00
Champagne	50.00	* Sauce, 4"	10.00
Compote		Spooner	25.00
Cov, hs, 7½"	110.00	Sugar, cov	55.00
Cov, hs, 8½"	120.00	Tumbler	40.00
Cov, ls, 6"	95.00	Wine	45.00

CABLE (Cable with Ring)

Flint, c1860. Made by Boston and Sandwich Glass Co. to commemorate the laying of the Atlantic Cable. Also found with amber stained panels and in opaque colors (rare).

	Clear		Clear
Bowl		Honey Dish	15.00
8", ftd	45.00	Lamp, 8¾"	
9"	70.00	Glass Base	135.00
Butter, cov	100.00	Marble Base	100.00
Cake Stand, 9"	100.00	Miniature Lamp, Cable with	
Celery Vase	70.00	Ring	500.00
Champagne	250.00	Pitcher, water, rare	500.00
Compote, open		Plate, 6"	75.00
hs, 5½"	65.00	Salt, individual, flat	35.00
ls, 7"	50.00	Salt, master	
ls, 9"	55.00	Cov.	95.00
ls, 11"	75.00	Ftd	45.00
Creamer.	200.00	Sauce, flat	15.00
Decanter, qt, ground stopper	295.00	Spooner	40.00
Egg Cup		Sugar, cov	120.00
Cov.	225.00	Syrup	225.00
Open	60.00	Tumbler, ftd	200.00
Goblet	70.00	Wine	175.00

CACTUS

Non-flint made by Indiana Tumbler and Goblet Co. c1895. Made in clear and chocolate. Pattern made in opalescent vaseline and aqua by Fenton Art Glass in 1950.

	Clear		Clear
Bowl		Pitcher, water	175.00
7¼" d	50.00	Plate, 7½"	80.00
8¼"	70.00	Sauce	
Butter, cov	125.00	Flat, 5¼"	32.50
Cake Stand	165.00	Footed	45.00
Celery Vase	80.00	Spooner	50.00
Compote, cov, hs, 8¼"	125.00	Sugar, cov	80.00
Creamer, cov	80.00	Syrup	65.00
Cruet, os	100.00	* Toothpick	50.00
Mug	50.00	Tumbler	45.00
Nappy	50.00	Vase, 6"	60.00

CADMUS

Non-flint made by Beaumont Glass Co., Grafton, WV, in the mid 1880s.

	Clear		Clear
Bowl.	15.00	Goblet	20.00
Butter, cov	35.00	Sauce	8.00
Compote, open		Spooner.	15.00
High std	25.00	Sugar, cov	25.00
Jelly	20.00	Tumbler	20.00
Creamer.	25.00	Wine	18.00

CANADIAN

Non-flint possibly made by Burlington Glass Works, Hamilton, Ontario, Canada, c1870.

	Clear		Clear
Bowl, 7" d, 4½" h, ftd	65.00	Butter, cov	85.00
Bread Plate, 10"	45.00	Cake Stand, 9¼"	85.00

	Clear			Clear
Celery Vase	65.00	Pitcher		
Compote		Milk		90.00
Cov, hs, 6".	90.00	Water		125.00
Cov, hs, 7".	100.00	Plate, 6", handles		30.00
Cov, hs, 8".	110.00	Sauce		
Cov, ls, 6"	50.00	Flat		15.00
Cov, ls, 8"	75.00	Footed		20.00
Open, ls, 7"	35.00	Spooner		45.00
Creamer	65.00	Sugar, cov		90.00
Goblet	45.00	Wine		45.00
Mug, small	45.00			

CANDLEWICK (Cole, Banded Raindrop)

Non-flint, unknown maker, c1880.

	Clear	Amber	Milk
Bowls	15.00	18.00	18.00
Butter, cov	35.00	45.00	45.00
Cake Stand	35.00	40.00	40.00
Celery	25.00	35.00	35.00
Compote			
Cov	45.00	60.00	60.00
Open	20.00	35.00	35.00
Creamer	20.00	30.00	30.00
Cup and Saucer	25.00	30.00	30.00
Goblet	20.00	25.00	24.00
Plate	10.00	15.00	15.00
Relish, sq	20.00	25.00	25.00
Salt & Pepper			
Shaker, pr	30.00	40.00	40.00
Sauce			
Flat	5.00	10.00	10.00
Footed	10.00	15.00	15.00

CANE (Cane Insert, Hobnailed Diamond and Star)

Non-flint made by Gillinder and Sons Glass Co., Philadelphia, PA, and by McKee Bros. Glass Co., c1885. Goblets and toddy plates with inverted "buttons" are known.

	Amber	Apple Green	Blue	Clear	Vaseline
Bowl, 9½", oval	15.00	—	—	—	—
Butter, cov	45.00	60.00	75.00	40.00	60.00
Celery Vase	38.00	40.00	50.00	32.50	40.00
Compote, open, ls, 5¾".	28.00	30.00	35.00	25.00	35.00
Cordial	—	—	—	25.00	—
Creamer	35.00	40.00	50.00	25.00	30.00
Finger Bowl	20.00	30.00	35.00	15.00	30.00
Goblet	25.00	40.00	35.00	20.00	40.00
Honey Dish	—	—	—	15.00	—
Match Holder, kettle.	18.00	—	35.00	30.00	35.00
Pickle	25.00	20.00	25.00	15.00	20.00
Pitcher, milk	60.00	55.00	65.00	40.00	55.00
Pitcher, water	80.00	85.00	80.00	48.00	85.00
Plate, toddy, 4½".	20.00	25.00	30.00	16.50	20.00
Relish	25.00	26.00	25.00	15.00	20.00
Salt & Pepper	60.00	50.00	80.00	30.00	70.00
Sauce, flat	—	10.00	—	7.00	—
Slipper	30.00	—	25.00	15.00	30.00
Spooner	42.00	35.00	30.00	20.00	30.00
Sugar, cov	45.00	45.00	45.00	25.00	45.00
Tray, water	35.00	40.00	50.00	30.00	45.00
Tumbler	24.00	30.00	35.00	20.00	25.00
Waste Bowl, 7½".	32.50	30.00	35.00	20.00	30.00
Wine	35.00	40.00	35.00	20.00	35.00

CAPE COD

Non-flint attributed to Boston and Sandwich Glass Co., Sandwich, MA, c1870.

	Clear		Clear
Bowl, 6", handled	30.00	Marmalade Jar, cov	85.00
Bread Plate	45.00	Pitcher	
Butter, cov	50.00	Milk.	65.00
Celery Vase	45.00	Water	75.00
Compote		Plate	
Cov, hs, 6" d	50.00	5", handles	30.00
Cov, hs, 8".	100.00	10"	45.00
Cov, hs, 12".	175.00	Platter, open handles.	45.00
Cov, ls, 6"	50.00	Sauce, ftd	12.50
Open, hs, 7"	50.00	Spooner	30.00
Creamer.	35.00	Sugar, cov	35.00
Decanter	160.00	Wine	35.00
Goblet	45.00		

CARDINAL (Blue Jay, Cardinal Bird)

Non-flint attributed to Ohio Flint Glass Co., Lancaster, OH, c1875. Shards have been found at Burlington Glass Works, Hamilton, Ontario, Canada. There were two butter dishes made, one in the regular pattern and one with three birds in the base— labeled in script Red Bird (cardinal), Pewit, and Titmouse. The latter is less common. Summit Art Glass Co., OH, reproduced the goblet in clear, blue, and green.

	Clear		Clear
Bowl, berry	65.00	Pitcher, water	150.00
Butter, cov		Sauce	
Regular.	65.00	Flat, 4"	10.00
Three birds in base	120.00	Footed, 4½" or 5½"	15.00
Cake Stand	75.00	Spooner	38.00
Creamer.	40.00	Sugar, cov	60.00
* Goblet	35.00		
Honey Dish, 3½"			
Cov.	45.00		
Open	20.00		

CAROLINA (Inverness, Mayflower)

Made by Bryce Bros., Pittsburgh, PA, c1890 and later by U. S. Glass Co., as part of the States series, c1903. Ruby stained pieces often are souvenir marked. Some clear pieces found with gilt or purple stain.

	Clear	Ruby Stained		Clear	Ruby Stained
Bowl, berry	15.00	—	Plate, 7½".	10.00	—
Butter, cov	35.00	—	Relish.	10.00	—
Cake Stand	35.00	—	Salt Shaker.	15.00	35.00
Compote			Sauce		
Open, hs, 8"	38.50	—	Flat.	8.00	—
Open, hs, 9½" . . .	20.00	—	Footed	10.00	—
Open, jelly.	10.00	—	Spooner	20.00	—
Creamer.	20.00	—	Sugar, cov	25.00	—
Goblet	25.00	45.00	Tumbler	10.00	—
Mug	20.00	35.00	Wine	20.00	35.00
Pitcher, milk	45.00	—			

CATHEDRAL (Orion, Waffle and Fine Cut)

Non-flint pattern made by Bryce Bros. Pittsburgh, PA, in the 1880s and by U. S. Glass Co. in 1891. Also found in ruby stained (add 50%).

	Amber	Amethyst	Blue	Clear	Vaseline
Bowl, berry, 8".	40.00	60.00	50.00	45.00	45.00
Butter, cov	60.00	110.00	40.00	45.00	60.00

	Amber	Amethyst	Blue	Clear	Vaseline
Cake Stand	50.00	75.00	65.00	40.00	65.00
Celery Vase	35.00	60.00	40.00	30.00	40.00
Compote					
Cov, hs, 8"	80.00	125.00	100.00	70.00	90.00
Open, hs, 9½" . . .	50.00	85.00	65.00	55.00	—
Open, ls, 7"	45.00	80.00	35.00	25.00	50.00
Open, jelly	—	—	—	25.00	—
Creamer					
Flat, sq	50.00	85.00	—	35.00	50.00
Tall	45.00	80.00	50.00	30.00	45.00
Cruet, os	80.00	—	—	45.00	—
Goblet	50.00	70.00	50.00	40.00	60.00
Lamp, 12¾" h	—	—	185.00	—	—
Pitcher, water	75.00	110.00	75.00	60.00	100.00
Relish, fish shape . .	40.00	50.00	50.00	—	45.00
Salt, boat shape . . .	20.00	30.00	25.00	15.00	25.00
Sauce					
Flat	15.00	30.00	20.00	15.00	20.00
Footed	15.00	35.00	20.00	15.00	20.00
Spooner	40.00	65.00	50.00	35.00	45.00
Sugar, cov	70.00	100.00	60.00	50.00	60.00
Tumbler	40.00	40.00	35.00	25.00	40.00
Wine	40.00	60.00	55.00	30.00	50.00

CHAIN

Non-flint, unknown maker, c1880.

	Clear		Clear
Butter, cov	35.00	Sauce, flat	8.00
Celery Vase	35.00	Spooner	25.00
Compote, cov	45.00	Sugar, cov	35.00
Creamer	20.00	Wine	20.00
Goblet	25.00		
Plate			
7" d	15.00		
11" d	25.00		

CHAIN AND SHIELD (Shield and Chain)

Non-flint, unknown maker, c1875.

	Clear		Clear
Bread Plate, handled	30.00	Pitcher, water	50.00
Butter, cov	45.00	Sauce, flat	10.00
Cordial	30.00	Spooner	20.00
Creamer	30.00	Sugar, cov	40.00
Goblet	30.00	Wine	35.00

CHAIN WITH STAR

Non-flint made by Bryce Bros., Pittsburgh, PA, c1882, and by U. S. Glass Co., c1891. Shards have been found at Burlington Glass Works, Hamilton, Ontario, Canada.

	Clear		Clear
Bowl, 9½"	30.00	Goblet	25.00
Bread Plate, 11", handles . .	30.00	Pickle, oval	10.00
Butter, cov	35.00	Pitcher, water	55.00
Cake Stand		Plate, 7"	25.00
8¾"	30.00	Relish	10.00
10½"	35.00	Salt Shaker	25.00
Celery Vase	25.00	Sauce, flat	10.00
Compote		Spooner	24.00
Cov, hs	50.00	Sugar, cov	35.00
Open, hs	30.00	Syrup	45.00
Creamer	25.00	Wine	25.00

CHAMPION (Fans with Cross Bars, Seagirt)

Made by McKee & Bros. Glass Co., Pittsburgh, PA, 1894–1917. Made in clear, amber, and ruby stained with limited production in emerald green. Pieces are often found with gold trim.

	Amber Stained	Clear	Ruby Stained
Bowl, sq or round			
Berry, master....	55.00	—	65.00
Berry, individual..	—	—	20.00
Butter, cov	100.00	45.00	100.00
Cake Stand	100.00	35.00	90.00
Celery Vase	—	—	100.00
Compote			
Cov..........	—	55.00	—
Open, fluted top..	150.00	40.00	225.00
Creamer........	—	25.00	60.00
Cruet, os	150.00	30.00	195.00
Cup	—	—	25.00
Goblet	65.00	25.00	65.00
Ice Bucket	125.00	40.00	—
Marmalade Jar	—	25.00	—
Pickle Dish, 8"....	—	15.00	—
Pitcher, water	150.00	70.00	175.00
Plate, 8" or 10"....	—	25.00	—
Rose Bowl	—	25.00	—
Salt Dip	—	10.00	65.00
Salt Shaker......	35.00	15.00	35.00
Spooner........	40.00	20.00	45.00
Sugar, cov	75.00	40.00	85.00
Syrup..........	150.00	75.00	—
Toothpick........	65.00	20.00	70.00
Tray, water	—	45.00	—
Tumbler	40.00	15.00	45.00
Wine	—	20.00	—

CHANDELIER (Crown Jewel)

Non-flint made by O'Hara Glass Co., Pittsburgh, PA, c1880 and continued by U. S. Glass Co. Also attributed to Canadian manufacturer. Sauce bowls made in amber ($35.00).

	Etched	Plain		Etched	Plain
Banana Stand....	—	100.00	Pitcher, water	125.00	115.00
Bowl, 8" d, 3¼" h ..	35.00	37.50	Salt, master	—	30.00
Butter, cov	85.00	65.00	Salt & Pepper.....	75.00	65.00
Cake Stand, 10" ...	85.00	65.00	Sauce, flat	—	15.00
Celery Vase	40.00	40.00	Sponge Dish......	—	30.00
Compote			Spooner.........	30.00	35.00
Cov, hs........	80.00	75.00	Sugar, cov	75.00	85.00
Open, hs, 8"	70.00	68.00	Sugar Shaker.....	125.00	110.00
Open, hs, 9½"...	70.00	68.00	Tray, water	70.00	50.00
Creamer.........	60.00	45.00	Tumbler	45.00	35.00
Finger Bowl	40.00	30.00	Violet Bowl	—	40.00
Goblet	60.00	65.00			
Inkwell, dated hard					
Rubber top	—	85.00			

CHERRY

Non-flint pattern made by Bakewell, Pears and Co., Pittsburgh, PA, c1870. This design was patented by William M. Kirchner on April 5, 1870. Made in clear and milk glass.

	Clear		Clear
Butter Dish, cov	65.00	Goblet	35.00
Celery Vase	40.00	Sauce	15.00
Champagne	35.00	Spooner...............	35.00
Compote, cov, hs, 8" d.....	75.00	Sugar, cov	50.00
Creamer, ah	45.00	Wine	30.00

CHERRY THUMBPRINT (Cherry and Cable, Paneled Cherry)

Non-flint pattern made by Northwood Glass Co. c1907. Some pieces are decorated with colored cherries and gilt cable. Some items have been reproduced.

	Clear	Decorated		Clear	Decorated
Bowl, berry	15.00	30.00	Sauce, ftd	15.00	20.00
Butter, cov	45.00	95.00	Spooner	35.00	50.00
Creamer	35.00	60.00	Sugar, cov	65.00	85.00
Cup, pedestal	15.00	30.00	Tumbler	30.00	45.00
Pitcher, water	80.00	110.00			

CLASSIC

Clear and frosted non-flint produced by Gillinder and Sons, Philadelphia, PA, c1882. Pieces with log feet instead of a flat or collared base are worth more.

	Clear		Clear
Bowl, 7", oov, log foot	145.00	Pitcher, water	
Butter, cov, log feet	185.00	Collared	200.00
Celery Vase		Log feet	250.00
Collared	115.00	Plate	
Log feet	125.00	Jas G. Blaine	185.00
Compote		Pres. Cleveland	180.00
Cov, 6½", collared	150.00	Thomas H. Hendricks	170.00
Cov, 6½", log feet	250.00	John A. Logan	225.00
Cov, 7½"d, log feet	225.00	Warrior	165.00
Cov, 8½", collared	175.00	Sauce	
Cov, 12½", collared	325.00	Flat	25.00
Open, 7¾", log feet	100.00	Log feet	30.00
Creamer		Spooner	
Collared	100.00	Collared	95.00
Log feet	150.00	Log feet	125.00
Creamer	125.00	Sugar, cov	
Goblet	250.00	Collared	150.00
Marmalade Jar, cov	350.00	Log feet	185.00
Pitcher, milk, log feet	450.00	Sweetmeat Jar	175.00

CLASSIC MEDALLION (Cameo #1)

A pattern of 1870–80, unknown maker.

	Clear		Clear
Bowl		Creamer	35.00
6¾", ftd	38.00	Pitcher, water	80.00
8", straight sides	30.00	Sauce, ftd	15.00
Butter, cov	40.00	Spooner	25.00
Celery Vase	30.00	Sugar, cov	40.00
Compote			
Cov, hs	50.00		
Open, 7"d, 3¾"h	30.00		

CLEAR DIAGONAL BAND (California State)

Non-flint, c1880. Shards have been found at Burlington Glass Works, Hamilton, Ontario, Canada. Also has been found in light amber.

	Clear		Clear
Bowl, Cov	30.00	Compote	
Bread Plate, Eureka	40.00	Cov, hs	45.00
Butter, cov	40.00	Cov, ls	30.00
Cake Stand	40.00	Creamer	25.00
Celery Vase	25.00	Dish, oval	10.00

	Clear		Clear
Goblet	15.00	Salt & Pepper	30.00
Marmalade Jar	35.00	Sauce, flat	5.00
Pitcher, water	40.00	Spooner	15.00
Plate	15.00	Sugar, cov	30.00
Relish, oval	10.00	Wine	20.00

CLEAR RIBBON

Made by George Duncan and Sons, Pittsburgh, PA, No. 150, c1878.

	Clear		Clear
Bread Plate, motto, GUT-DODB, ftd	40.00	Dish, cov, oblong	
		6"	25.00
Butter, cov	50.00	8"	30.00
Cake Stand, 9"	35.00	Goblet, fancy foot	35.00
Celery Vase	20.00	Pickle	15.00
Compote		Pitcher, water	60.00
Cov, hs	65.00	Sauce, ftd	10.00
Open, ls	25.00	Spooner	25.00
Creamer	30.00	Sugar, cov	40.00

CLEMATIS (Fuchsia)

Non-flint made in the late 1870s.

	Clear		Clear
Butter, cov	40.00	Sauce, flat	10.00
Creamer	35.00	Spooner	25.00
Goblet	30.00	Sugar, cov	45.00
Lamp, 12", iron base	50.00		

COIN—COLUMBIAN (Spanish Coin)

Non-flint, c1890. Prices listed for clear; frosted 50% higher.

	Clear		Clear
Butter, cov	125.00	Salt & Pepper Shakers, pr	95.00
Cake Stand	400.00	Sauce	12.00
Celery	75.00	Spooner	45.00
Compote		Sugar	
Cov, 8"	75.00	Cov	60.00
Open, 7"	60.00	Open	35.00
Creamer	65.00	Syrup, gold coins	225.00
Cruet	65.00	* Toothpick	25.00
* Goblet	55.00	Tray, water	125.00
Lamp, oil 9½"	125.00	* Tumbler	25.00
Pitcher		Wine	70.00
Milk, gilt	175.00		
Water	75.00		

COLORADO (Lacy Medallion)

Non-flint States pattern made by U. S. Glass Co. in 1898. Made in amethyst stained, ruby stained, and opaque white with enamel floral trim, all of which are scarce. Some pieces found with ornate silver frames or feet. Purists consider these two separate patterns, with the Lacy Medallion restricted to souvenir pieces. Reproductions have been made.

	Blue	Clear	Green
Banana Stand	65.00	35.00	50.00
Bowl			
6"	35.00	25.00	30.00

	Blue	Clear	Green
7½", ftd	40.00	25.00	35.00
8½", ftd	65.00	45.00	60.00
Butter, cov	200.00	60.00	125.00
Cake Stand	70.00	55.00	65.00
Celery Vase	65.00	35.00	75.00
Compote			
Open, ls, 5"	35.00	20.00	30.00
Open, ls, 6"	45.00	20.00	42.00
Open, ls, 9¼"	95.00	35.00	65.00
Creamer			
Individual	45.00	30.00	40.00
Regular	95.00	45.00	70.00
Mug	40.00	20.00	30.00
Nappy	40.00	20.00	35.00
Pitcher			
Milk	250.00	—	100.00
Water	375.00	95.00	185.00
Plate			
6"	50.00	18.00	45.00
8"	65.00	20.00	60.00
Punch Cup	30.00	18.00	25.00
Salt Shaker	65.00	30.00	40.00
Sauce, ruffled	30.00	15.00	25.00
Sherbet	50.00	25.00	45.00
Spooner	65.00	40.00	60.00
Sugar			
Cov, regular	75.00	60.00	70.00
Open, individual	35.00	24.00	30.00
* Toothpick	60.00	30.00	45.00
Tray, calling card	45.00	25.00	35.00
Tumbler	35.00	18.00	30.00
Vase, 12"	85.00	35.00	60.00
Violet Bowl	60.00	—	—
Wine	—	25.00	40.00

COMET

Flint, possibly made by Boston and Sandwich Glass Co. in the early 1850s.

	Clear		Clear
Butter, cov	200.00	Pitcher, water	500.00
Compote, open, ls	140.00	Spooner	95.00
Creamer	175.00	Sugar, cov	175.00
Goblet	135.00	Tumbler	110.00
Mug	135.00	Whiskey	165.00

CONNECTICUT

Non-flint, one of the States patterns made by U. S. Glass Co. c1900. Found in plain and engraved. Two varieties of ruby stained toothpicks ($90.00) have been identified.

	Clear		Clear
Biscuit Jar	25.00	Dish, 8", oblong	20.00
Bowl		Lamp, enamel dec.	85.00
4"	10.00	Lemonade, handled	20.00
8"	15.00	Pitcher, water	40.00
Butter, cov	35.00	Relish	12.00
Cake Stand	40.00	Salt & Pepper	35.00
Celery Tray	20.00	Spooner	25.00
Celery Vase	25.00	Sugar, cov	35.00
Compote		Sugar Shaker	35.00
Cov, hs	40.00	Toothpick	55.00
Open, hs, 7"	25.00	Tumbler, water	18.00
Creamer	28.00	Wine	35.00

CORD AND TASSEL

Non-flint made by LaBelle Glass Co., Bridgeport, OH, and patented by Andrew Baggs in 1872. Also made by Central Glass Co. and other companies.

	Clear		Clear
Bowl, oval.............	20.00	Goblet	35.00
Butter, cov	65.00	Lamp, ah, pedestal	100.00
Cake Stand, 10"	65.00	Mug, ah	65.00
Castor Bottle...........	25.00	Mustard Jar, cov	45.00
Celery Vase	35.00	Pitcher, water, ah	95.00
Compote		Salt & Pepper...........	45.00
Cov, hs, 8"............	100.00	Sauce	10.00
Open, ls	35.00	Spooner..............	35.00
Cordial	45.00	Sugar, cov	65.00
Creamer...............	25.00	Syrup................	125.00
Egg Cup..............	35.00	Tumbler, water	45.00
Dish, oval, vegetable	25.00	Wine	35.00

CORD DRAPERY

Made by National Glass Co., Greentown, IN, 1899–1903. Made by Indiana Glass Co., Dunkirk, IN, after 1907.

	Amber	Blue	Clear	Emerald Green
Bowl, 7½"........	25.00	25.00	20.00	30.00
Butter, cov	85.00	85.00	80.00	175.00
Cake Stand	50.00	55.00	45.00	75.00
Compote				
Open, 6"	45.00	60.00	48.00	85.00
Open, 7".......	75.00	75.00	60.00	95.00
Open, jelly......	—	55.00	45.00	—
Creamer........	65.00	95.00	45.00	85.00
Cruet, os	265.00	100.00	90.00	125.00
Cup	18.00	18.00	15.00	25.00
Goblet	50.00	50.00	55.00	65.00
Jelly, cov	85.00	95.00	65.00	115.00
Pickle, 9¼", oval ...	40.00	—	25.00	—
Pitcher, water	175.00	195.00	65.00	200.00
Plate	35.00	40.00	25.00	40.00
Relish..........	25.00	25.00	22.00	30.00
Sauce, flat	15.00	15.00	10.00	15.00
Spooner........	50.00	60.00	45.00	65.00
Sugar, cov	125.00	95.00	60.00	100.00
Syrup..........	295.00	—	120.00	—
Sweetmeat, cov, 6½" d, 5¼" h	165.00	—	—	—
Toothpick	500.00	500.00	80.00	500.00
Tumbler	45.00	50.00	40.00	65.00
Wine	95.00	110.00	90.00	120.00

CORDOVA

Non-flint made by O'Hara Glass Co., Pittsburgh, PA. It was exhibited for the first time at the Pittsburgh Glass Show, December 16, 1890. Toothpick has been found in ruby stained (valued at $35.00).

	Clear	Emerald Green		Clear	Emerald Green
Bowl, Berry, cov ...	30.00	—	Finger Bowl	16.00	—
Butter, cov, handled	50.00	—	Inkwell, metal lid ...	80.00	—
Cake Stand	45.00	—	Mug, handled	20.00	35.00
Celery Vase	45.00	—	Nappy, handled, 6"d	12.00	—
Cologne Bottle	30.00	—	Pitcher		
Compote			Milk...........	30.00	—
Cov, hs	40.00	—	Water	50.00	—
Open, hs.......	35.00	—	Punch Bowl	90.00	—
Creamer.........	35.00	45.00	Punch Cup	15.00	30.00

	Clear	Emerald Green		Clear	Emerald Green
Salt Shaker	20.00	—	Toothpick	15.00	20.00
Spooner	35.00	45.00	Tumbler	18.00	—
Sugar, cov	40.00	80.00	Vase	12.00	—
Syrup	125.00	40.00			

COTTAGE (Dinner Bell, Fine Cut Band)

Non-flint made by Adams & Co., Pittsburgh, PA, in the late 1870s and by U. S. Glass Co. in the 1890s. Known to have been made in emerald green, amber, light blue, and amethyst. Add 50% for amber, 75% for other colors.

	Clear	Ruby Stained		Clear	Ruby Stained
Banana Stand	55.00	—	Dish, oval, deep	20.00	—
Bowl			Finger Bowl	25.00	—
7 ½, oval	15.00	—	* Goblet	25.00	—
9½, oval	20.00	—	Pitcher		
Butter, cov			Milk	36.00	—
Flat	45.00	—	Water	50.00	—
Footed	45.00	—	Plate		
Cake Stand			5"	10.00	20.00
9"	38.00	—	6"	15.00	—
10"	42.00	—	7"	15.00	—
Celery Vase	35.00	—	8"	15.00	—
Champagne	65.00	75.00	9"	20.00	—
Compote			Relish	10.00	—
Cov, hs 6"	75.00	—	Salt Shaker	35.00	—
Cov, hs 7"	85.00	—	Saucer	15.00	40.00
Cov, hs hs, 8"	90.00	—	Spooner	20.00	—
Cov, hs, 8¼"	80.00	—	Sugar, cov	45.00	—
Open, hs, 8¼"d	65.00	—	Syrup	85.00	—
Jelly	35.00	45.00	Tray, water	35.00	—
Creamer	35.00	50.00	Tumbler	25.00	—
Cruet, os	55.00	—	Waste Bowl	20.00	—
Cup and Saucer	35.00	—	Wine	35.00	—

CROESUS

Made in clear by Riverside Glass Works, Wheeling, WV, in 1897. Produced in amethyst and green by McKee & Bros. Glass in 1899. Some pieces trimmed in gold; prices are for examples with gold in very good condition. Reproduced.

	Amethyst	Clear	Green
Bowl			
4", ftd	60.00	10.00	30.00
6¼", ftd	180.00	65.00	115.00
8", flat	150.00	—	120.00
8", ftd	100.00	25.00	115.00
8", ftd, cov	130.00	35.00	115.00
10", ftd	150.00	—	120.00
* Butter, cov	160.00	85.00	170.00
Cake Stand, 10"	160.00	40.00	140.00
Celery Vase	265.00	65.00	135.00
Compote			
Cov, hs, 5"	110.00	30.00	115.00
Cov, hs, 6"	110.00	30.00	115.00
Cov, hs, 7"	115.00	30.00	125.00
Open, hs, 5"	60.00	20.00	60.00
Open, hs, 6"	65.00	20.00	60.00
Open, hs, 7"	75.00	25.00	75.00
Compote, jelly	200.00	20.00	175.00
Condiment Set (cruet, salt & pepper on small tray)	200.00	175.00	175.00
* Creamer			
Individual	175.00	60.00	100.00
Regular	150.00	55.00	120.00
Cruet, os	300.00	125.00	150.00

	Amethyst	Clear	Green
Pitcher, water	325.00	80.00	200.00
Plate, 8″, ftd	75.00	20.00	65.00
Relish, boat shaped.	70.00	30.00	60.00
Salt & Pepper	115.00	40.00	125.00
Sauce			
Flat.	40.00	15.00	35.00
Footed	45.00	20.00	40.00
Spooner	80.00	60.00	70.00
Sugar, cov	170.00	85.00	150.00
*Toothpick	100.00	25.00	85.00
Tray, condiment . . .	75.00	25.00	30.00
*Tumbler	65.00	20.00	50.00

CRYSTALINA

Made by Hobbs Glass Co., Pittsburgh, PA, in 1880; later carried on by U. S. Glass Co. Made in clear with ruby stained edge on all pieces. Some items also known in emerald green and cobalt blue (add 33%).

	Clear		Clear
Bowl, berry, 8″, square.	20.00	Platter, 19″	30.00
Bread Tray	30.00	Relish, leaf shape	15.00
Butter, cov	50.00	Sauce	
Butter, pats, leaf shape	10.00	Leaf shape, handles.	8.00
Celery Tray, leaf shape	40.00	Square	8.00
Creamer		Spooner	15.00
Individual, small.	15.00	Sugar	
Regular.	20.00	Cov.	30.00
Cup, short handle, 4″		Open, called "Berry	
underplate.	50.00	sugar"	20.00
Pickle, leaf shape	15.00		
Plate			
7″, shape of leaf.	20.00		
10″, round	25.00		

CRYSTAL WEDDING (Collins, Crystal Anniversary)

Non-flint made by Adams Glass Co., Pittsburgh, PA, c1890 and by U. S. Glass Co. in 1891. Also found in frosted, amber stained, and cobalt blue (rare). Heavily reproduced in clear, ruby stained, and milk with enamel trim.

	Clear	Ruby Stained		Clear	Ruby Stained
Banana Stand.	95.00	—	Pickle.	25.00	40.00
Bowl			Pitcher		
4½″, individual			Milk, round	110.00	125.00
berry	15.00	—	Milk, sq	125.00	200.00
6″, sq, cov.	65.00	75.00	Water, round	110.00	210.00
7″, sq, cov.	75.00	85.00	Water, sq.	165.00	225.00
8″, sq, master			Plate, 10″	25.00	40.00
berry	50.00	85.00	Relish.	20.00	40.00
8″, sq, cov.	60.00	95.00	Salt		
Butter, cov	75.00	125.00	Individual.	25.00	40.00
Cake Plate, sq	45.00	85.00	Master	35.00	65.00
Cake Stand, 10″ . . .	65.00	—	Salt Shaker.	65.00	75.00
Celery Vase	45.00	75.00	Sauce	15.00	20.00
Compote			Spooner	30.00	60.00
* Cov, hs, 7 x 13″ . .	100.00	110.00	Sugar, cov	70.00	85.00
Open, hs, 7″, sq. .	60.00	65.00	Syrup	150.00	200.00
Open, ls, 5″, sq . .	50.00	55.00	Tumbler	35.00	45.00
Creamer.	50.00	75.00	Vase		
Cruet	125.00	200.00	Footed, twisted . .	25.00	—
* Goblet	55.00	85.00	Swung	25.00	—
Nappy, handle.	25.00	—	Wine	45.00	70.00

CUPID AND VENUS (Guardian Angel)

Non-flint made by Richards and Hartley Glass Co., Tarentum, PA, in the late 1870s. Also made in vaseline, rare.

	Amber	Clear		Amber	Clear
Bowl			Cruet, os	—	135.00
8", cov, ftd	—	35.00	Goblet	—	75.00
9", oval	—	32.00	Marmalade Jar, cov	—	85.00
Bread Plate	75.00	40.00	Mug		
Butter, cov	—	55.00	Miniature	—	40.00
Cake Plate	—	45.00	Medium, 2½"	—	35.00
Cake Stand	—	60.00	Large, 3½"	—	40.00
Celery Vase	—	40.00	Pitcher		
Champagne	—	90.00	Milk	175.00	75.00
Compote			Water	195.00	65.00
Cov, hs, 8"	—	100.00	Plate, 10", round . . .	75.00	40.00
Cov, ls, 7"	—	90.00	Sauce		
Cov, ls, 9"	—	100.00	Flat	—	10.00
Open, ls, 8½",			Footed, 3½", 4"		
scalloped	135.00	35.00	and 4½"	—	15.00
Open, hs, 9¼" . . .	—	45.00	Spooner	—	35.00
Cordial, 3½"	—	85.00	Sugar, cov	—	65.00
Creamer	—	35.00	Wine, 0¾"	—	86.00

CURRANT

Non-flint made by Campbell, Jones and Co., Pittsburgh, PA, and patented in 1871 by Mary B. Campbell. Variations in stems and bases suggest more than one manufacturer. Researchers have found shards at Boston and Sandwich Glass Co., Sandwich, MA, and Burlington Glass Works, Ontario, Canada.

	Clear		Clear
Bowl, 7", vegetable	18.00	Jam Jar, cov	45.00
Butter, cov	75.00	Pitcher	
Cake Stand		Milk, ah	125.00
9¼"	60.00	Water, ah	95.00
11"	85.00	Plate, oval	
Celery Vase	48.00	5" x 7"	25.00
Compote		6" x 9"	30.00
Cov, hs, 8"	100.00	Relish	15.00
Cov, hs, 9"	135.00	Salt, ftd	30.00
Cov, hs, 12"	195.00	Sauce, ftd, 4"	12.00
Cov, ls, 8"	45.00	Spooner	25.00
Cordial	45.00	Sugar, cov	55.00
Creamer, ah	45.00	Tumbler, ftd	30.00
Egg Cup	25.00	Wine	25.00
Goblet	30.00		

CURRIER AND IVES

Non-flint made by Bellaire Glass Co., Findlay, OH, c1889–98. Known to have been made in colors, but rarely found. A decanter is known in ruby stained.

	Clear		Clear
Bowl, oval, 10", canoe		Plate, 10"	20.00
shaped	30.00	Relish	18.00
Butter, cov	50.00	Salt Shaker	30.00
Cake Stand, 10"	75.00	Sauce, oval	12.00
Compote		Spooner	30.00
Cov, hs, 7½"	95.00	Sugar, cov	45.00
Open, hs, 7½", scalloped	50.00	Syrup	75.00
Creamer	30.00	Tray	
Cup and Saucer	30.00	Water, Balky Mule	65.00
Decanter	35.00	Wine, Balky Mule	50.00
Dish, oval, boat shaped, 8"	25.00	Tumbler	45.00
Goblet, knob stem	30.00	Water Bottle, 12" h, os	55.00
Lamp, 9½", hs	75.00	Wine, 3¼"	18.00
Pitcher			
Milk	65.00		
Water	70.00		

CURTAIN (Sultan)

Clear non-flint made by Bryce Bros., Pittsburgh, PA, in the late 1870s.

	Clear		Clear
Bowl		Cruet, os	45.00
7½".	20.00	Finger Bowl	30.00
8"	25.00	Goblet	30.00
Butter, cov	55.00	Mug	25.00
Cake Stand		Pickle	10.00
8"	40.00	Pitcher, water	75.00
9½"	45.00	Plate, 7", sq	20.00
Castor Set, salt, pepper, and		Salt Shaker	25.00
mustard, stand	115.00	Sauce, 4¾"	8.00
Celery Tray	30.00	Spooner	25.00
Celery Vase	30.00	Sugar, cov	35.00
Compote, open, hs, 10"	45.00	Tray, water	35.00
Creamer	25.00	Tumbler	20.00

CURTAIN TIE BACK

Clear non-flint made by Adams & Co., Pittsburgh, PA, in the mid 1880s.

	Clear		Clear
Bowl, 7½", sq	20.00	Relish	10.00
Bread Plate	35.00	Salt & Pepper, pr	35.00
Butter, cov	40.00	Sauce	
Celery Vase	25.00	Flat	5.00
Compote, cov, hs	40.00	Footed	8.00
Creamer	25.00	Spooner	30.00
Goblet		Sugar, cov	35.00
Fancy base	30.00	Tray, water	30.00
Flat base	20.00	Tumbler	15.00
Pickle	12.00	Wine	20.00
Pitcher, water	45.00		

CUT LOG (Cat's Eye and Block, Ethol)

Non-flint made by Greensburg Glass Co. in 1888, and by Westmoreland Specialty Glass Co., c1896. Also reported in camphor glass, but rare.

	Clear		Clear
Biscuit Jar	95.00	Goblet	45.00
Bowl, 10", deep, ftd,		Mug, large	45.00
scalloped	40.00	Mustard Jar	35.00
Butter, cov	65.00	Olive Dish	20.00
Cake Stand		Pitcher, water, ah	75.00
9"	45.00	Relish	25.00
10"	55.00	Salt & Pepper, pr	60.00
Celery Tray	20.00	Salt, master	85.00
Celery Vase	40.00	Sauce	
Compote		Flat	20.00
Cov, hs, 7¼"	85.00	Footed	25.00
Cov, hs, 12½"	90.00	Spooner	35.00
Cov, jelly, 6¼"	45.00	Sugar	
Open, hs, 8"	55.00	Cov, regular	55.00
Open, hs, 10"	70.00	Cov, individual	30.00
Creamer		Open, individual	20.00
Individual	15.00	Tumbler	45.00
Regular, 5"	40.00	Wine	30.00
Cruet, os	50.00		

DAHLIA

Non-flint attributed to Bryce, Higbee and Co., Pittsburgh, PA, c1885. Shards have been found at Burlington Glass Works, Hamilton, Ontario, and Diamond Flint Glass Co., Montreal, Quebec, Canada.

	Amber	Apple Green	Blue	Clear	Vaseline
Bowl.	30.00	25.00	25.00	18.00	30.00
Bread Plate	55.00	50.00	60.00	45.00	55.00
Butter, cov	80.00	70.00	85.00	40.00	80.00
Cake Plate	60.00	45.00	60.00	24.00	60.00
Cake Stand, 9"	72.50	50.00	50.00	25.00	72.50
Champagne	65.00	85.00	75.00	55.00	75.00
Compote					
Cov, hs, 7".	90.00	85.00	85.00	55.00	80.00
Open, hs, 8"	60.00	45.00	45.00	30.00	60.00
Cordial	55.00	50.00	50.00	35.00	55.00
Creamer	40.00	35.00	35.00	25.00	40.00
Egg Cup					
Double	80.00	65.00	65.00	50.00	80.00
Single	55.00	40.00	40.00	25.00	55.00
Goblet	55.00	85.00	75.00	40.00	65.00
Mug					
Large	55.00	55.00	55.00	35.00	55.00
Small	50.00	45.00	40.00	30.00	50.00
Pickle	35.00	30.00	30.00	20.00	35.00
Pitcher					
Milk	70.00	55.00	55.00	45.00	70.00
Water	100.00	90.00	90.00	55.00	90.00
Plate					
7"	45.00	40.00	40.00	20.00	45.00
9", handles	35.00	45.00	50.00	18.00	50.00
Platter	50.00	45.00	45.00	30.00	50.00
Relish, 9½" l	20.00	20.00	20.00	15.00	25.00
Salt, individual, ftd . .	35.00	30.00	30.00	5.00	35.00
Sauce					
Flat	15.00	12.00	15.00	10.00	15.00
Footed	20.00	15.00	15.00	10.00	20.00
Spooner	50.00	45.00	50.00	35.00	60.00
Sugar, cov	75.00	60.00	60.00	40.00	75.00
Syrup	75.00	—	—	55.00	—
Wine	45.00	40.00	45.00	25.00	45.00

DAISIES IN OVAL PANELS (Bull's Eye and Fan)

Non-flint made by U. S. Glass Co., Pittsburgh, PA, c1904. Some pieces gilted.

	Amethyst Stain	Clear	Emerald Green	Pink Stain	Sapphire Blue Stain
Bowl					
5", pinched ends	—	—	18.00	—	—
8", berry	—	15.00	20.00	—	30.00
Butter, cov	—	45.00	65.00	—	—
Cake Stand	—	25.00	—	—	—
Creamer					
Individual	—	10.00	—	—	—
Regular	—	25.00	30.00	—	35.00
Custard Cup	—	10.00	—	—	—
Goblet	25.00	22.50	45.00	25.00	45.00
Lemonade Mug, 5"	—	20.00	—	—	—
Pitcher					
Lemonade, ftd . . .	—	55.00	—	—	—
Water, tankard . . .	55.00	40.00	100.00	50.00	100.00
Relish	20.00	15.00	35.00	20.00	35.00
Sauce	25.00	10.00	20.00	25.00	30.00
Spooner	25.00	21.50	45.00	25.00	45.00
Sugar, cov	40.00	35.00	60.00	30.00	35.00
Toothpick	—	35.00	40.00	65.00	—
Tumbler	55.00	15.00	45.00	40.00	35.00
Wine	22.00	20.00	40.00	40.00	25.00

DAISY AND BUTTON

Non-flint made in the 1880s by several companies in many different forms. In continuous production since inception. Original manufacturers include: Bryce

Brothers, Doyle & Co., Hobbs, Brockunier & Co., George Duncan & Sons, Boston & Sandwich Glass Co., Beatty & Sons, and U.S. Glass Co. Reproductions have existed since the early 1930s in original and new colors. Reproductions, too, have been made by several companies, including L. G. Wright, Imperial Glass Co., Fenton Art Glass Co., and Degenhart Glass Co. Also found in amberina, amber stain, and ruby stained.

	Amber	Apple Green	Blue	Clear	Vaseline
Bowl, triangular. . . .	40.00	45.00	45.00	25.00	65.00
Bread Plate, 13″ . . .	35.00	60.00	35.00	20.00	40.00
Butter, cov					
Round.	70.00	90.00	70.00	65.00	95.00
Square	110.00	115.00	110.00	100.00	120.00
Butter Pat.	30.00	40.00	35.00	25.00	35.00
Canoe					
4″	12.00	24.00	15.00	10.00	24.00
8½″.	30.00	35.00	30.00	25.00	35.00
12″	60.00	35.00	28.00	20.00	40.00
14″	30.00	40.00	35.00	25.00	40.00
* Castor Set					
4 bottle, glass std	90.00	85.00	95.00	65.00	75.00
5 bottle, metal std	105.00	100.00	110.00	100.00	95.00
Celery Vase	48.00	55.00	40.00	30.00	55.00
* Compote					
Cov, hs, 6″.	35.00	50.00	45.00	25.00	50.00
Open, hs, 8″	75.00	65.00	60.00	40.00	65.00
* Creamer.	35.00	40.00	40.00	18.00	35.00
* Cruet, os	100.00	80.00	75.00	45.00	80.00
Egg Cup.	20.00	30.00	25.00	15.00	30.00
Finger Bowl	30.00	50.00	35.00	30.00	42.00
* Goblet	40.00	50.00	40.00	25.00	40.00
* Hat, 2½″.	30.00	35.00	40.00	20.00	40.00
Ice Cream Tray, 14 × 9 × 2″. . . .	75.00	50.00	55.00	35.00	55.00
Ice Tub.	—	35.00	—	—	75.00
Inkwell	40.00	50.00	45.00	30.00	45.00
Parfait	25.00	35.00	30.00	20.00	35.00
Pickle Castor	125.00	90.00	150.00	75.00	150.00
Pitcher, water					
Bulbous, reed handle	125.00	95.00	90.00	75.00	90.00
Tankard	62.00	65.00	62.00	60.00	65.00
* Plate					
5″, leaf shape . . .	20.00	24.00	16.00	12.00	25.00
6″, round.	10.00	22.00	15.00	6.50	24.00
7″, square	24.00	35.00	25.00	15.00	35.00
Punch Bowl, stand	90.00	100.00	95.00	85.00	100.00
* Salt & Pepper.	30.00	40.00	30.00	20.00	35.00
* Sauce, 4″	18.00	25.00	18.00	15.00	25.00
* Slipper					
5″.	45.00	48.00	50.00	45.00	50.00
11½″.	40.00	50.00	30.00	35.00	50.00
* Spooner.	40.00	40.00	45.00	35.00	45.00
* Sugar, cov	45.00	50.00	45.00	35.00	50.00
Syrup.	45.00	50.00	45.00	30.00	45.00
* Toothpick					
Round.	40.00	55.00	25.00	40.00	45.00
Urn	25.00	30.00	25.00	15.00	30.00
* Tray	65.00	65.00	60.00	35.00	60.00
Tumbler	18.00	30.00	35.00	15.00	25.00
Vase, wall pocket . .	125.00	—	—	—	—
* Wine	15.00	25.00	20.00	10.00	45.00

DAISY AND BUTTON WITH CROSSBARS (Daisy and Thumbprint Crossbar, Daisy and Button with Crossbar and Thumbprint Band, Daisy with Crossbar, Mikado)

Non-flint made by Richards and Hartley, Tarentum, PA, c1885. Reissued by U.S. Glass Co. after 1891. Shards have been found at Burlington Glass Works, Hamilton, Ontario, Canada.

	Amber	Blue	Clear	Vaseline
Bowl				
6"	20.00	30.00	15.00	25.00
9"	40.00	40.00	25.00	35.00
Bread Plate	30.00	45.00	25.00	35.00
Butter, cov				
Flat	55.00	55.00	45.00	55.00
Footed	—	75.00	25.00	60.00
Celery Vase	36.00	40.00	30.00	50.00
Compote				
Cov, hs, 8"	55.00	65.00	45.00	55.00
Open, hs, 8"	45.00	50.00	30.00	45.00
Open, ls, 7"	30.00	—	20.00	45.00
Creamer				
Individual	25.00	30.00	18.00	30.00
Regular	42.50	45.00	35.00	40.00
Cruet, os	75.00	85.00	35.00	100.00
Goblet	40.00	40.00	25.00	48.00
Mug, 3" h	15.00	18.00	12.50	20.00
Pitcher				
Milk	65.00	80.00	45.00	90.00
Water	95.00	85.00	65.00	125.00
Salt & Pepper	40.00	50.00	30.00	45.00
Sauce				
Flat	15.00	18.00	10.00	15.00
Footed	18.00	25.00	15.00	24.00
Spooner	35.00	35.00	25.00	35.00
Sugar, cov				
Individual	25.00	35.00	10.00	25.00
Regular	50.00	60.00	25.00	55.00
Syrup	100.00	125.00	65.00	125.00
Toothpick	40.00	40.00	28.00	35.00
Tumbler	20.00	25.00	18.00	25.00
Wine	30.00	35.00	25.00	30.00

DAISY AND BUTTON WITH NARCISSUS
(Daisy and Button with Clear Lily)

Non-flint made by Indiana Glass Co. Dunkirk, IN, c1910. Sometimes found with flowers flashed with cranberry flashing and pieces trimmed in gold. Some pieces have been reproduced.

	Clear	Flashed Color		Clear	Flashed Color
* Bowl, 6" w, 9¼" l,			Salt Shaker	18.00	—
oval, ftd	25.00	—	Sauce		
Butter, cov	50.00	—	Flat	10.00	—
Celery Vase	20.00	—	Footed, 4"	15.00	—
Compote, open, ls . .	35.00	—	Spooner	30.00	—
Creamer	25.00	—	Sugar, cov	38.00	42.50
Decanter, os	40.00	62.50	Tray, water, 10"	30.00	40.00
Goblet	25.00	—	Tray, wine	32.50	42.50
Pitcher, water	50.00	70.00	Tumbler	18.00	20.00
Punch Cup	10.00	18.00	* Wine	22.00	25.00

DAISY AND BUTTON WITH THUMBPRINT PANEL (Daisy and Button with Amber Stripes, Daisy and Button with Thumbprint, Daisy and Button Thumbprint)

Non-flint pattern made by Adams & Co., Pittsburgh, PA, c1886. It was reissued by U. S. Glass, Pittsburgh, PA, c1891. It was made in clear, amber, blue, green, and vaseline and can be found with amber and ruby stain.

	Amber	Blue	Clear	Ruby Stained
Bowl, 6" d	15.00	20.00	10.00	25.00
Butter Dish, cov . . .	15.00	15.00	40.00	70.00
Cake Stand, hs	55.00	60.00	45.00	75.00
Celery Vase, 10" h .	55.00	60.00	35.00	70.00

	Amber	Blue	Clear	Ruby Stained
Compote, open, hs, 8" d.	40.00	45.00	30.00	50.00
Creamer, ah, 5¼" h.	35.00	40.00	25.00	50.00
Goblet	35.00	40.00	25.00	40.00
Sauce, 4½" w, sq, ftd.	15.00	20.00	15.00	25.00
Spooner	35.00	40.00	30.00	55.00
Sugar, cov	45.00	50.00	40.00	65.00
Tumbler	30.00	35.00	15.00	35.00
Wine	30.00	35.00	25.00	45.00

DAISY AND BUTTON WITH V ORNAMENT (Van Dyke)

Made by A. J. Beatty & Co., Steubenville, OH, 1886–87. Reissued by U. S. Glass Co., c1892.

	Amber	Blue	Clear	Vaseline
Bowl				
9"	30.00	40.00	25.00	35.00
10"	30.00	40.00	25.00	35.00
Butter, cov	75.00	95.00	50.00	85.00
Celery Vase	50.00	55.00	30.00	55.00
Creamer	30.00	50.00	30.00	50.00
Finger Bowl	30.00	45.00	25.00	55.00
Goblet	35.00	45.00	25.00	50.00
Ice Cream Tray, 16 x 9 x 2"	75.00	—	—	—
Match Holder	30.00	40.00	35.00	25.00
Mug	20.00	30.00	20.00	35.00
Pickle Castor	120.00	120.00	60.00	100.00
Pitcher, water	65.00	90.00	40.00	60.00
Punch Cup	12.00	20.00	12.50	25.00
Sauce, flat	20.00	20.00	12.00	30.00
Sherbet	15.00	20.00	15.00	10.00
Spooner	40.00	40.00	35.00	45.00
Sugar, cov	50.00	75.00	45.00	65.00
Toothpick	35.00	40.00	30.00	35.00
Tray, water	55.00	65.00	20.00	55.00
Tumbler	25.00	30.00	15.00	35.00
Wine	30.00	35.00	25.00	20.00

DAKOTA (Baby Thumbprint, Thumbprint Band)

Non-flint made by Ripley and Co., Pittsburgh, PA, in the late 1880s and early 1890s. Later reissued by U. S. Glass Co. as one of the States patterns. Prices listed are for etched fern and berry pattern; also found with fern and no berry, and oak leaf etching, and scarcer grape etching. Other etchings known include fish, swan, peacock, bird and insect, bird and flowers, ivy and berry, stag, spider and insect in web, buzzard on dead tree, and crane catching fish. Sometimes ruby stained with or without souvenir markings. There is a four-piece table set available in a "hotel" variant, prices are about 20% more than the regular type.

	Clear Etched	Clear Plain	Ruby Stained
Basket, 10 x 2"	200.00	175.00	200.00
Bottle, 5½"	75.00	65.00	—
Bowl, berry	45.00	35.00	—
Butter, cov	65.00	40.00	125.00
Cake Cover, 8" d.	300.00	200.00	—
Cake Stand			
9½"	60.00	35.00	—
10½"	65.00	45.00	—
Celery Tray	35.00	25.00	—
Celery Vase	40.00	30.00	—
Compote			
Cov, hs, 5"	60.00	50.00	—
Cov, hs, 6"	65.00	50.00	—
Cov, hs, 7"	70.00	55.00	—

	Clear Etched	Clear Plain	Ruby Stained
Cov, hs, 8″	75.00	60.00	—
Cov, hs, 9″	100.00	80.00	—
Cov, hs, 10″	125.00	100.00	—
Open, ls, 5″	40.00	30.00	—
Open, ls, 6″	45.00	35.00	—
Open, ls, 7″	45.00	35.00	—
Open, ls, 8″	50.00	40.00	—
Open, ls, 9″	65.00	55.00	—
Open, ls, 10″	75.00	65.00	—
Condiment Tray . . .	—	75.00	—
Creamer	55.00	30.00	60.00
Cruet	90.00	55.00	135.00
Goblet	35.00	25.00	75.00
Pitcher			
Milk	100.00	80.00	200.00
Tankard	125.00	95.00	225.00
Water	95.00	75.00	190.00
Plate, 10″	85.00	75.00	—
Salt Shaker	65.00	50.00	125.00
Sauce			
Flat, 4″ d	20.00	15.00	25.00
Footed, 5″ d	25.00	15.00	30.00
Spooner	30.00	25.00	65.00
Sugar, cov	65.00	55.00	85.00
Tray, water, 13″ d . .	100.00	75.00	—
Tumbler	35.00	30.00	55.00
Waste Bowl	65.00	50.00	75.00
Wine	30.00	20.00	55.00

DART

Clear non-flint made in OH in the 1880s.

	Clear		Clear
Bowl	10.00	Goblet	28.00
Butter, cov	25.00	Pitcher, water	35.00
Compote		Sauce, ftd	12.50
Cov, hs, 8½″ d, 12½″ h . . .	60.00	Spooner	20.00
Open, jelly	18.00	Sugar, cov	35.00
Creamer	25.00	Tumbler	15.00

DEER AND DOG (Frosted Dog)

Non-flint made by unknown American manufacturer, c1870. Shards have been found at Burlington Glass Works, Hamilton, Ontario, Canada. Pattern identified by frosted dog finial. Found in both etched and non-etched styles, deduct 33% for clear.

	Etched		Etched
Butter, cov	125.00	Mug	40.00
Celery Vase	95.00	Pitcher, water, ah	150.00
Compote, cov, 7″, ls, non-		Sauce, ftd	20.00
etched	150.00	Spooner	60.00
Creamer	75.00	Sugar, cov	125.00
Goblet	65.00	Wine	75.00
Marmalade Jar, cov	125.00		

DEER AND PINE TREE (Deer and Doe)

Non-flint made by Belmont Glass Co. and McKee & Bros. Glass Co. c1886. Souvenir mugs with gilt found in clear and olive green. Also made in canary (vaseline). The goblet has been reproduced since 1938. L. G. Wright Glass, Co., has reproduced the goblet using new molds in clear.

	Amber	Apple Green	Blue	Clear
Bread Plate	100.00	125.00	125.00	75.00
Butter, cov	125.00	425.00	125.00	95.00
Cake Stand	—	—	—	75.00
Celery Vase	—	—	—	75.00
Compote				
Cov, hs, 8", sq . . .	—	—	—	100.00
Open, hs, 7"	—	—	—	45.00
Open, hs, 9"	—	—	—	55.00
Creamer	95.00	85.00	90.00	65.00
Finger Bowl	—	—	—	55.00
* Goblet	—	—	—	55.00
Marmalade Jar	—	—	—	90.00
Mug	40.00	45.00	50.00	40.00
Pickle	—	—	—	30.00
Pitcher				
Milk	—	—	—	90.00
Water	125.00	125.00	125.00	125.00
Platter, 8 x 13"	75.00	—	80.00	60.00
Sauce				
Flat	—	—	—	20.00
Footed	—	—	—	25.00
Spooner	—	—	—	65.00
Sugar, cov	—	—	—	85.00
Tray, water	100.00	—	90.00	60.00

DELAWARE (American Beauty, Four Petal Flower)

Non-flint made by U. S. Glass Co., Pittsburgh, PA, 1899–1909. Also made by Diamond Glass Co., Montreal, Quebec, Canada, c1902. Also found in amethyst (scarce), clear with rose trim, custard, and milk glass. Prices are for pieces with perfect gold trim.

	Clear	Green w/Gold	Rose w/Gold
Banana Bowl	40.00	55.00	65.00
Bowl			
8"	30.00	40.00	50.00
9"	25.00	60.00	75.00
Bottle, os	80.00	150.00	185.00
Bride's Basket, SP			
frame	75.00	115.00	165.00
Butter, cov	50.00	115.00	150.00
Claret Jug, tankard			
shape	110.00	195.00	200.00
Celery Vase, flat . . .	75.00	90.00	95.00
Creamer	45.00	65.00	70.00
Cruet, os	90.00	200.00	250.00
Finger Bowl	25.00	50.00	75.00
Lamp Shade,			
electric	85.00	—	100.00
Pin Tray	30.00	55.00	95.00
Pitcher, water	50.00	150.00	125.00
Pomade Box,			
jeweled	100.00	250.00	350.00
Puff Box, bulbous,			
jeweled	100.00	200.00	315.00
Punch Cup	18.00	30.00	35.00
Sauce, 5½", boat . .	15.00	35.00	30.00
Spooner	45.00	50.00	55.00
Sugar, cov	65.00	85.00	100.00
Toothpick	35.00	125.00	150.00
Tumbler	20.00	40.00	45.00
Vase			
6"	25.00	45.00	70.00
8"	25.00	55.00	75.00
9½"	40.00	80.00	85.00

DEW AND RAINDROP (Dewdrop and Raindrop, Dewdrop and Rain)

Non-flint made by Kokomo Glass Co, Kokomo, IN, c1901. Federal Glass and others made this pattern using a lesser quality glass and without the tiny dewdrops on stems. Prices listed are for the earlier, more brilliant pattern. A ruby stained creamer and water pitcher are documented.

	Clear		Clear
Bowl, 8″	40.00	Sauce, flat, 4″ d	15.00
Butter, cov	65.00	* Sherbet	10.00
* Cordial	45.00	Spooner	35.00
Creamer	35.00	Sugar	
* Goblet	30.00	Cov	35.00
Mug	35.00	Open	25.00
Pitcher, water	65.00	Tumbler	35.00
Salt & Pepper Shakers, pr . .	40.00	* Wine	20.00

DEWDROP IN POINTS

Non-flint made by Brilliant Glass Works, Brilliant, OH, in the late 1870s and by Greensburg Glass Co., Greensburg, PA, after 1889.

	Clear		Clear
Bread Plate	25.00	Pitcher, water	35.00
Butter, cov	40.00	Plate, 12″	20.00
Cake Stand	40.00	Platter, 9 x 11¾″	25.00
Compote		Sauce	
Cov, hs	75.00	Flat	10.00
Open, hs	25.00	Footed	15.00
Open, ls	22.50	Spooner	20.00
Creamer	30.00	Sugar, cov	40.00
Goblet	25.00	Wine	25.00
Pickle	15.00		

DEWDROP WITH STAR (Star and Dewdrop)

Non-flint made by Campbell, Jones and Co., Pittsburgh, PA, in 1877. There was no goblet made in this pattern. This pattern has been reproduced in color.

	Clear		Clear
Bowl		Honey Dish, underplate	75.00
6″	8.00	Lamp, patented 1876	85.00
7″	15.00	Pickle, oval	15.00
9″, ftd	20.00	Pitcher, water, ah	125.00
Bread Plate motto, sheaf of		* Plate	
wheat center	85.00	5″	12.00
Butter, cov, dome lid	50.00	7″	15.00
Cake Stand	40.00	9″	20.00
Celery Vase	40.00	Relish	15.00
Cheese Dish, cov, dome lid .	135.00	* Salt, ftd	20.00
Compote		Sauce	
Cov, hs, dome lid	75.00	Flat, 4″ d	10.00
Cov, ls, 5″	60.00	* Footed, 4½″ d	15.00
Open, hs	35.00	Spooner	35.00
Cordial	35.00	Sugar, cov, domed lid	50.00
Creamer, ah	35.00		

DEWEY (Flower Flange)

Made by Indiana Tumbler and Goblet Co., Greentown, IN, in 1894. Later made by U. S. Glass Co. until 1904. Some experimental colors were made, including a Nile green opaque mug ($75.00). Imperial Glass Co. has reproduced the butter dish, some of which are marked "IG."

	Amber	Chocolate	Clear	Green	Vaseline
Bowl, 8", ftd	65.00	200.00	50.00	65.00	70.00
* Butter, cov	75.00	200.00	45.00	65.00	95.00
Creamer					
Individual, 4" h,					
cov	45.00	85.00	25.00	45.00	55.00
Regular, 5" h	65.00	275.00	35.00	65.00	75.00
Cruet, os	110.00	500.00	75.00	145.00	125.00
Mug	55.00	350.00	35.00	55.00	60.00
Parfait	65.00	150.00	45.00	65.00	75.00
Pitcher, water	90.00	—	55.00	175.00	175.00
Plate, 7½", ftd	35.00	—	30.00	40.00	65.00
Relish.	42.00	—	20.00	42.00	45.00
Salt Shaker.	55.00	400.00	35.00	55.00	65.00
Sauce, flat	25.00	65.00	5.00	25.00	30.00
Spooner	40.00	175.00	25.00	40.00	50.00
Sugar, cov					
Individual.	45.00	100.00	25.00	45.00	65.00
Regular.	50.00	150.00	35.00	55.00	75.00
Tray, serpentine					
Large	55.00	—	35.00	55.00	65.00
Small	45.00	400.00	25.00	45.00	55.00
Tumbler	55.00	—	40.00	45.00	65.00

DIAGONAL BAND (Diagonal Band and Fan)

Made c1875–85, unknown maker. Shards have been found at Burlington Glass Works, Hamilton, Ontario, Canada.

	Amber	Apple Green	Clear
Bread Plate	30.00	35.00	25.00
Butter, cov	60.00	80.00	35.00
Cake Stand	40.00	55.00	30.00
Celery Vase	45.00	50.00	25.00
Compote			
Cov, hs, 7".	65.00	80.00	55.00
Cov, ls, 8"	65.00	70.00	45.00
Open, hs, 7½" . . .	45.00	50.00	20.00
Creamer.	40.00	50.00	30.00
Goblet	30.00	45.00	30.00
Pitcher			
Milk.	50.00	85.00	35.00
Water	65.00	95.00	40.00
Plate, 6"	—	—	15.00
Relish, 6⅞" oval . . .	15.00	20.00	10.00
Sauce			
Flat.	—	—	6.00
Footed	—	15.00	15.00
Spooner	25.00	40.00	20.00
Sugar, cov	40.00	50.00	30.00
Wine	35.00	45.00	20.00

DIAMOND AND SUNBURST (Diamond Sunburst, Plain Sunburst)

Non-flint made by Bryce, Walker and Co, Pittsburgh, PA, c1882. Patented by John Bryce in 1874. Shards have been found at Burlington Glass Works, Hamilton, Ontario, Canada.

	Clear		Clear
Butter, cov	40.00	Creamer.	35.00
Butter Pat.	10.00	Decanter, os	45.00
Cake Stand	35.00	Egg Cup.	25.00
Celery Vase	25.00	Goblet	25.00
Champagne	25.00	Pickle.	10.00
Compote		Pitcher, water	50.00
Cov, hs	50.00	Relish.	10.00
Open, hs.	28.50	Salt, ftd	15.00

	Clear		Clear
Sauce, flat	10.00	Syrup.................	45.00
Spooner..............	20.00	Tumbler	25.00
Sugar		Wine	30.00
Cov................	40.00		
Open	20.00		

DIAMOND POINT (Diamond Point with Ribs, Pineapple, Sawtooth, Stepped Diamond Point)

Flint originally made by Boston and Sandwich Glass Co. c1850 and by the New England Glass Co., East Cambridge, MA, c1860. Many other companies manufactured this pattern throughout the nineteenth century. Rare in color.

	Flint	Non-Flint		Flint	Non-Flint
Ale Glass, 6¼" h...	85.00	—	Egg Cup		
Bowl			Cov...........	75.00	50.00
7", cov	60.00	20.00	Open	40.00	20.00
8", cov	60.00	20.00	Goblet	45.00	35.00
8", open	45.00	15.00	Honey Dish.......	15.00	—
Butter, cov	95.00	50.00	Lemonade	55.00	—
Cake Stand, 14" ...	185.00	—	Mustard, cov......	25.00	—
Candlesticks, pr ...	145.00	—	Pitcher		
Castor Bottle......	25.00	10.00	Pint...........	185.00	—
Celery Vase	75.00	30.00	Quart	275.00	—
Champagne	85.00	35.00	Plate		
Claret...........	90.00	—	6"	30.00	—
Compote			8"	50.00	—
Cov, hs, 8"......	135.00	60.00	Salt, master, cov ...	75.00	—
Open, hs 10½",			Sauce, flat	15.00	—
flared........	100.00	—	Spill Holder.......	45.00	—
Open, hs, 11",			Spooner.........	45.00	25.00
scalloped rim ..	110.00	—	Sugar, cov	65.00	—
Open, ls, 7½" ...	50.00	40.00	Syrup...........	150.00	—
Cordial..........	165.00	—	Tumbler, bar......	65.00	35.00
Creamer, ah	115.00	—	Whiskey, ah	85.00	—
Decanter, qt, os. ...	165.00	—	Wine	75.00	30.00

DIAMOND QUILTED (Quilted Diamond)

Non-flint, c1880. Heavily reproduced.

	Amber	Amethyst	Blue	Clear	Vaseline
Bowl					
6"	10.00	20.00	—	—	—
7"	18.00	—	—	—	25.00
Butter, cov	50.00	100.00	100.00	40.00	75.00
Celery Vase	35.00	60.00	50.00	40.00	40.00
Champagne	—	36.00	—	21.00	38.00
Compote					
Cov, hs, 8"......	140.00	120.00	120.00	45.00	90.00
Cov, ls, 8"	—	—	100.00	—	—
Open, ls, 9"	—	—	—	15.00	35.00
Creamer.........	45.00	40.00	70.00	25.00	55.00
* Goblet	40.00	40.00	40.00	30.00	35.00
Mug............	—	30.00	40.00	—	—
Pitcher, water	75.00	85.00	80.00	50.00	75.00
* Salt					
Individual......	20.00	25.00	20.00	10.00	20.00
Master	35.00	40.00	40.00	20.00	35.00
Sauce					
Flat...........	12.00	—	16.50	8.00	18.00
Footed	16.00	18.00	18.00	12.00	22.00
Spooner.........	35.00	40.00	40.00	30.00	50.00
Sugar, cov	50.00	75.00	55.00	40.00	60.00
Tray............	55.00	70.00	75.00	30.00	65.00
* Tumbler	45.00	40.00	40.00	25.00	32.50
Vase, 9"	—	—	—	48.00	—
* Wine	20.00	40.00	35.00	15.00	20.00

DIAMOND SPEARHEAD

Made by Dugan Glass Co., Indiana, PA, c1900. No cruet reported. A cake stand has been found, but it was not listed in early catalogs. Also made in canary opalescent, prices same as blue opalescent. A cake stand (10″, $65.00), toothpick holder ($75.00), and a carafe ($180.00), are known in canary opalescent.

	Clear	Cobalt Blue Opal	Green Opal	Sapphire Blue Opal	White Opal
Bowl, berry	20.00	—	40.00	40.00	35.00
Butter, cov	40.00	150.00	85.00	75.00	—
Carafe	—	—	180.00	—	—
Celery Vase	20.00	—	45.00	40.00	35.00
Compote					
Cov, hs	—	—	35.00	30.00	32.00
Cov, ls, jelly	—	—	60.00	50.00	—
Creamer	20.00	70.00	35.00	30.00	32.00
Cup and Saucer . . .	—	—	60.00	60.00	—
Goblet	—	—	90.00	90.00	—
Mug	20.00	—	55.00	65.00	—
Pitcher, water	50.00	200.00	195.00	75.00	—
Plate, 10″	—	—	80.00	—	—
Relish	—	—	25.00	20.00	—
Sauce	—	—	15.00	10.00	—
Spooner	20.00	—	50.00	40.00	—
Sugar, cov	30.00	—	50.00	45.00	—
Syrup	—	230.00	195.00	65.00	—
Toothpick	—	125.00	85.00	—	—

DIAMOND THUMBPRINT (Diamond and Concave)

Flint attributed to Boston and Sandwich Glass Co. and other factories in the 1850s. Compotes, sugar bowls, and other pieces are being reproduced for Sandwich Glass Museum by Viking Glass Co., each piece embossed with the "S.M." trademark.

	Clear		Clear
Ale Glass, 6¼″	90.00	* Goblet	350.00
Bitters Bottle, orig pewter		Honey Dish	25.00
pourer, applied lip, po-		Mug, ah	200.00
lished pontil	450.00	Pitcher, ah	
* Butter, cov	200.00	Milk	450.00
Celery Vase, scalloped top . .	185.00	Water	500.00
Champagne	285.00	Sauce, flat	15.00
* Compote, cov, 8″	300.00	* Spooner	85.00
Cordial	325.00	* Sugar, cov	150.00
* Creamer	225.00	Sweetmeat Jar, cov	250.00
Decanter		Tray, rect, 11 × 7″	100.00
Pint, os	175.00	Tumbler, bar	125.00
Quart, os	225.00	Whiskey, ah	300.00
Egg Cup	85.00	* Wine	250.00
Finger Bowl	100.00		

DICKINSON

Flint made by Boston and Sandwich Glass Co., Sandwich, MA, c1860.

	Clear		Clear
Butter, cov	80.00	Goblet	45.00
Creamer, ah	55.00	Sauce	10.00
Compote		Spooner	40.00
Open, hs, 5½″	65.00	Sugar, cov	95.00
Open, ls, 7¼″	55.00		

DOLLY MADISON (Jefferson's #271)

Made by Jefferson Glass Co., Follansbee, WV, c1907. Also found in non-opalescent colors, (25% less).

	Clear	Blue Opal	Green Opal	White Opal
Bowl, berry, 9¼" . . .	35.00	50.00	45.00	35.00
Butter, cov	40.00	120.00	125.00	75.00
Creamer.	35.00	65.00	90.00	80.00
Pitcher, water	45.00	150.00	140.00	125.00
Sauce	18.00	45.00	50.00	45.00
Spooner.	30.00	75.00	85.00	75.00
Sugar, cov	45.00	65.00	100.00	45.00
Tumbler	30.00	40.00	60.00	40.00

DOUBLE DAISY (Rosette Band)

Non-flint pattern whose maker has not been identified, c1893.

	Clear	Ruby Stained		Clear	Ruby Stained
Buttor Dich, oov, daisy finial.	40.00	100.00	Salt, master	25.00	45.00
			Sauce	15.00	30.00
Compote, cov, hs . .	85.00	225.00	Spooner	25.00	50.00
Creamer, ah, 5½" h .	35.00	70.00	Sugar, cov	40.00	85.00
Goblet	40.00	75.00	Tumbler	20.00	40.00
Pitcher, water, tankard, ah	90.00	185.00	Wine	30.00	60.00

DOYLE'S SHELL (Shell #2, Cube and Fan #2, Knight)

Made by Doyle and Co., Pittsburgh, PA, in 1866 and continued by U. S. Glass Co. to c1892.

	Clear	Emerald Green		Clear	Emerald Green
Bowl, berry	15.00	—	Pitcher, water	45.00	—
Butter, cov	45.00	55.00	Pickle dish	15.00	—
Cake Stand	30.00	—	Salt Shaker.	15.00	—
Celery Tray, long, flat	20.00	25.00	Spooner	20.00	25.00
			Sugar, oov	30.00	35.00
Celery Vase	20.00	—	Tray, water	35.00	—
Creamer.	20.00	30.00	Tumbler	10.00	15.00
Goblet	20.00	30.00	Waste Bowl.	15.00	25.00
Mug	15.00	20.00	Wine	20.00	—
Nappies, handled . .	15.00	—			

DRAPERY (Lace)

Non-flint made by Doyle and Co., Pittsburgh, PA, in the 1870s. Reissued by U. S. Glass Co., after 1891. Originally designed and patented by Thomas B. Atterbury, 1870. Shards have been found at Boston and Sandwich Glass Co., Sandwich, MA. Pieces with fine stippling have applied handles; pieces with coarse stippling have pressed handles. Pine cone shaped finials.

	Clear		Clear
Butter, cov	45.00	Pitcher, water, ah	85.00
Compote, ls	55.00	Plate, 6"	30.00
Creamer, ah	30.00	Sauce, flat	10.00
Dish, oval	30.00	Spooner	25.00
Egg Cup.	25.00	Sugar, cov	40.00
Goblet	35.00	Tumbler	30.00

DUNCAN BLOCK (Block, Waffle Variant)

Non-flint pattern made by George Duncan & Sons, Pittsburgh, PA, c1887. The pattern was continuously produced until the merger with U. S. Glass in 1891. It was made in clear and sometimes is found with ruby staining and copper wheel engraving. Prices listed below are for plain clear pieces.

	Clear		Clear
Bowl, crimped rim, 8″ d	25.00	Pitcher, water, tankard	45.00
Butter Dish, cov	45.00	Sauce, ftd, 4″ d	10.00
Celery Tray	25.00	Spooner	25.00
Creamer	25.00	Sugar, cov	35.00
Egg Cup	15.00	Tumbler	15.00
Goblet	20.00	Wine	15.00

EGG IN SAND (Bean, Stippled Oval)

Non-flint, c1885. Has been reported in colors, but rare.

	Clear		Clear
Bread Plate, octagonal	25.00	Salt & Pepper	65.00
Butter, cov	40.00	Sauce	10.00
Compote, cov, jelly	45.00	Spooner, flat rim	30.00
Creamer	30.00	Sugar, cov	35.00
Dish, swan center	40.00	Tray, water	40.00
Goblet	35.00	Tumbler	33.00
Pitcher, water	45.00	Wine	35.00
Relish	15.00		

EGYPTIAN (Parthenon)

Non-flint, made by Adams & Co., Pittsburgh, PA, in 1882.

	Clear		Clear
Bowl, 8½″	50.00	Creamer	50.00
Bread Plate		Goblet	45.00
Cleopatra	65.00	Honey Dish	14.00
* Mormon Temple	300.00	Pickle, oval	20.00
Butter, cov	85.00	Pitcher, water	185.00
Celery Vase	75.00	Plate, 12″, handles,	
Compote		Pyramids	90.00
Cov, hs, 7″, Sphinx base . .	250.00	Relish	20.00
Cov, hs, 8″ d (11″ h),		Sauce, ftd, 4½″	18.50
Sphinx base	275.00	Spooner	40.00
Open, hs, 7½″, Sphinx		Sugar, cov	80.00
base	75.00		

ELECTRIC

Made by U. S. Glass Co. c1891. Colors would be 20% more than the price given. It was made in about forty pieces.

	Clear		Clear
Biscuit Jar, covered	50.00	Goblet	25.00
Bowl, Berry	15.00	Jam Jar	40.00
Butter, covered	45.00	Mug	15.00
Cake Stand	35.00	Pitcher, water	55.00
Compote		Relish	15.00
Cov	45.00	Salt Shaker, single	30.00
Jelly, open	15.00	Spooner	25.00
Creamer		Sugar, covered	40.00
Individual	25.00	Syrup Jug	50.00
Table	30.00	Tray, water	45.00
Tankard	30.00	Tumbler	15.00

EMPRESS

Made by Riverside Glass Works, Wellsburg, WV, c1898. Also found in amethyst (rare). Clear and emerald green pieces trimmed in gold; prices are for pieces with gold in very good condition.

	Clear	Emerald Green		Clear	Emerald Green
Bowl, 8½".......	—	45.00	Punch Cup, ftd	20.00	35.00
Breakfast Set, individual creamer			Salt Shaker.......	30.00	50.00
Sauce, 4½" d	15.00	25.00
and sugar	40.00	85.00	Spooner.........	40.00	70.00
Butter, cov	50.00	100.00	Sugar, cov	45.00	125.00
Celery Vase	55.00	—	Sugar Shaker	55.00	110.00
Creamer.........	40.00	80.00	Syrup...........	60.00	300.00
Cruet..........	50.00	175.00	Toothpick	—	150.00
Oil Lamp, atypical ..	60.00	225.00	Tumbler	32.50	55.00
Pitcher, water	65.00	150.00			

ENGLISH (Diamond with Diamond Point)

Non-flint pattern made by Westmoreland Glass Co., 1896. Made in clear, emerald green, and milk glass.

	Clear		Clear
Butter Dish, cov	35.00	Pitcher, water	40.00
Celery	40.00	Spooner...............	20.00
Compote, cov, hs	60.00	Sugar, cov	35.00
Creamer, 3½" h.........	25.00	Tumbler	20.00
Goblet	30.00		

ESTHER (Tooth and Claw)

Non-flint made by Riverside Glass Works, Wellsburg, WV, c1896. Some green pieces have gold trim. Also found in ruby stained and amber stained with etched or enamel decoration.

	Clear	Green	Ruby Stained
Bowl, 8"	25.00	50.00	60.00
Butter, cov	65.00	100.00	150.00
Cake Stand, 10½"..	60.00	80.00	95.00
Celery Vase	40.00	90.00	85.00
Cheese Dish, cov ..	85.00	135.00	125.00
Compote, jelly, hs ..	30.00	75.00	55.00
Cracker Jar.......	85.00	225.00	200.00
Creamer.........	45.00	70.00	75.00
Cruet, os	45.00	245.00	265.00
Goblet	45.00	95.00	75.00
Jam Jar, cov......	40.00	125.00	75.00
Pitcher, water	65.00	165.00	250.00
Plate, 10"	25.00	60.00	60.00
Relish...........	20.00	25.00	40.00
Salt Shaker.......	20.00	35.00	25.00
Spooner.........	35.00	50.00	60.00
Sugar, cov	55.00	70.00	100.00
Syrup...........	65.00	200.00	175.00
Toothpick	45.00	85.00	100.00
Tumbler	25.00	50.00	55.00
Wine	35.00	55.00	45.00

EUGENIE

Flint pattern made by McKee & Brothers, Pittsburgh, PA, c1859 in clear.

	Clear		Clear
Bowl, cov, 7" d	55.00		
Celery Vase	90.00	Goblet	150.00
Champagne	85.00	Sugar, cov	225.00
Compote, cov, hs, 7" d.....	125.00	Tumbler	45.00
Creamer..............	175.00	Wine	40.00

EUREKA

Flint made by McKee & Bros. Glass Co., Pittsburgh, PA, in the late 1860s. Pieces have applied handles and bud finials. Made in flint and non-flint.

	Clear		Clear
Bowl		Creamer	45.00
6", round	25.00	Egg Cup	30.00
7", oval	30.00	Goblet	30.00
8", oval	35.00	Pitcher, water	95.00
Butter, cov	60.00	Salt, ftd	30.00
Champagne	35.00	Sauce, flat	10.00
Compote		Spooner	40.00
Cov, hs	85.00	Sugar, cov	50.00
Open, hs	50.00	Tumbler, ftd	25.00
Cordial	40.00	Wine	25.00

EVERGLADES (Carnelian)

Made by Harry Northwood Co., Wheeling, WV, c1903. Add 200% to white opal prices for green opalescent.

	Blue Opal	Canary Opal	Custard	White Opal
Banana Dish	175.00	170.00	—	150.00
Bowl, berry, master	175.00	100.00	150.00	80.00
Butter, cov	200.00	150.00	300.00	125.00
Compote, jelly	85.00	90.00	200.00	67.50
Creamer	90.00	75.00	145.00	45.00
Cruet, os	325.00	300.00	550.00	175.00
Pitcher, water	350.00	375.00	500.00	200.00
Salt Shaker	95.00	75.00	125.00	—
Sauce	35.00	25.00	50.00	25.00
Spooner	75.00	65.00	125.00	45.00
Sugar, cov	175.00	145.00	165.00	75.00
Tumbler	65.00	65.00	110.00	25.00

EXCELSIOR

Flint attributed to several firms, including Boston and Sandwich Glass Co., Sandwich, MA; McKee Bros., Pittsburgh, PA, and Ihmsen & Co., Pittsburgh, PA, 1850s–60s. Quality and design vary. Prices are for high quality flint. Very rare in color.

	Clear		Clear
Ale Glass	50.00	Egg Cup	
Bar Bottle	85.00	Double	55.00
Bowl, 10", open	125.00	Single	40.00
Bitters Bottle	95.00	Goblet, Maltese Cross	50.00
Butter, cov	100.00	Lamp, hand	95.00
Candlestick, 9½" h	125.00	Mug	30.00
Celery Vase, scalloped top	85.00	Pickle Jar, cov	45.00
Champagne	60.00	Pitcher, water	350.00
Claret	45.00	Salt, master	30.00
Compote		Spillholder	75.00
Cov, ls	125.00	Spooner	60.00
Open, hs	85.00	Sugar, cov	90.00
Cordial	40.00	Syrup	125.00
Creamer	85.00	Tumbler, bar	50.00
Decanter		Whiskey, Maltese Cross	65.00
Pint	85.00	Wine	45.00
Quart	85.00		

EYEWINKER (Cannon Ball, Crystal Ball, Winking Eye)

Non-flint made in Findlay, OH, in 1889. Reportedly made by Dalzell, Gilmore and Leighton Glass Co., which was organized in 1883 in West Virginia and moved to Findlay in 1888. Made only in clear glass; reproduced in color by several companies, including L. G. Wright Co. A goblet and toothpick were not originally made in this pattern.

	Clear		Clear
Banana Stand, hs	135.00	* Honey Dish	40.00
Bowl		Lamp, kerosene	125.00
6½"	25.00	Nappy, folded sides, 7¼"	30.00
9", cov	75.00	* Pitcher, water	95.00
* Butter, cov	70.00	Plate	
Cake Stand, 8"	55.00	7"	30.00
Celery Vase	45.00	9", sq, upturned sides	65.00
* Compote		10", upturned sides	85.00
Cov, hs, 6½"	60.00	Salt Shaker	35.00
Cov, hs, 9½"	90.00	Sauce	15.00
Open, 7¼", fluted	65.00	Spooner	35.00
Open, 4½", jelly	45.00	* Sugar, cov	55.00
Creamer	65.00	Syrup, pewter top	125.00
Cruet	65.00	* Tumbler	45.00

FANCY LOOPS

Non flint, made by A. H. Heisey Co., Newark, OH, c1897. Made in clear and emerald green, occasionally found with ruby stain. Original molds did not include Heisey trademark.

	Clear		Clear
Butter, cov	60.00	Sauce, flat	15.00
Creamer	35.00	Spooner	35.00
Goblet	40.00	Sugar, cov	55.00
Pitcher, water, tankard	80.00	Tumbler	30.00
Relish	20.00	Wine	25.00

FAN WITH DIAMOND (Shell)

Non-flint, made by McKee & Bros. Glass Co., Pittsburgh, PA, c1880.

	Clear		Clear
Bowl, oval, flat		Egg Cup	25.00
6 x 8"	25.00	Goblet	30.00
6¾ x 9"	25.00	Pitcher, water	
Butter, cov	50.00	Applied Strap Handle	75.00
Compote, cov		Pressed Handle	50.00
HS, 8¼"	50.00	Sauce, flat, 4"	12.00
LS, pattern on base		Spooner	25.00
7½"	50.00	Sugar	
8⅜"	50.00	Cov	50.00
Creamer		Open, buttermilk type	20.00
Applied Handle	45.00	Syrup, ah, bird finial	100.00
Pressed Handle	30.00	Wine	35.00

FEATHER (Cambridge Feather, Feather and Quill, Fine Cut and Feather, Indiana Feather, Indiana Swirl, Prince's Feather, Swirl, Swirl and Feather)

Non-flint made by McKee & Bros. Glass Co., Pittsburgh, PA, 1896–1901; Beatty-Brady Glass Co., Dunkirk, IN, c1903; and Cambridge Glass Co., Cambridge, OH, c1902–03. Later the pattern was reissued with variations and quality differences. Also found in amber stain.

	Clear	Emerald Green		Clear	Emerald Green
Banana Boat, ftd	75.00	175.00	Bowl, round		
Bowl, oval			4"	15.00	—
8½"	25.00	—	4½"	15.00	—
9¼"	18.00	75.00	6"	20.00	—

	Clear	Emerald Green		Clear	Emerald Green
7″	25.00	75.00	Creamer	40.00	85.00
8″	30.00	85.00	Cruet, os	45.00	250.00
Bowl, sq			Dishes, nest of 3: 7″,		
4½″	15.00	—	8″, and 9″	40.00	—
8″	30.00	—	Goblet	55.00	150.00
Butter, cov	55.00	150.00	Honey Dish	15.00	—
Cake Plate	65.00	—	Marmalade Jar	125.00	—
Cake Stand			Pickle Castor	145.00	—
8″	40.00	125.00	Pitcher		
9½″	50.00	125.00	Milk	50.00	165.00
11″	70.00	175.00	Water	75.00	250.00
Celery Vase	35.00	85.00	Plate, 10″	35.00	75.00
Champagne	65.00	—	Relish	18.00	—
Compote			Salt Shaker	35.00	70.00
Cov, hs, 8½″	125.00	250.00	Sauce	12.00	—
Cov, ls, 4¼″,			Spooner	25.00	60.00
jelly	100.00	150.00	Sugar, cov	45.00	80.00
Cov, ls, 8¼″	150.00	—	Syrup	125.00	300.00
Open, ls, 4″	15.00	—	Toothpick	85.00	165.00
Open, ls, 6″	20.00	—	Tumbler	45.00	85.00
Open, ls, 7″	30.00	—	* Wine		
Open, ls, 8″	35.00	—	Scalloped border	40.00	—
Cordial	125.00	—	Straight border	25.00	—

FEATHER DUSTER (Rosette Medallion, Huckel)

Made by U. S. Glass Co., Pittsburgh, PA, in 1895 and probably by another company c1895.

	Clear	Emerald Green		Clear	Emerald Green
Bowl, Berry, 8″	15.00	20.00	Plate, 9″	20.00	—
Butter, cov	40.00	—	Relish	15.00	—
Cake Stand, 10″	35.00	—	Spooner, plain form	20.00	—
Celery Vase	20.00	—	Sugar, cov	35.00	—
Compote			Tray, "Gold Standard		
Cov, hs, 8″	50.00	—	Tray", full-length		
Open ls, shallow			portrait of Mc-		
bowl, 9″	25.00	—	Kinley, Feather		
Creamer	25.00	—	Duster border,		
Goblet	30.00	—	1896	200.00	—
Mug	15.00	—	Tumbler	15.00	20.00
Pitcher, water, ½			Waste Bowl	20.00	—
gallon	45.00	55.00	Water Tray, round	—	75.00

FESTOON

Non-flint, 1890–94. No goblet or wine was made in this pattern.

	Clear		Clear
Bowl		Pickle Castor, cov	110.00
7 x 4½″, rect	25.00	Pitcher, water	65.00
8″, round	25.00	Plate, 7″, 8″, 9″	30.00
9″, rect	30.00	Relish, 9 x 5½″	30.00
Butter, cov	40.00	Sauce, flat	7.50
Cake Stand, 10″	40.00	Spooner	35.00
Compote, open, hs	65.00	Sugar, cov	50.00
Creamer	35.00	Tray, water, 10″	35.00
Finger Bowl	30.00	Tumbler	22.00
Marmalade Jar, cov	60.00	Waste Bowl	30.00
Mug	35.00		

FINECUT (Flower in Square)

Non-flint made by Bryce Bros., Pittsburgh, PA, c1885, and by U. S. Glass Co. in 1891.

	Amber	Blue	Clear	Vaseline
Bowl, 8¼"........	15.00	20.00	10.00	15.00
Bread Plate	50.00	60.00	25.00	50.00
Butter, cov	55.00	75.00	45.00	60.00
Cake Stand	—	—	35.00	—
Celery Tray......	—	45.00	25.00	40.00
Celery Vase, SP holder . . .	—	—	—	115.00
Creamer.........	38.00	40.00	35.00	75.00
Goblet	45.00	55.00	22.00	42.00
Pitcher, water	100.00	100.00	60.00	115.00
Plate				
6".............	—	20.00	8.00	—
7".............	25.00	40.00	15.00	20.00
10"............	30.00	50.00	21.00	45.00
Relish...........	15.00	25.00	10.00	20.00
Sauce, flat	14.00	15.00	10.00	14.00
Spooner.........	30.00	45.00	18.00	40.00
Sugar, cov	45.00	55.00	35.00	45.00
Tray, water	50.00	55.00	25.00	50.00
Tumbler	—	—	18.00	28.00
Wine	—	—	24.00	30.00

FINECUT AND BLOCK (Button and Oval Medallion, Nailhead and Panel)

Non-flint made by King, Son & Co., Pittsburgh, PA, c1890 and by Model Flint Glass Co., Findlay, OH, c1894. Made in clear, solid colors of amber, blue, and yellow (all comparable in price), and in clear with color blocks. Heavily reproduced by Fenton.

	Clear	Solid Colored Pieces	Colored Block: Amber	Colored Block: Blue	Colored Block: Yellow or Pink
Bowl, 9", handle ...	35.00	40.00	40.00	40.00	40.00
Butter, cov					
Flat...........	65.00	—	—	—	—
Footed	75.00	100.00	125.00	125.00	125.00
Cake Stand					
Large	40.00	—	—	—	—
Small	35.00	—	—	—	—
Celery Tray......	30.00	45.00	50.00	60.00	65.00
Compote					
Cov, ls........	35.00	—	—	—	—
Opon, lo, 8½" ...	30.00	—	45.00	40.00	45.00
Open jelly	18.00	50.00	75.00	75.00	75.00
Cordial	—	—	—	75.00	75.00
Creamer.........	45.00	65.00	70.00	60.00	75.00
Custard Cup......	15.00	25.00	35.00	30.00	35.00
Egg Cup.........	20.00	25.00	45.00	35.00	45.00
Finger Bowl	20.00	40.00	55.00	55.00	55.00
Goblet					
Lady's.........	45.00	—	—	50.00	—
* Regular.......	32.00	65.00	60.00	65.00	60.00
Perfume Bottle	65.00	75.00	95.00	95.00	95.00
Pickle Jar, cov.	40.00	—	—	—	—
Pitcher					
Milk..........	45.00	85.00	95.00	95.00	125.00
Water	45.00	85.00	95.00	95.00	125.00
Plate, 5¾".......	12.50	—	—	—	—
Punch Cup	12.00	—	—	20.00	—
Relish, rect.......	12.00	—	55.00	50.00	55.00
Salt, individual	12.00	—	—	—	—
Salt, master	—	—	35.00	—	—
Sauce					
Flat..........	10.00	15.00	15.00	15.00	15.00
Footed	10.00	15.00	15.00	15.00	15.00
Spooner........	30.00	45.00	55.00	65.00	50.00
Sugar, cov	45.00	—	120.00	130.00	120.00
Tray					
Ice Cream......	55.00	—	—	—	—
Water	60.00	—	—	—	—
Tumbler	20.00	50.00	50.00	45.00	45.00
* Wine	30.00	—	45.00	45.00	45.00

FINECUT AND PANEL

Non-flint made by many Pittsburgh factories in the 1880s, including Bryce Bros. and Richard and Hartley Glass Co. Reissued in the early 1890s by U. S. Glass Co. An aqua wine is known.

	Amber	Blue	Clear	Vaseline
Bowl				
7″............	25.00	35.00	15.00	30.00
8″, oval........	40.00	—	18.00	30.00
Bread Plate......	50.00	45.00	30.00	—
Butter, cov.......	65.00	75.00	40.00	60.00
Cake Stand, 10″...	50.00	75.00	30.00	50.00
Compote				
Cov, hs......	125.00	135.00	75.00	130.00
Open, hs.......	65.00	65.00	35.00	60.00
Creamer........	35.00	50.00	25.00	40.00
Goblet..........	40.00	48.00	20.00	35.00
Pitcher				
Milk..........	65.00	—	—	50.00
Water........	85.00	85.00	40.00	45.00
Plate, 6″........	12.00	20.00	10.00	15.00
Platter..........	30.00	50.00	25.00	30.00
Relish..........	20.00	25.00	15.00	20.00
Sauce, ftd.......	15.00	25.00	8.00	15.00
Spooner........	35.00	45.00	20.00	30.00
Sugar, cov......	37.50	42.50	30.00	32.50
Tray, water.......	60.00	55.00	30.00	60.00
Tumbler........	25.00	30.00	20.00	38.00
Waste Bowl.......	30.00	35.00	20.00	35.00
Wine..........	30.00	35.00	20.00	35.00

FINE RIB

Flint made by New England Glass Co., East Cambridge, MA, in the 1860s and by McKee & Bros. Glass Co., Pittsburgh, PA, 1868–69. Later made in non-flint, which has limited collecting interest and is priced at approximately one third the value of flint.

	Clear		Clear
Ale Glass..............	50.00	* Honey Dish, 3½″d........	16.00
Bitters Bottle............	65.00	Lamp.................	150.00
Bowl		Lemonade Glass........	65.00
Cov, 5½″ d..........	50.00	Mug.................	55.00
Cov, 7″ d.............	65.00	Pitcher, ah	
Open, 6″ d...........	35.00	Milk.............	250.00
Open, 8″ d...........	35.00	Water.............	350.00
Butter, cov............	75.00	Plate, 6″ or 7″..........	20.00
Castor Set.............	200.00	Salt	
Celery Vase............	85.00	Cov, ftd.............	85.00
Champagne............	125.00	Individual, ftd..........	35.00
Compote		Individual, flat, round....	30.00
Cov, hs, 8″...........	110.00	Sauce, 4″ d............	15.00
Open, hs, 7¾″.........	60.00	Spooner..............	65.00
Open, ls, 9″..........	75.00	Sugar, cov............	75.00
Cordial...............	85.00	Tumbler..............	75.00
Creamer, ah............	125.00	Tumble-Up.............	125.00
Decanter, quart bar lip.....	75.00	Whiskey, handled........	75.00
Egg Cup..............	40.00	Wine................	50.00
* Goblet................	60.00		

FISHSCALE (Coral)

Non-flint made by Bryce Bros., Pittsburgh, PA, in the mid 1880s and by U. S. Glass Co. 1891–98. Also attributed to Burlington Glass Works, Hamilton, Ontario, Canada.

	Clear		Clear
Bowl		Cov, 9½″.............	55.00
Cov, 7″..............	45.00	Open, 8″.............	20.00

	Clear			Clear
Bread Plate	30.00	Pitcher		
Butter, cov	45.00	Milk		35.00
Cake Plate	55.00	Water		55.00
Cake Stand		Plate		
9"	30.00	7", round		25.00
10½"	35.00	9", square		30.00
Celery Vase	30.00	Relish		15.00
Compote		Salt Shaker		65.00
Cov, hs, 8"	85.00	Sauce		
Open, hs, 8"	30.00	Flat		12.00
Open, hs, 9"	40.00	Footed		15.00
Open, jelly	20.00	Spooner		25.00
Creamer	30.00	Sugar, cov		50.00
Goblet	25.00	Tray, attached Daisy & But-		
Lamp, finger	75.00	ton shoe		50.00
Mug, large	35.00	Tumbler		75.00
Pickle Scoop	15.00	Waste Bowl		35.00

FLAMINGO HABITAT

Non-flint, maker unknown, c1870, etched pattern

	Clear			Clear
Bowl, 10", oval	40.00	Creamer		40.00
Butter, cov	65.00	Goblet		45.00
Celery Vase	45.00	Sauce, ftd		15.00
Champagne	45.00	Spooner		25.00
Cheese Dish, blown	110.00	Sugar, cov		50.00
Compote		Tumbler		30.00
Cov, 4½"	75.00	Wine		45.00
Cov, 6½"	95.00			
Open, 5", jelly	35.00			
Open, 6"	40.00			

FLAT DIAMOND (Lippman)

Non-flint made by Richards and Hartley, Tarentum, PA, c1880. Reissued by U. S. Glass Co. after 1891. Shards also have been found at Burlington Glass Works, Hamilton, Ontario, Canada.

	Clear			Clear
Butter, cov	45.00	Spooner		20.00
Celery Vase	35.00	Sugar		
Creamer	40.00	Cov		45.00
Goblet	25.00	Open		20.00
Pitcher, water	45.00	Wine		25.00
Sauce				
Flat	5.00			
Footed	8.00			

FLEUR-DE-LIS AND DRAPE (Fleur-de-Lis and Tassel)

Non-flint made by Adams & Co., Pittsburgh, PA, c1888. Reissued by U. S. Glass Co. c1892. Made in clear, emerald green, and milk white.

	Clear	Emerald Green		Clear	Emerald Green
Bowl	15.00	30.00	7"	35.00	45.00
Butter, cov	45.00	55.00	8"	45.00	60.00
Cake Stand	35.00	55.00	Open, hs		
Claret	35.00	50.00	5"	25.00	30.00
Compote			6"	25.00	30.00
Cov, ls			7"	30.00	35.00
5"	30.00	40.00	8"	30.00	40.00
6"	35.00	40.00	Creamer	25.00	40.00

	Clear	Emerald Green		Clear	Emerald Green
Cruet, os	45.00	85.00	Plate, 8"	20.00	35.00
Cup	15.00	25.00	Salt Shaker	20.00	35.00
Cup and Saucer	25.00	35.00	Spooner	25.00	40.00
Goblet	25.00	45.00	Sugar, cov	30.00	55.00
Honey Dish, cov	40.00	55.00	Syrup, metal top	50.00	125.00
Mustard Jar, cov	35.00	50.00	Tumbler	20.00	30.00
Pitcher			Waste Bowl	30.00	40.00
Milk	40.00	60.00	Water Tray, 11½"	24.00	50.00
Water	50.00	65.00	* Wine	25.00	45.00

FLORIDA (Emerald Green Herringbone, Paneled Herringbone)

Non-flint made by U. S. Glass Co., in the 1890s. One of the States patterns. Goblet reproduced in green and other colors.

	Clear	Emerald Green		Clear	Emerald Green
Berry Set	75.00	110.00	Pitcher, water	50.00	75.00
Bowl, 7¾"	10.00	15.00	Plate		
Butter, cov	50.00	85.00	7½"	12.00	18.00
Cake Stand			9¼"	15.00	25.00
Large	60.00	75.00	Relish		
Small	30.00	40.00	6", sq	10.00	15.00
Celery Vase	30.00	35.00	8½", sq	15.00	22.00
Compote, open, hs,			Salt Shaker	25.00	50.00
6½", sq	—	40.00	Sauce	5.00	7.50
Creamer	30.00	45.00	Spooner	20.00	35.00
Cruet, os	40.00	110.00	Sugar, cov	32.00	50.00
* Goblet, 5¾" h	25.00	40.00	Syrup	60.00	175.00
Mustard Pot, attach-			Tumbler	20.00	30.00
ed underplate, cov	25.00	45.00	Wine	25.00	50.00
Nappy	15.00	25.00			

FLOWER BAND (Bird Finial, Frosted Flower Band)

Non-flint pattern whose maker has not been identified, c1870. Made in clear and clear with a frosted band. A goblet was reproduced by Fenton, Williamstown, WV, in various colors.

	Clear	Frosted Band		Clear	Frosted Band
Butter Dish, cov, love-			Goblet	65.00	95.00
birds finial	100.00	150.00	Sauce, flat	10.00	20.00
Celery Vase	60.00	85.00	Spooner	45.00	65.00
Compote, cov, hs, 8"			Sugar, cov, lovebirds		
d	135.00	165.00	finial	100.00	150.00
Creamer, 6" h	65.00	95.00			

FLOWER POT (Flower Plant, Potted Plant)

Non-flint made in the 1880s. There are occasional pieces found in amber and vaseline.

	Clear		Clear
Bread Plate	45.00		
Butter, cov	50.00	Pitcher	
Cake Stand, 10½"	48.00	Milk	40.00
Compote		Water	55.00
Cov, 7"	45.00	Salt Shaker	20.00
Open, 7¼"	20.00	Sauce, ftd	8.50
Creamer	30.00	Spooner	25.00
Goblet	35.00	Sugar, cov	40.00

FLUTE

More than fifteen Flute variants were produced in flint and non-flint glass from the 1850s through the 1880s. Some of the flint variants are Beaded Flute, Bessimer Flute, New England Flute—all with comparable prices. Prices listed are for flint.

	Clear		Clear
Ale Glass	50.00	Goblet	25.00
Bitters Bottle	75.00	Honey Dish	15.00
Butter, cov, ls	60.00	Lamp	75.00
Candlestick, 4"	50.00	Mug	35.00
Claret	45.00	Pitcher, water	90.00
Compote		Sauce, flat	15.00
Open, ls, 8½"	40.00	Sugar, cov	50.00
Open, ls, 9½"	45.00	Tumbler	15.00
Creamer	45.00	Whiskey, handle	30.00
Decanter, bar lip	75.00	Wine	25.00
Egg Cup			
Double	50.00		
Single	30.00		

FLUTED SCROLLS (Klondyke)

Made by Harry Northwood and Co., Indiana, PA, c1898. Sometimes with burnished gold trim. Pattern known as Jackson in custard.

	Blue Opal	Custard	Vaseline Opal	White Opal
Bowl, berry	100.00	100.00	75.00	—
Butter, cov	135.00	200.00	185.00	65.00
Creamer	75.00	100.00	125.00	45.00
Cruet, os	100.00	175.00	85.00	—
Pitcher, water	210.00	190.00	175.00	—
Puff Box	50.00	—	55.00	—
Salt Shaker	45.00	—	40.00	20.00
Sauce	30.00	45.00	25.00	—
Spooner	100.00	100.00	100.00	65.00
Sugar, cov	95.00	115.00	150.00	80.00
Tray	40.00	—	30.00	25.00
Tumbler	75.00	—	65.00	—

FRANCES WARE

Made by Hobbs, Brockunier & Co., Wheeling, WV, c1880. A clear frosted hobnail or swirl pattern glass with amber stained top rims. It may be pressed or mold blown. Swirl pieces are noted, otherwise they are hobnail.

	Clear	Frosted/ Amber Stain		Clear	Frosted/ Amber Stain
Bowl, 7½"	50.00	75.00	Sauce, 4", sq	18.00	32.00
Box, 5¼", round,			Spooner	45.00	60.00
cov	45.00	65.00	Sugar, cov	60.00	85.00
Butter, cov	80.00	110.00	Sugar Shaker, swirl .	65.00	125.00
Creamer	50.00	85.00	Syrup, swirl	85.00	175.00
Cruet, os	35.00	175.00	Toothpick	75.00	125.00
Finger Bowl, 4"	40.00	50.00	Tray		
Mustard, cov, swirl . .	—	135.00	Leaf shape, 12" .	75.00	125.00
Pitcher			Rect, rounded		
8½"	90.00	150.00	edges, 14 x		
11"	150.00	185.00	9½"	110.00	150.00
Salt Shaker			Water, oval	75.00	150.00
Hobnail	50.00	65.00	Tumbler	35.00	45.00
Swirl	30.00	75.00			

FROSTED CIRCLE

Produced by Bryce Bros., Pittsburgh, PA, c1885. Later made by U. S. Glass Co. in the late 1890s. Reproduced.

	Clear Circle	Frosted Circle		Clear Circle	Frosted Circle
Bowl, cov			Cup and Saucer . . .	25.00	40.00
7"	20.00	25.00	* Goblet	35.00	45.00
8"	25.00	30.00	Juice	15.00	30.00
Butter, cov	55.00	65.00	Pitcher, water	55.00	80.00
Cake Stand			Plate, 7"	35.00	50.00
8"	30.00	35.00	Punch Cup	15.00	20.00
9½"	40.00	50.00	Salt Shaker	25.00	35.00
Champagne	35.00	55.00	Sauce	8.50	10.00
Compote			Spooner	30.00	35.00
Cov, 7", hs.	30.00	65.00	Sugar, cov	42.50	50.00
Cov, 8", hs.	45.00	75.00	Sugar Shaker	40.00	65.00
Open, 7", hs	20.00	30.00	Syrup	95.00	135.00
Open, 10", hs . . .	45.00	55.00	Tumbler	25.00	35.00
Creamer	35.00	45.00	Wine	35.00	45.00
Cruet, os	45.00	65.00			

FROSTED LEAF

Flint pattern made 1860–70. Imperial Glass, Bellaire, OH, has been authorized by the Smithsonian Institution, Washington, D.C., to reproduce several pieces, embossed with the "S. I." mark.

	Clear		Clear
* Butter, cov	135.00	Lamp, oil	500.00
Celery Vase	145.00	Pitcher, water	400.00
Champagne	160.00	Salt, individual	50.00
Compote, cov	250.00	Sauce, flat	25.00
* Creamer	300.00	* Spooner	85.00
Decanter, os, qt.	250.00	* Sugar, cov	175.00
Egg Cup	100.00	Tumbler	150.00
Goblet	95.00	* Wine	125.00

FROSTED STORK (Flamingo, Frosted Crane)

Non-flint made by Crystal Glass Co., Bridgeport, OH, c1880. Shards have been identified at the Burlington Glass Works, Hamilton, Ontario, Canada. Reproduced by A.A. Importing Co. Inc., St. Louis, MO. Details of the stork's activities differ from scene to scene on the same piece.

	Clear		Clear
Bowl, 9"	50.00	Platter, 11½ x 8"	
* Bread Plate, oval.	70.00	101 border	70.00
Butter, cov	80.00	Scenic border	70.00
Creamer	45.00	Relish.	45.00
Finger Bowl	50.00	Sauce, flat	20.00
* Goblet	65.00	Spooner	40.00
Jam Jar, cov.	125.00	Sugar, cov	95.00
Pickle, cov, stork finial	125.00	Tray, water	100.00
Pitcher, water	200.00	Waste Bowl.	50.00

GALLOWAY (Mirror Plate, U.S. Mirror, Virginia, Woodrow)

Non-flint made by U. S. Glass Co., Pittsburgh, PA, c1904–19. Jefferson Glass Co., Toronto, Canada, produced it from 1900–25. Clear glass with and without gold trim; also known with rose stain and ruby stain.

	Clear w/ Gold	Rose Stained		Clear w/ Gold	Rose Stained
Basket, no gold. . . .	75.00	125.00	Pitcher		
Bowl			Milk.	60.00	80.00
6½", belled	20.00	35.00	Tankard	75.00	125.00
8½", oval.	35.00	45.00	Water, ice lip	65.00	175.00
8½", round	30.00	50.00	Plate, 8", round. . . .	40.00	65.00
9", rect	30.00	45.00	Punch Bowl	160.00	225.00
11" d, round	45.00	65.00	Punch Bowl Plate,		
Butter, cov	65.00	125.00	20"	80.00	125.00
Cake Stand	65.00	90.00	Punch Cup	10.00	15.00
Carafe, water	55.00	85.00	Relish.	20.00	30.00
Celery Vase	35.00	75.00	Rose Bowl	25.00	60.00
Champagne	60.00	175.00	Salt, master	35.00	60.00
Compote			Salt & Pepper, pr. . .	40.00	75.00
Cov, hs, 6".	90.00	125.00	Sauce		
Open, hs, 5½" . . .	25.00	40.00	Flat, 4"	10.00	20.00
Open, hs, 10",			Footed, 4½".	10.00	20.00
scalloped	55.00	75.00	Sherbet	25.00	30.00
Creamer.	30.00	50.00	Spooner	30.00	80.00
Cruet	45.00	125.00	Sugar, cov	55.00	75.00
Egg Cup.	40.00	60.00	Sugar Shaker	40.00	100.00
Finger Bowl	40.00	65.00	Syrup.	65.00	135.00
Goblet	75.00	95.00	* Toothpick	30.00	55.00
Lemonade	35.00	45.00	Tumbler	35.00	45.00
Mug	40.00	50.00	Vase, swung.	30.00	—
Nappy, tricorn	25.00	50.00	Waste Bowl.	40.00	65.00
Olive, 6"	20.00	30.00	Water Bottle	40.00	85.00
Pickle Castor, sp holder and lid . . .	65.00	200.00	Wine	45.00	65.00

GARDEN OF EDEN (Fish, Lotus, Lotus and Serpent, Lotus with Serpent, Turtle)

Non-flint, c1870.

	Clear		Clear
Bowl, 4½" x 7", oval	15,00	Mug	45.00
Bread Tray, motto	35.00	Pickle, oval.	15.00
Butter, covered	75.00	Pitcher, water	65.00
Cake Stand, 11½".	50.00	Plate, 6½", handled.	20.00
Celery	25.00	Salt, Master	30.00
Compote, cov, hs, 10"	80.00	Spooner	25.00
Creamer.	40.00	Sugar, covered	50.00
Dish, oval.	12.00	Toothpick	45.00
Goblet	80.00		

GARFIELD DRAPE (Canadian Drape)

Non-flint issued in 1881 by Adams & Co., Pittsburgh, PA, after the assassination of President Garfield.

	Clear		Clear
Bread Plate		Honey Dish.	15.00
Memorial, portrait of Garfield	65.00	Goblet	40.00
"We Mourn Our Nation's		Pitcher	
Loss", portrait.	75.00	Milk.	70.00
Butter, cov	60.00	Water, ah.	75.00
Cake Stand, 9½".	75.00	Water, strap handle	100.00
Celery Vase	45.00	Relish, oval.	20.00
Compote		Sauce	
Cov, hs, 8".	100.00	Flat.	8.50
Cov, ls, 6"	85.00	Footed	12.00
Open, hs, 8½"	40.00	Spooner	35.00
Creamer.	40.00	Sugar, cov	60.00
		Tumbler	35.00

GEORGIA (Peacock Feather)

Non-flint made by Richards and Hartley Glass Co., Tarentum, PA, and reissued by U. S. Glass Co. in 1902 as part of the States series. Rare in blue. (Chamber lamp, pedestal base, $275.00.) No goblet known in pattern.

	Clear		Clear
Bonbon, ftd	25.00	Creamer	35.00
Bowl, 8"	30.00	Cruet, os	55.00
Butter, cov	45.00	Decanter	70.00
Cake Stand, 10"	50.00	Lamp	
Castor Set, 2 bottles	60.00	Chamber, pedestal	85.00
Celery Tray, 11¾"	35.00	Hand, oil, 7"	80.00
Children's		Mug	25.00
Cake Stand	35.00	Nappy	25.00
Creamer	35.00	Pitcher, water	70.00
Compote		Plate, 5¼"	15.00
Cov, hs, 5"	35.00	Relish	15.00
Cov, hs, 6"	40.00	Salt Shaker	40.00
Cov, hs, 7"	45.00	Sauce	10.00
Cov, hs, 8"	50.00	Spooner	35.00
Open, hs, 5"	20.00	Sugar, cov	45.00
Open, hs, 6"	25.00	Syrup, metal lid	65.00
Open, hs, 7"	30.00	Tumbler	35.00
Open, hs, 8"	35.00		
Condiment Set, tray, oil cruet, salt & pepper	75.00		

GIANT BULL'S EYE (Bull's Eye and Spearhead)

Made by Bellaire Glass Co., Findlay, OH, c1889 and continued by U. S. Glass Co. after 1891.

	Clear		Clear
Bowl, 8"	25.00	Decanter, os	50.00
Brandy Bottle, os, tall, narrow	55.00	Goblet	45.00
		Lamp, handled	125.00
Butter, cov	45.00	Pitcher, water	75.00
Cake Stand	30.00	Relish	15.00
Cheese Dish, cov	45.00	Tray, wine, 7¼"	45.00
Claret Jug, tankard shape	60.00	Tumbler	30.00
Compote, cov	75.00	Vase	35.00
Creamer	30.00	Wine	30.00
Cruet, os	60.00		

GIBSON GIRL

Non-flint made by Kokomo Glass Co., c1904.

	Clear		Clear
Butter, cov	75.00	Salt Shaker	50.00
Creamer	85.00	Spooner	50.00
Pitcher, water	175.00	Sugar, cov	75.00
Plate, 10"	75.00	Tumbler	65.00

GONTERMAN

Non-flint pattern made by George Duncan & Sons, Pittsburgh, PA, c1887–90. Made as an acid-finished body with amber stain.

	Acid Finish w/ Amber Stain		Acid Finish w/ Amber Stain
Bowl, 7" d	85.00	Goblet	350.00
Butter Dish, cov	125.00	Pitcher, water	200.00
Cake Stand, hs, 10" d	100.00	Sauce, flat, 4" d	20.00
Celery Vase	95.00	Spooner	75.00
Compote, cov, hs, 5" d	100.00	Sugar, cov	100.00
Creamer	110.00		

GOOSEBERRY

Non-flint of the 1880s. Attributed to Boston and Sandwich Glass Co. and others in clear and milk glass. Reproduced in clear and milk glass.

	Clear	Milk Glass		Clear	Milk Glass
Butter, cov	50.00	75.00	Pitcher, water, ah	165.00	225.00
Compote			Sauce	10.00	15.00
Cov, hs, 6".	60.00	65.00	Spooner	25.00	30.00
Cov, hs, 7".	70.00	75.00	Sugar, Cov	45.00	55.00
Cov, hs, 8".	75.00	90.00	Syrup, ah	75.00	135.00
Creamer	30.00	50.00	Tumbler	35.00	40.00
* Goblet	35.00	45.00			
Mug	35.00	40.00			

GOTHIC (Cathedral)

Flint attributed to Union Glass Co., Somerville, MA, c1860. Shards have been found at Boston and Sandwich Glass Co.

	Clear		Clear
Bowl, 7"	70.00	Egg Cup	50.00
Butter, cov	85.00	Goblet	65.00
Castor Set, pewter frame	125.00	Plate	125.00
Celery Vase	90.00	Salt, master	60.00
Champagne	165.00	Sauce, flat	15.00
Compote		Spooner	40.00
Cov, hs, 8".	110.00	Sugar, cov	85.00
Open, ls, 7".	65.00	Tumbler	95.00
Creamer, ah	75.00	Wine	125.00

GRAND (Diamond Medallion, Fine Cut and Diamond, Fine Cut Medallion)

Non-flint made by Bryce, Higbee and Co., Pittsburgh, PA, in 1885. Also attributed to Diamond Glass Co., Ltd., Montreal, Canada. Stemware comes in plain and ringed stems.

	Clear		Clear
Bowl, 6", cov	30.00	Creamer	25.00
Bread Plate, 10"	25.00	Goblet	25.00
Butter, cov		Pitcher, water	40.00
Flat	35.00	Plate, 10"	25.00
Footed	45.00	Relish, 7½", oval	12.00
Cake Stand		Salt Shaker	30.00
8"	30.00	Sauce	
10"	35.00	Flat	10.00
Celery Vase, pedestal	25.00	Footed	12.00
Compote		Spooner	20.00
Cov, hs, 5½"	60.00	Sugar, cov	35.00
Cov, hs, 7½"	75.00	Syrup, metal top	90.00
Open, hs, 9"	65.00	Waste Bowl, collared	30.00
Cordial	50.00	Wine	25.00

GRAPE AND FESTOON WITH STIPPLED LEAF

Non-flint made by Doyle and Company, Pittsburgh, PA, in the early 1870s.

	Clear		Clear
Bowl	15.00	Compote	
Butter, cov	50.00	Cov, hs, 8".	115.00
Buttermilk Goblet	30.00	Open, ls, 8".	75.00
Celery Vase	40.00	Creamer, ah	50.00

	Clear		Clear
Egg Cup	30.00	Plate, 6"	18.00
Goblet	35.00	Relish	12.50
Lamp, oil, 7½"	65.00	Salt, ftd	24.00
Mug	20.00	Sauce, flat, 4"	10.00
Pitcher		Spooner	35.00
Milk, ah	75.00	Sugar, cov	50.00
Water, ah	90.00	Wine	45.00

GRAPE BAND (Ashburton with Grape Band, Early Grape Band, Grape Vine)

Issued in flint by Bryce, Walker and Co., Pittsburgh, PA, in the late 1850s; non-flint in 1869.

	Flint	Non-Flint		Flint	Non-Flint
Butter, cov	75.00	50.00	Pickle	—	15.00
Compote			Pitcher, water	—	85.00
Cov, hs	—	50.00	Plate, 6"	—	20.00
Open, hs	—	25.00	Salt Dip	—	20.00
Cordial	65.00	—	Spooner	—	30.00
Creamer, ah	—	50.00	Sugar, cov	—	45.00
Egg Cup	—	20.00	Tumbler	35.00	20.00
Goblet	40.00	25.00	Wine	35.00	25.00

GRASSHOPPER (Long Spear)

Maker unknown; over forty pieces documented. Pieces without the grasshopper bring 40–50% less. Creamer and sugar known in vaseline and blue. Footed sauces and covered compote known in vaseline. Goblet is modern.

	Amber	Clear		Amber	Clear
Bowl			Plate		
Cov	55.00	35.00	8½", ftd	—	25.00
Open, ftd	—	25.00	9", ftd	—	20.00
Butter, cov	90.00	65.00	10½", ftd	100.00	25.00
Celery Vase	90.00	50.00	Salt Dip	—	40.00
Compote			Salt Shaker	—	35.00
Cov, hs, 7"	—	50.00	Sauce		
Cov, hs, 8½"	—	65.00	Flat	—	15.00
Creamer	60.00	40.00	Footed	—	18.00
Marmalade Jar, cov	—	125.00	Spooner	75.00	40.00
Pickle	—	20.00	Sugar, cov	80.00	70.00
Pitcher, water	125.00	75.00			

HAIRPIN (Sandwich Loop)

Flint made at Boston and Sandwich Glass Co., Sandwich, MA, c1850. Finials are acorn shaped, handles are applied.

	Clear		Clear
Bowl, 6¼" d	100.00	Salt, cov, ftd	85.00
Celery Vase	40.00	Sauce, flat	15.00
Champagne	80.00	Spooner	40.00
Compote, cov hs	225.00	Sugar, cov	95.00
Creamer, ah	55.00	Tumbler	50.00
Decanter, os, qt	90.00	Whiskey, handled	45.00
Egg Cup	30.00	Wine	50.00
Goblet	40.00		

HALLEY'S COMET (Etruria)

Clear non-flint made by Model Flint Glass Co., Findlay, OH, c1890 and by National Glass Co., Pittsburgh, PA, 1891–1902. The tail of the comet forms continuous loops. Found with copper wheel engraving and/or ruby stain.

	Clear		Clear
Bowl		Goblet	35.00
4", cov, 3 ftd	40.00	Mustard, cov, ftd	45.00
8"	25.00	Pitcher, water	100.00
9"	25.00	Punch Cup	25.00
Butter, cov	80.00	Relish	25.00
Cake Stand	75.00	Salt & Pepper, pr.	45.00
Celery Vase	30.00	Spooner	45.00
Compote		Sugar, cov	65.00
Cov, hs, 10"	60.00	Syrup	85.00
Open, hs, 8"	40.00	Tumbler	25.00
Creamer	35.00	Wine	25.00
Cruet, os	60.00		

HAMILTON (Cape Cod)

Flint made by Cape Cod Glass Co., Sandwich, MA, c1860. Shards have been found at Boston and Sandwich Glass Co. Other companies also may have made it. Non-flint values are 33% less.

	Clear		Clear
Butter, cov	75.00	Lamp, hand	85.00
Castor Set, 4 bottles, pewter		Pitcher, water	175.00
std	175.00	Plate, 6"	45.00
Celery Vase	60.00	Salt, ftd	30.00
Compote		Sauce, 4½" d	10.00
Cov, hs	95.00	Spooner	35.00
Open, ls, 6" scallop rim . .	80.00	Sweetmeat Dish, hs, cov . .	95.00
Creamer, ah	75.00	Sugar, cov	75.00
Decanter, os	150.00	Tumbler, water or bar	85.00
Egg Cup, frosted leaf	50.00	Whiskey, ah	95.00
Goblet	45.00	Wine	90.00
Honey Dish	15.00		

HAMILTON WITH LEAF (Hamilton with Vine)

Flint pattern made by Cape Cod Glass Co., Sandwich, MA, c1860.

	Clear	Frosted Leaf		Clear	Frosted Leaf
Butter Dish, cov . . .	85.00	115.00	Sauce, flat, 4" d . . .	10.00	20.00
Celery Vase	50.00	65.00	Sugar, cov	65.00	95.00
Compote, open, hs,			Sweetmeat Dish,		
8" d	65.00	95.00	cov	90.00	145.00
Egg Cup	65.00	80.00	Tumbler, bar	85.00	135.00
Goblet	45.00	65.00	Whiskey, ah	100.00	125.00
Honey Dish	15.00	20.00	Wine	75.00	95.00
Salt, master, ftd	45.00	60.00			

HAND (Early Pennsylvania)

Made by O'Hara Glass Co., Pittsburgh, PA, c1880. Covered pieces have a hand holding bar finial, hence the name.

	Clear		Clear
Bowl		Compote	
9"	30.00	Cov, hs, 7"	60.00
10"	40.00	Cov, hs, 8"	95.00
Butter, cov	85.00	Open, hs, 7¾"	35.00
Cake Stand	55.00	Cordial, 3½"	85.00
Celery Vase	48.00	Creamer	40.00

	Clear		Clear
Goblet	45.00	Spooner	30.00
Honey Dish	10.00	Sugar, cov	75.00
Marmalade Jar, cov	75.00	Syrup	125.00
Mug	40.00	Tray	55.00
Pickle	20.00	Tumbler	85.00
Pitcher, water	75.00	Wine	55.00
Sauce			
Flat	12.00		
Footed	15.00		

HARP (Lyre)

Flint made by Bryce Bros., Pittsburgh, PA, in the late 1840s and early 1850s. Also found in McKee catalog of 1859.

	Clear		Clear
Bowl, cov, 6½" d	150.00	Nappy	100.00
Butter, cov	150.00	Salt, master	75.00
Compote, cov, ls, 6"	200.00	Spill Holder	85.00
Goblet, rare	1,000.00	Spooner	95.00
Honey Dish	20.00	Sweetmeat Jar, cov	200.00
Lamp			
Hand	200.00		
Stand	225.00		

HARTFORD

Made by Fostoria Glass Co., Moundsville, WV, until about 1930.

	Clear	Emerald Green		Clear	Emerald Green
Basket, flat, handle,			Olive, flat, 5½" sq,		
turned up sides	20.00	28.00	turned up sides	15.00	25.00
Bowl			Relish, oval	15.00	25.00
6", sq, collared			Salt & Pepper	45.00	65.00
base	15.00	12.00	Salt, individual	6.00	20.00
7" and 8"	15.00	15.00	Sauce		
Butter, cov, sq	40.00	55.00	4½", flat	8.00	8.00
Celery Vase	30.00	40.00	4½", footed	10.00	12.00
Creamer	25.00	35.00	Sugar, cov	35.00	45.00
Dish, 9", rect	15.00	20.00	Syrup, metal top	45.00	75.00
Finger Bowl	10.00	15.00	Tumbler, small	15.00	20.00

HARTLEY (Paneled Diamond Cut with Fan)

Non-flint made by Richards and Hartley, Tarentum, PA, in the 1880s and by U. S. Glass Co. in 1891. Trilobed form has either plain or engraved panels. Twenty-three pieces documented.

	Amber	Blue or Vaseline	Clear
Bowl, berry			
7", ftd	30.00	35.00	15.00
9"	30.00	35.00	15.00
Bread Plate, trilobed	30.00	40.00	20.00
Butter, cov	50.00	60.00	40.00
Cake Stand, 10"	45.00	50.00	40.00
Celery Vase	30.00	40.00	25.00
Compote			
Cov, ls, 7¾"	65.00	75.00	45.00
Open, 7" and 8"	30.00	40.00	18.00
Creamer	30.00	35.00	20.00
Dish, centerpiece	40.00	45.00	20.00
Goblet	35.00	40.00	25.00

	Amber	Blue or Vaseline	Clear
Pitcher			
Milk, qt	80.00	85.00	75.00
Water, ½ gal	90.00	90.00	85.00
Plate	45.00	50.00	30.00
Relish.	18.00	20.00	15.00
Spooner	28.00	30.00	18.00
Sugar, cov	40.00	50.00	30.00
Tumbler	30.00	35.00	20.00
Wine	40.00	45.00	20.00

HARVARD YARD (Harvard #1)

Made by Tarentum Glass Co., Tarentum, PA, in 1896. Also found in clear with gold, emerald green, pink, and ruby stained.

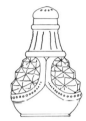

	Clear		Clear
Bowl.	20.00	Plate, 10″	15.00
Butter, cov	30.00	Salt Dip	15.00
Cake Stand	30.00	Sauce	5.00
Cordial	25.00	Spooner	20.00
Creamer	18.00	Sugar, cov	25.00
Egg Cup.	15.00	Toothpick	15.00
Goblet	25.00	Tray, oval	35.00
Jug	45.00	Tumbler	20.00
Pitcher, water	40.00	Wine	15.00

HAWAIIAN LEI

Made by J. B. Higbee Co. during the 1900s. Also may have been made in Canada. Available in clear children's table set and cake plate; some children's pieces reproduced in clear, light blue, pink, and cobalt blue. Some pieces are marked with company trademark—a small bee embossed in glass with HIG/bee, but similar fake trademark reproduced from the 1970s to present.

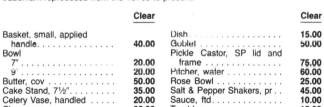

	Clear		Clear
Basket, small, applied		Dish	15.00
handle.	40.00	Goblet	50.00
Bowl		Pickle Castor, SP lid and	
7″	20.00	frame	75.00
9″	20.00	Pitcher, water	60.00
Butter, cov	50.00	Rose Bowl	25.00
Cake Stand, 7½″	35.00	Salt & Pepper Shakers, pr . .	45.00
Celery Vase, handled	20.00	Sauce, ftd.	10.00
Champagne	35.00	Tumbler	15.00
Compote, open, hs, 8″	35.00	Vase, tall, flared rim.	20.00
Creamer	45.00	Wine	25.00

HEART WITH THUMBPRINT (Bull's Eye in Heart, Columbia, Columbian, Heart and Thumbprint)

Non-flint made by Tarentum Glass Co. 1898–1906. Some emerald green pieces have gold trim. Made experimentally in custard, blue custard, opaque Nile green, and cobalt.

	Clear	Emerald Green	Ruby Stain
Banana Boat.	75.00	—	125.00
Barber Bottle	115.00	—	—
Bowl			
7″ sq	35.00	100.00	85.00
9½″ sq	35.00	125.00	90.00
10″ scalloped. . . .	45.00	100.00	80.00
Butter, cov	125.00	175.00	125.00
Cake Stand, 9″	150.00	—	175.00
Carafe, water	100.00	—	150.00

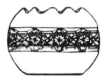

	Clear	Emerald Green	Ruby Stain
Card Tray	20.00	55.00	80.00
Celery Vase	65.00	—	90.00
Compote, open, hs			
7½", scalloped	150.00	—	175.00
8½"	100.00	—	185.00
Cordial, 3" h	125.00	175.00	150.00
Creamer			
Individual	30.00	45.00	35.00
Regular	60.00	110.00	175.00
Cruet	75.00	—	—
Finger Bowl	45.00	85.00	65.00
Goblet	58.00	125.00	110.00
Hair Receiver, lid	60.00	100.00	85.00
Ice Bucket	60.00	—	—
Lamp			
Finger	65.00	125.00	—
Oil, 8"	50.00	160.00	—
Mustard, SP cov	95.00	100.00	—
Nappy, triangular	30.00	60.00	—
Pitcher, water	200.00	—	—
Plate			
6"	25.00	45.00	35.00
10"	45.00	85.00	75.00
Powder Jar, SP cov	65.00	—	—
Punch Cup	20.00	35.00	30.00
Rose Bowl			
Large	60.00	—	90.00
Small	30.00	—	75.00
Salt & Pepper, pr	95.00	—	—
Sauce, 5"	20.00	35.00	30.00
Spooner	50.00	85.00	75.00
Sugar			
Individual	25.00	35.00	35.00
Table, cov	85.00	90.00	—
Syrup	95.00	—	—
Tray, 8¼" l, 4¼" w	30.00	65.00	35.00
Tumbler	45.00	85.00	60.00
Vase			
6"	35.00	65.00	55.00
10"	65.00	100.00	85.00
Wine	45.00	150.00	125.00

HEAVY GOTHIC (Whitton)

Made by Columbia Glass Co., Findlay, OH, c1890 and continued by U. S. Glass Co., Pittsburgh, PA, after 1891.

	Clear	Ruby Stained		Clear	Ruby Stained
Bowl, cov			Open, 7½" d,		
5" d	30.00	65.00	flared	25.00	55.00
7" d	40.00	75.00	Creamer, 4¼" h	25.00	50.00
Bowl, open			Dish, oblong, flat		
5½" d, belled	15.00	25.00	7" l	10.00	20.00
6½" d, flared	15.00	25.00	9" l	15.00	25.00
9" d, belled	20.00	35.00	Goblet, 6¼" h	25.00	50.00
10" d, flared	30.00	45.00	Honey Dish, cov, un-		
Butter, cov, 5¼" d	40.00	125.00	derplate, 4" d	45.00	90.00
Cake Stand, hs			Lamp, oil	90.00	—
9" d	45.00	60.00	Pickle Jar, cov	50.00	110.00
10" d	50.00	65.00	Pitcher, water, ½ gal	45.00	225.00
Celery Vase	25.00	90.00	Salt Shaker, orig top	15.00	45.00
Claret	35.00	65.00	Sauce		
Compote, hs			4" d, flat, belled	8.00	15.00
Cov, 5" d	30.00	90.00	4" d, ftd	10.00	20.00
Cov, 8" d	45.00	110.00	4½" d, flat,		
Open, 6½" d,			scalloped	10.00	20.00
belled	20.00	40.00	5" d, flat, belled	10.00	20.00

	Clear	Ruby Stained		Clear	Ruby Stained
Spooner	20.00	55.00	Sugar Shaker	50.00	150.00
Sugar, cov			Syrup, orig top	50.00	175.00
Breakfast	25.00	45.00	Tumbler	20.00	35.00
Table	35.00	65.00	Wine	15.00	35.00

HEAVY PANELLED FINECUT (Sequoia)

Made by George Duncan and Sons, Pittsburgh, PA, c1880 and by U. S. Glass Co. in 1891. Some handled pieces, such as platter or bread tray, have small leaves on handles. Also found in amber, blue, and vaseline.

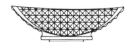

	Clear		Clear
Bowl, berry, 10"	15.00	Pitcher, water	50.00
Bread Tray	30.00	Platter	30.00
Butter, cov	40.00	Spooner	20.00
Cake Stand	35.00	Sugar, cov	35.00
Castor Set, 5-bottle	75.00	Tumbler, Bar	20.00
Celery Boat, 11"	30.00	Tray, small, shaped like large	
Compote, cov, hs, 8"	55.00	platter, with leaves on han-	
Creamer	35.00	dles, 6½" x 4⅜"	15.00
Goblet	20.00		

HENRIETTA (Big Block, Diamond Block, Hexagon Block)

Non-flint pattern made by the Columbia Glass Co., Findlay, OH, c1889. Reissued by U. S. Glass Co., Pittsburgh, PA, c1891–92. Made in clear, emerald green, and ruby stain. Some pieces are found with copper wheel engraving. Prices listed for plain clear pieces.

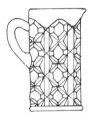

	Clear		Clear
Bowl, 8" d	20.00	Pitcher, water, tankard, ah	50.00
Bread Plate	20.00	Rose Bowl	20.00
Butter Dish, cov, 5½" h	35.00	Salt, master	15.00
Cake Stand, hs, 10" d	40.00	Sauce, 4½" d	10.00
Celery Tray, 8" l	20.00	Spooner	25.00
Compote, open, hs,		Sugar, cov	30.00
scalloped	25.00	Tumbler, 3⅝" h	20.00
Creamer	25.00	Vase, 5" h	25.00

HEXAGON BLOCK

Non-flint pattern made by Hobbs, Brockunier & Co., Wheeling, WV, c1889. Reissued by U. S. Glass Co., Pittsburgh, PA, after 1891 merger. Made in clear, clear with amber or ruby stain, plain or etched with Fern and Berry pattern or Bird and Flower pattern. Prices listed below are for plain pieces.

	Amber or Ruby Stained	Clear		Amber or Ruby Stained	Clear
Bowl, berry, 9" d	40.00	25.00	Goblet	50.00	35.00
Butter Dish, cov	125.00	40.00	Sauce, flat, 4" d	20.00	10.00
Celery Vase, ftd	75.00	35.00	Spooner, ftd	45.00	25.00
Compote, cov, hs, 7"			Sugar, cov, ftd	70.00	45.00
d, deep bowl	90.00	45.00	Tumbler	35.00	15.00
Creamer, ah, ftd	65.00	40.00			

HICKMAN (La Clede)

Non-flint made by McKee & Bros. Glass Co., Pittsburgh, PA, c1897. Also made in ruby stain (rare). Documented in light green and two shades of amber.

	Clear	Emerald Green		Clear	Emerald Green
Banana Stand, ftd . .	65.00	—	Dish, 4" sq	15.00	—
Bonbon, 9", sq	15.00	—	Goblet	30.00	40.00
Bottle, pepper	25.00	—	Ice Bucket	60.00	—
Bowl			Lemonade	15.00	—
Round, or with			Mustard Jar, under-		
scalloped top			plate, cov	45.00	—
4"	12.00	—	Nappy, 5"	10.00	—
4½"	12.00	—	Olive, 4", handle . . .	10.00	20.00
5"	15.00	20.00	Pickle	15.00	20.00
6"	15.00	25.00	Pitcher, water	55.00	—
7"	15.00	—	Plate, 9¼"	15.00	—
8"	20.00	—	Punch Bowl	175.00	375.00
Square, 7"	15.00	18.00	Punch Cup	10.00	15.00
Butter, cov	35.00	60.00	Punch Glass, ftd . . .	30.00	—
Celery	25.00	35.00	Relish	20.00	15.00
Champagne	25.00	—	Rose Bowl	25.00	30.00
Cologne Bottle, fac-			Salt, individual, flat,		
eted stopper	30.00	—	sloping sides	10.00	—
Compote			Salt Shaker, single		
Cov, hs, 7"	75.00	—	Round, long cut		
Open, hs, 8"	45.00	—	neck	15.00	—
Open, ls, 4½",			Round, squat	20.00	30.00
jelly	40.00	45.00	Square	20.00	—
Condiment Set, han-			Sauce	8.50	10.00
dled tray, cruet,			Spooner	27.00	—
pepper bottle,			Sugar, cov	42.00	50.00
open salt	85.00	110.00	Sugar Shaker	45.00	—
Cordial	25.00	—	Toothpick	45.00	75.00
Creamer	25.00	35.00	Tumbler	30.00	—
Cruet, os	45.00	—	Vase, 10¼"	12.00	45.00
Cup, Custard	12.00	—	Wine	30.00	35.00

HIDALGO (Frosted Waffle)

Non-flint made by Adams & Co., Pittsburgh, PA, in the 1880s and by U. S. Glass Co. in 1891. This pattern comes etched and clear, and also with part of pattern frosted. Add 20% for frosted. Rare in color and ruby stained.

	Amber Stained	Clear		Amber Stained	Clear
Bowl, 10", sq	35.00	20.00	Pickle, boat shaped.	18.00	12.00
Bread Plate, cupped,			Pitcher		
sq, 10"	75.00	60.00	Milk	—	40.00
Butter, cov	—	50.00	Water	—	45.00
Celery Vase	35.00	20.00	Plate, 10"	—	35.00
Compote			Salt, master, sq	—	25.00
Cov, hs, 7½"	85.00	65.00	Salt & Pepper	—	40.00
Cov, ls, 6"	—	50.00	Sauce, handled	—	10.00
Open, hs, 10" . . .	—	45.00	Spooner	—	20.00
Open, hs, 11" . . .	—	50.00	Sugar, cov	—	48.00
Creamer	—	40.00	Sugar Shaker	—	45.00
Cruet	—	65.00	Syrup	—	60.00
Cup and Saucer . . .	—	40.00	Tray, water	—	55.00
Egg Cup	—	30.00	Tumbler	—	25.00
Goblet	40.00	20.00	Waste Bowl	—	25.00
Nappy, handled, sq .	—	18.00			

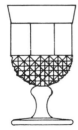

HINOTO (Diamond Point with Panels)

Flint, possibly made by Boston and Sandwich Glass Co. in the late 1850s. Rare in color.

	Clear		Clear
Butter, cov	90.00	Creamer, ah	75.00
Celery Vase	65.00	Egg Cup	35.00
Champagne	75.00	Goblet	60.00
Cologne Bottle, os	48.00	Pitcher, tankard	110.00

	Clear		Clear
Salt	35.00	Tumbler	45.00
Spooner	35.00	Whiskey	50.00
Sugar, cov	75.00	Wine	65.00

HOBB'S BLOCK (Divided Squares)

Non-flint pattern made by Hobbs, Brockunier & Co., Wheeling, WV, c1888. Reissued by U. S. Glass Co., Pittsburgh, PA, after 1891 merger. Made in clear, opaque blue, opaque white, clear with amber stain, clear with acid finish and amber stain.

	Amber Stain	Clear		Amber Stain	Clear
Bowl, oval, 9" d	40.00	30.00	Sauce, flat, 4½" d	15.00	10.00
Butter Dish, cov	55.00	35.00	Spooner	30.00	25.00
Celery Tray	45.00	25.00	Sugar, cov	45.00	35.00
Creamer, oval, ah	40.00	30.00	Tumbler	30.00	15.00
Goblet	100.00	40.00			
Pitcher, water, tankard, ah	90.00	45.00			

HOBNAIL BAND

Non-flint, c1990. Sometimes hobnails are ruby stained.

	Clear	Ruby Stained		Clear	Ruby Stained
Bowl, 9¼"	15.00	—	Coaster	8.00	—
Butter, cov	40.00	55.00	Creamer	25.00	—
Candlesticks, ball top, pr	35.00	—	Cup and Saucer	30.00	—
			Custard Cup	10.00	—
Celery Tray	18.00	—	Goblet	15.00	—
Champagne	12.00	—	Pitcher, water	40.00	75.00

HOBNAIL, OPALESCENT

Made by several companies with variations in forms of pieces c1880–1900. Pieces are found round in shape, with frilled tops, pieces on three feet, pieces on four feet, square in shape or octagonal in shape. Highly reproduced. Fenton Glass still makes this pattern.

	Blue Opal	Green Opal	Vaseline Opal	White Opal
Bar Bottle	—	150.00	—	—
Butter, cov				
Flat	100.00	110.00	105.00	85.00
Four Feet	110.00	115.00	110.00	90.00
* Celery Vase	85.00	120.00	100.00	65.00
* Creamer				
Flat	95.00	115.00	110.00	85.00
Four Feet	100.00	120.00	115.00	95.00
Cruet, os	—	350.00	125.00	50.00
Mug	35.00	55.00	50.00	30.00
Pitcher, water	100.00	275.00	120.00	95.00
Sauce, flat	25.00	35.00	30.00	20.00
Spooner				
Flat	25.00	40.00	30.00	20.00
Four Feet	35.00	40.00	30.00	25.00
Sugar, cov				
Flat	40.00	60.00	55.00	30.00
Four Feet	45.00	65.00	60.00	35.00
* Sugar, open	20.00	25.00	15.00	—
Syrup	85.00	200.00	165.00	75.00
Toothpick	30.00	50.00	50.00	30.00
Tray, water, 11½"	35.00	40.00	30.00	—
Tumbler	40.00	65.00	50.00	30.00
* Wine	24.00	28.00	17.50	—

HOBNAIL, POINTED

Non-flint, c1880. Also found in apple green, dark green, and vaseline.

	Amber	Blue	Clear
Bone Dish	25.00	30.00	20.00
* Bowl.	25.00	30.00	20.00
Butter, cov	48.00	50.00	42.50
Cake Stand, 10" . . .	40.00	45.00	35.00
Celery Vase	30.00	35.00	20.00
Compote, open, hs, 8"	45.00	50.00	40.00
Cordial	25.00	30.00	20.00
Creamer.	30.00	35.00	25.00
Goblet	30.00	35.00	25.00
Inkwell	30.00	35.00	25.00
Pickle.	15.00	20.00	12.00
* Pitcher, water	40.00	45.00	35.00
Plate, 7"	14.00	16.00	12.00
Salt, individual	10.00	15.00	5.00
* Sauce, flat	15.00	12.00	10.00
Spooner.	25.00	30.00	20.00
* Sugar, open	20.00	25.00	15.00
Tray, water, 11½" . .	35.00	40.00	30.00
* Wine	24.00	28.00	17.50

HOBNAIL WITH FAN

Non-flint, made by Adams & Co., Pittsburgh, PA, c1880. Also made in ruby stained.

	Amber	Blue	Clear
Bowl, berry	35.00	40.00	25.00
Butter, cov	55.00	60.00	40.00
Celery Vase	35.00	40.00	30.00
Creamer.	40.00	45.00	25.00
Dish, oblong	—	—	24.00
Goblet	35.00	40.00	20.00
Salt, individual	15.00	18.00	10.00
Sauce, flat, 4¾" . . .	15.00	18.00	6.00
Sugar, cov	45.00	50.00	30.00
Tray, 12" l.	30.00	35.00	20.00

HOLLY

Non-flint, possibly made by Boston and Sandwich Glass Co. in the late 1860s and early 1870s.

	Clear		Clear
Bowl, cov, 8" d	150.00	Pitcher, water, ah	225.00
Butter, cov	150.00	Salt	
Cake Stand, 11"	125.00	Flat, oval.	65.00
Celery Vase	110.00	Ftd	60.00
Compote, cov, hs	165.00	Sauce, flat	20.00
Creamer, ah	125.00	Spooner	60.00
Egg Cup.	65.00	Sugar, cov	125.00
Goblet	100.00	Tumbler	125.00
Pickle, oval.	30.00	Wine	125.00

HONEYCOMB

A popular pattern made in flint and non-flint glass by numerous firms c1850–1900, resulting in many minor pattern variations. Found with copper wheel engraving. Rare in color.

	Flint	Non-Flint		Flint	Non-Flint
Ale Glass	50.00	25.00	Honey Dish, cov	15.00	25.00
Barber Bottle	45.00	25.00	Lamp		
Bowl, cov, 7¼" pat'd			All Glass	—	85.00
1869, acorn finial	100.00	45.00	Marble base	—	90.00
10"	—	40.00	Lemonade	40.00	20.00
Butter, cov	65.00	45.00	Mug, half pint	25.00	15.00
Cake Stand	55.00	35.00	Pitcher, water, ah	165.00	60.00
Castor Bottle	25.00	18.00	Plate, 6"	—	12.50
Celery Vase	45.00	20.00	Pomade Jar, cov	50.00	20.00
Champagne	50.00	25.00	Relish	30.00	20.00
Claret	35.00	35.00	Salt, master, cov,		
Compote, cov, hs			ftd	35.00	30.00
6½" x 8½" h	100.00	50.00	Salt Shaker, orig top	—	35.00
9¼ x 11½" h	110.00	65.00	Sauce	12.00	7.50
Compote, open, hs			Spillholder	35.00	20.00
7 x 5" h	35.00	25.00	Spooner	65.00	35.00
7 x 7" h	60.00	40.00	Sugar		
7½", scalloped	45.00	25.00	Frosted rosebud		
8 x 6¼" h	65.00	40.00	finial	—	50.00
Compote, open, ls,			Regular	75.00	45.00
6" d, Saucer Bowl	35.00	25.00	Tumbler		
7½", scalloped	40.00	25.00	Bar	35.00	—
Cordial, 3½"	35.00	25.00	Flat	40.00	12.50
Creamer, ah	35.00	20.00	Footed	45.00	15.00
Decanter			Vase		
Pint	55.00	18.50	7½"	45.00	—
Quart, os	70.00	65.00	10½"	75.00	—
Egg Cup	20.00	15.00	Whiskey, handled	125.00	—
Finger Bowl	45.00	—	Wine	35.00	15.00
Goblet	25.00	15.00			

HONEYCOMB WITH STAR (Starred Honeycomb)

Non-flint made by Fostoria Glass Co., Moundsville, WV, c1905. Clear and gold trimmed.

	Clear		Clear
Butter, covered	40.00	Cruet	50.00
Cake Stand	30.00	Nappy, handled	10.00
Celery	20.00	Spooner	15.00
Compote, covered, high std	45.00	Sugar, covered	35.00
Creamer	30.00	Tumbler	15.00

HORN OF PLENTY (Comet, Peacock Tail)

Flint and non-flint made by Bryce, McKee & Co., Pittsburgh, PA, c1850. Also produced by McKee & Bros., Pittsburgh, PA, 1850–60. Shards have been found at Boston and Sandwich Glass Co., Sandwich, MA. Applied handles. Reproductions made by Fostoria and L. G. Wright c1938.

	Clear Flint		Clear Flint
Bar Bottle, pewter spout, 8"	135.00	Open, hs, 8"	125.00
Bowl, 8½"	145.00	Open, hs, 9¼"	200.00
Butter, cov		Open, hs, 10½"	250.00
Conventional finial	125.00	Open, ls, 8"	55.00
Shape of Acorn	130.00	Open, ls, 9"	85.00
Butter Pat	20.00	Cordial	150.00
Cake Stand	395.00	Creamer, ah	
Celery Vase	185.00	5½"	225.00
Champagne	145.00	7"	175.00
Compote		Decanter, os	
Cov, hs, 6¼"	175.00	Pint	475.00
Cov, hs, 8¼" d, 5¾" h,		Quart	485.00
oval	350.00	Egg Cup	40.00
Open, hs, 7"	130.00	* Goblet	75.00

	Clear Flint		Clear Flint
* Lamp	200.00	Spill Holder	65.00
Mug, small, applied handle	150.00	Spooner	45.00
Pepper Sauce Bottle, pewter		Sugar, cov	150.00
top	200.00	* Tumbler	75.00
Pitcher, water	600.00	Whiskey	
Plate, 6"	100.00	Applied handle	235.00
Relish, 7" l, 5" w	45.00	Shot glass, 3"	100.00
Salt, master, oval, flat	75.00	Wine	125.00
Sauce, 4½"	15.00		

HORSESHOE (Good Luck, Prayer Rug)

Non-flint made by Adams & Co., Pittsburgh, PA, and others in the 1880s.

	Clear		Clear
Bowl, cov, oval		Marmalade Jar, cov	110.00
7"	150.00	Pitcher	
8"	195.00	Milk	110.00
Bread Plate, 14 x 10"		Water	85.00
Double horseshoe handles	65.00	Plate	
Single horseshoe handles	40.00	7"	45.00
Butter, cov	95.00	10"	55.00
Cake Plate	40.00	Relish	
Cake Stand		5 x 7"	20.00
9"	70.00	8", Wheelbarrow, pewter	
10"	80.00	wheels	75.00
Celery Vase, knob stem	40.00	Salt	
Cheese, cov, woman		Individual, horseshoe shape	20.00
churning	275.00	Master, horseshoe shape	100.00
Compote		Master, wheelbarrow, pew-	
Cov, hs, 7", horseshoe		ter wheels	75.00
finial	95.00	Sauce	
Cov, hs, 8 x 12¼"	125.00	Flat	10.00
Cov, hs, 11"	135.00	Footed	15.00
Creamer, 6½"	55.00	Spooner	35.00
Doughnut Stand	75.00	Sugar, cov	65.00
Finger Bowl	80.00	Vegetable Dish, oblong	35.00
Goblet		Waste Bowl	45.00
Knob Stem	40.00	Wine	150.00
Plain Stem	38.00		

HUBER (Flaring Huber, Straight Huber)

Flint and non-flint made by Bakewell-Pears; Cape Cod Glass Co., George A. Duncan & Sons; King, Son & Co.,; J. B. Lyon & Co.; McKee & Bros.; New England Glass Co.; and Richard and Hartley in the 1860s. Non-flint values would be 35% of prices shown. Rare in color. Etching adds value.

	Clear		Clear
Ale Glass	20.00	Stopper, pt	85.00
Bitters Bottle	50.00	Stopper, qt	85.00
Bowl		Egg Cup	
6"	40.00	Handle	40.00
7", cov	70.00	Regular	30.00
Butter, cov	85.00	Goblet	35.00
Celery	65.00	Jar, ftd, 6" d	75.00
Champagne	35.00	Lemonade	25.00
Claret	50.00	Mug	35.00
Compote		Pitcher, water	150.00
Cov, hs, 8"	100.00	Plate, 7½"	30.00
Cov, hs, 10"	100.00	Salt, ftd	25.00
Cov, ls, 8"	100.00	Sauce, flat	15.00
Open, 7"	60.00	Spooner	35.00
Open, 8", engraved	75.00	Sugar, cov	70.00
Cordial	40.00	Tumbler	
Creamer	80.00	Jelly	25.00
Decanter		Water	20.00
Bar Lip, pt	70.00	Whiskey	35.00
Bar Lip, qt	75.00	Wine	30.00

HUMMINGBIRD (Bird and Fan, Fern and Bird, Flying Robin, Hummingbird and Fern, Thunder Bird)

Non-flint, c1885. A clear water pitcher is known in a mold variant.

	Amber	Blue	Canary	Clear
Butter, cov	110.00	110.00	85.00	60.00
Celery Vase	90.00	90.00	65.00	45.00
Compote, hs, open	95.00	95.00	65.00	48.00
Creamer	75.00	75.00	60.00	40.00
Goblet	55.00	70.00	50.00	35.00
Pitcher				
Milk	65.00	95.00	—	50.00
Water	125.00	150.00	100.00	85.00
Sauce, ftd	25.00	30.00	30.00	18.00
Spooner	40.00	75.00	45.00	30.00
Sugar, cov	100.00	100.00	65.00	55.00
Tray, water	150.00	120.00	80.00	60.00
Tumbler, bar	75.00	75.00	45.00	30.00
Waste Bowl, 5¼"	—	—	—	35.00
Wine	—	—	—	65.00

IDYLL (Jefferson's #251)

Made by Jefferson Glass Co., Follansbee, WV, c1907. Often decorated with gold. Made in clear, green, blue crystal, and white, blue and green opalescent. Prices are for blue or green opal; white about 20% less; non-opalescent colors 50% less.

	Blue or Green Opal		Blue or Green Opal
Bowl, berry, 8"	65.00	Sauce	
Butter, covered	125.00	4½" d	20.00
Condiment Set, cruet, pr		6" d	35.00
shakers, tray	175.00	Spooner	75.00
Cruet	150.00	Sugar, cov	125.00
Pitcher, water	150.00	Toothpick	200.00
Salt & Pepper Shakers, pr	85.00	Tumbler	45.00

ILLINOIS (Clarissa, Star of the East)

Non-flint; One of the States patterns made by U. S. Glass Co. c1897. Most forms are square. A few items are known in ruby stained, including a salt ($50.00), and a lidless straw holder with the stain on the inside ($95.00).

	Clear	Emerald Green		Clear	Emerald Green
Basket, ah, 11½"	100.00	—	Olive	18.00	—
Bowl			Pitcher, milk		
5", round	20.00	—	Round, SP rim	175.00	—
6", sq	25.00	—	Square	65.00	—
8", round	25.00	—	Pitcher, water		
9", sq	35.00	—	Square	65.00	—
* Butter, cov	60.00	—	Tankard, round,		
Candlesticks, pr	95.00	—	SP rim	75.00	135.00
Celery Tray, 11"	40.00	—	Plate, 7", sq	25.00	—
Cheese, cov	75.00	—	Relish		
Compote, open			7½" x 4"	18.00	40.00
hs, 5"	40.00	—	8½ x 3"	18.00	—
hs, 9"	60.00	—	9 × 3", canoe	40.00	—
Creamer			Salt		
Individual	30.00	—	Individual	15.00	—
Table	40.00	—	Master	25.00	—
Cruet	65.00	—	Salt & Pepper, pr	40.00	—
Finger Bowl	25.00	—	Sauce	15.00	—
Marmalade Jar	135.00	—	Spooner	35.00	—

	Clear	Emerald Green		Clear	Emerald Green
Straw Holder, cov	175.00	400.00	Tray, 12 x 8", turned		
Sugar			up sides	50.00	—
Individual	30.00	—	Tumbler	30.00	40.00
Table, cov	55.00	—	Vase, 6", sq	35.00	45.00
Sugar Shaker	65.00	—	Vase, 9½"	—	125.00
Syrup, pewter top	95.00	—			
Toothpick					
Adv emb in base	45.00	—			
Plain	30.00	—			

INDIANA (Doric, Prison Windows)

Non-flint pattern made by U. S. Glass Co., Factory U, Glass City, IN, c1897. Made in clear and found rarely with ruby stain.

	Clear		Clear
Bowl, 6" d	15.00	Salt Shaker	20.00
Butter Dish, cov	45.00	Sauce, flat, 4" d	15.00
Celery Tray	25.00	Spooner	35.00
Compote, open, hs, jelly	30.00	Sugar, cov	45.00
Creamer	35.00	Tumbler	35.00
Pitcher, water, tankard	65.00		

INTAGLIO (Flower Spray with Scroll)

Made by Northwood Co., Indiana, PA, c1899. Also reported in custard trimmed in green and gold. Creamers in blue opalescent were used as premiums in 1901 by Arbuckle Coffee.

	Blue Opal	Custard	Vaseline Opal	White Opal
Bowl, berry	50.00	50.00	60.00	45.00
Butter, cov	165.00	235.00	170.00	150.00
Compote, jelly	45.00	100.00	60.00	35.00
Creamer	60.00	100.00	50.00	40.00
Cruet, os	100.00	210.00	110.00	95.00
Pitcher, water	200.00	185.00	225.00	125.00
Sauce	35.00	90.00	42.00	25.00
Spooner	75.00	115.00	80.00	50.00
Sugar, cov	150.00	100.00	100.00	85.00
Tumbler	65.00	70.00	58.00	45.00
Wine	—	—	—	20.00

INVERTED FAN AND FEATHER

Made by Northwood Co., Wheeling, WV, c1900. Also known in carnival and canary opalescent.

	Blue Opal	Clear Opal	Custard	Green w/ Gold	Pink Slag
Bowl, berry					
Individual	40.00	—	40.00	15.00	160.00
Master	125.00	100.00	225.00	110.00	740.00
Butter, cov	275.00	195.00	245.00	200.00	650.00
Compote, jelly	200.00	195.00	175.00	195.00	375.00
Creamer	80.00	65.00	175.00	85.00	450.00
Cruet	200.00	195.00	575.00	195.00	950.00
Lamp, individual	—	—	375.00	—	—
Pitcher, water	325.00	200.00	500.00	215.00	750.00
Rose Bowl, ftd	150.00	—	—	—	—
Salt Shaker, single	—	—	95.00	—	300.00
Spooner	100.00	75.00	100.00	75.00	—
*Sugar, cov	145.00	95.00	125.00	100.00	550.00
*Tumbler	80.00	25.00	80.00	35.00	450.00

INVERTED FERN

Flint attributed to Boston and Sandwich Glass Co. c1860. Goblets reproduced in color as well as non-flint clear.

	Clear		Clear
Bowl, 7″	45.00	Plate, 6″	100.00
Butter, cov	95.00	Pitcher, water	250.00
Champagne	125.00	Salt, master, ftd	35.00
Compote, open, hs, 8″	55.00	Sauce, flat	10.00
Creamer, ah	125.00	Spooner	40.00
Egg Cup	30.00	Sugar, cov	80.00
* Goblet, rayed base	45.00	Tumbler	95.00
Honey Dish	18.00	Wine	75.00

INVERTED STRAWBERRY

Non-flint made by Cambridge Glass Co. c1908. Ruby stained also found in souvenir types. No original toothpick made. Reproduced in carnival glass, amethyst, and green by Guernsey Glass Co., Cambridge, OH. Available in children's berry set and punch set.

	Clear	Ruby Stained		Clear	Ruby Stained
Basket, ah	65.00	—	* Pitcher, water	45.00	—
Bowl, 9″	25.00	—	* Plate, 10″	24.00	40.00
Butter, cov	65.00	—	Punch Cup	12.00	—
Celery Tray,			Relish, 7″	12.00	—
handled	30.00	—	Rose Bowl	30.00	—
Compote, open, hs,			Salt, individual	20.00	—
5″	38.00	—	Sauce, flat, 4″	18.00	—
Creamer	25.00	—	Spooner	25.00	—
* Cruet	45.00	—	Sugar, cov	45.00	—
Goblet	25.00	—	* Toothpick	25.00	—
Mug	20.00	30.00	* Tumbler	—	45.00
Nappy	15.00	—			

IOWA (Paneled Zipper)

Non-flint made by U. S. Glass Co. c1902. Part of the States pattern series. Available in clear glass with gold trim (add 20%) and ruby or cranberry stained. Also found in amber (goblet, $65.00), green, canary, and blue. Add 50% to 100% for color.

	Clear		Clear
Bowl, berry	12.00	Lamp	125.00
Bread Plate, motto	80.00	Olive	15.00
Butter, cov	40.00	Pitcher, water	50.00
Cake Stand	35.00	Punch Cup	15.00
Carafe	35.00	Salt Shaker, single	24.00
Compote, cov, 8″	40.00	Sauce, 4½″	6.50
Corn Liquor Jug, os	60.00	Spooner	30.00
Creamer	30.00	Sugar, cov	35.00
Cruet, os	30.00	Toothpick	20.00
Cup	15.00	Tumbler	25.00
Decanter, 1½ pts	40.00	Vase, 8″ h	20.00
Goblet	28.00	Wine	30.00

IRIS WITH MEANDER (Iris)

Made by Jefferson Glass Co., Steubenville, OH, c1903. Available in gold trim in clear, apple green, amethyst (toothpick, $50.00; water pitcher, $115.00), and blue. Also found in amber opalescent (rare) and green opalescent (usually found in berry sets and toothpicks).

	Blue Opal	Canary Opal	White Opal
Bowl, berry	95.00	80.00	50.00
Butter, cov	310.00	195.00	125.00
Compote, jelly, 5" . .	85.00	75.00	50.00
Creamer	145.00	100.00	60.00
Cruet, os	200.00	150.00	100.00
Pickle	30.00	30.00	20.00
Pitcher, water	225.00	200.00	125.00
Plate, 7"	50.00	60.00	35.00
Salt & Pepper	100.00	100.00	85.00
Sauce	30.00	30.00	30.00
Spooner	75.00	65.00	50.00
Sugar, cov	150.00	100.00	80.00
* Toothpick	85.00	60.00	50.00
Tumbler	60.00	45.00	30.00
Vase, 11"	60.00	35.00	25.00

IVANHOE

Originally made by Dalzell, Gilmore and Leighton Co., Findlay, OH, in 1897 in a large number of clear pieces.

	Clear		Clear
Butter, cov	40.00	Spooner	20.00
Compote, open, 7"	35.00	Sugar, cov	35.00
Creamer	25.00	Syrup Jug, metal top	75.00
Cruet, os	65.00	Tumbler	25.00
Pitcher, water	60.00		

IVY IN SNOW (Ivy in Snow-Red Leaves, Forest Ware)

Non-flint pattern made by Co-Operative Flint Glass Co., Beaver Falls, PA, in the 1890s. Phoenix Glass of Monaco, PA, also produced this pattern 1937–42 and was called Forest Ware. Ivy in Snow-Red Leaves is the name used for pieces where the leaves are ruby stained. Some pieces have a ruby stained band. Also known in amber stained. Widely reproduced pattern with many reproductions in white milk glass.

	Clear	Ruby Stained		Clear	Ruby Stained
Bowl			Mug	25.00	40.00
7"	20.00	—	Pitcher		
8 x 5½"	30.00	—	Milk	85.00	200.00
Butter, cov	55.00	—	Water	55.00	250.00
Cake Stand, 8"	45.00	—	Plate		
Celery Vase	30.00	75.00	6"	20.00	—
Champagne	35.00	55.00	7"	25.00	—
Compote			10"	30.00	—
Cov, hs, 6" d	45.00	75.00	Relish	20.00	30.00
Open, jelly	35.00	55.00	Sauce	15.00	20.00
Creamer			Spooner	35.00	60.00
Regular	30.00	75.00	Sugar, cov	50.00	75.00
Tankard	35.00	135.00	Syrup	70.00	275.00
Finger Bowl	25.00	—	Tumbler	25.00	45.00
Goblet	35.00	65.00	Wine	32.00	55.00
Marmalade Jar	35.00	—			

JACOB'S COAT

Non-flint, c1880. Colors are rare (add 50%).

	Clear		Clear
Bowl, 8"	20.00	Celery	25.00
Butter, cov	48.00	Creamer	24.00

	Clear		Clear
Goblet	30.00	Spooner	30.00
Milk	45.00	Sugar, cov	48.00
Water	45.00		

JACOB'S LADDER (Maltese)

Non-flint made by Portland Glass Co., Portland, ME, and Bryce Bros, Pittsburgh, PA, in 1876 and by U. S. Glass Co. in 1891. A few pieces found in amber, yellow, blue, pale blue, and pale green.

	Clear		Clear
Bowl		Creamer	35.00
6" x 8¾"	15.00	Cruet, os, ftd	85.00
6¾" x 9¾"	20.00	Goblet	60.00
7½" x 10¾"	20.00	Honey Dish, 3½"	10.00
9", berry, ornate SP holder,		Marmalade Jar	75.00
ftd	125.00	Mug	100.00
Butter, cov	65.00	Pitcher, water, ah	150.00
Cake Stand		Plate, 6¼"	20.00
8" or 9"	50.00	Relish 9½ x 5½"	15.00
11" or 12"	60.00	Salt, master, ftd	20.00
Castor Bottle	18.00	Sauce	
Castor Set, 4 bottles	100.00	Flat, 4", or 5"	8.00
Celery Vase	45.00	Footed, 4"	12.00
Cologne Bottle, Maltese		Spooner	35.00
cross stopper, ftd	85.00	Sugar, cov	80.00
Compote		Syrup	
Cov, hs, 6"	80.00	Knight's Head finial	125.00
Cov, hs 7½"	80.00	Plain top	100.00
Cov, hs, 9½"	125.00	Tumbler, bar	85.00
Open, hs, 7½"	35.00	Wine	35.00
Open, hs, 8½", scalloped	30.00		
Open, hs, 9½", scalloped	38.00		
Open, hs, 10"	40.00		

JASPER (Belt Buckle, Eleanor, Late Buckle)

Non-flint pattern made by Bryce Brothers, Pittsburgh, PA, c1880. Reissued by U. S. Glass Co., Factory B, Pittsburgh, PA, after 1891 merger.

	Clear		Clear
Bowl, 5" d	15.00	Pitcher, water	65.00
Butter Dish, cov	35.00	Sauce, ftd, 4" d	10.00
Cake Stand, hs, 9" d	25.00	Spooner	25.00
Compote, cov, hs, 8" d	55.00	Sugar, cov	35.00
Creamer, 6" h	25.00	Wine	25.00
Goblet	25.00		

JERSEY SWIRL (Swirl)

Non-flint made by Windsor Glass Co., Pittsburgh, PA, c1887. Heavily reproduced in color by L. G. Wright Co. The clear goblet is also reproduced.

	Amber	Blue	Canary	Clear
Bowl, 9¼"	55.00	55.00	45.00	35.00
Butter, cov	55.00	55.00	50.00	40.00
Cake Stand, 9"	75.00	70.00	45.00	30.00
* Celery Vase	42.00	42.00	35.00	30.00
* Compote, hs, 8"	50.00	50.00	45.00	35.00
Creamer	45.00	45.00	40.00	30.00
Cruet, os	—	—	—	25.00
* Goblet				
Buttermilk	40.00	40.00	35.00	30.00
Water	40.00	40.00	35.00	30.00
Marmalade Jar	—	—	—	50.00

	Amber	Blue	Canary	Clear
Pickle Castor, SP frame and lid	—	—	—	125.00
Pitcher, water	50.00	50.00	45.00	35.00
Plate, round				
6"	25.00	25.00	20.00	15.00
8"	30.00	30.00	25.00	20.00
10"	38.00	38.00	35.00	30.00
* Salt, Ind	20.00	20.00	18.00	15.00
Sauce, 4½", flat . . .	20.00	20.00	15.00	10.00
Spooner	30.00	30.00	25.00	20.00
Sugar, cov	40.00	40.00	35.00	30.00
Tumbler	30.00	30.00	25.00	20.00
* Wine	50.00	50.00	40.00	15.00

JEWEL AND FLOWER (Beaded Oval and Leaf)

Made by Northwood Glass Co., Wheeling, WV, c1908.

	Clear Opal	Blue Opal	Vaseline Opal
Bowl, berry	55.00	75.00	85.00
Butter, cov	75.00	95.00	250.00
Creamer	60.00	55.00	100.00
Cruet	75.00	95.00	100.00
Pitcher, water	125.00	140.00	150.00
Salt Shaker	35.00	50.00	50.00
Sauce, gold trim . . .	25.00	—	—
Spooner	50.00	80.00	80.00
Sugar, cov	75.00	90.00	100.00
Tumbler	45.00	50.00	75.00

JEWELED HEART

Made by Northwood Glass Co., Indiana, PA, and others, 1898–1910. Also made in clear, blue, and apple green. Some items have goofus coloring. A clear creamer is valued at $25.00; 6" plate, $18.00; and a clear with gold water pitcher is $75.00. A clear green toothpick is $45.00. No goblet or wine were originally made. Heavily reproduced.

	Green Opal	Sapphire Blue Opal	White Opal
Bowl, berry, ruffled edge	100.00	115.00	50.00
Butter, cov	130.00	135.00	100.00
* Creamer	90.00	100.00	50.00
Cruet	200.00	175.00	85.00
Pitcher, water	135.00	150.00	100.00
Salt Shaker	40.00	50.00	35.00
Sauce	25.00	30.00	20.00
Spooner	75.00	80.00	45.00
* Sugar, cov	100.00	85.00	55.00
Sugar Shaker	100.00	110.00	75.00
Syrup	125.00	140.00	125.00
* Toothpick	35.00	35.00	30.00
Tumbler	25.00	35.00	25.00

JUBILEE (Isis, Radiant Daisy and Button)

Non-flint made by McKee & Bros., Jeannette, PA, c1890–1904. Made in clear and ruby stained.

	Clear		Clear
Bowl	20.00	Plate, 9" d	20.00
Butter, cov	30.00	Spooner	15.00
Creamer	15.00	Sugar, cov	25.00
Goblet	18.00	Wine	20.00
Pitcher, water	35.00		

JUMBO

A non-flint novelty pattern made by Canton Glass Co., Canton, OH, and by Aetna Glass in 1884 as well as other companies, resulting in many variants. The unique motif was used to commemorate P. T. Barnum's famous elephant, "Jumbo."

	Clear		Clear
Butter, cov		Creamer, plain Jumbo	225.00
Oblong, plain Jumbo	400.00	Pitcher, water	550.00
Round, Barnum's head. . .	325.00	Sauce	50.00
Compote		Spoon Rack	350.00
Cov 7"	400.00	Spooner, Barnum's head . . .	100.00
Cov, 8"	500.00	Sugar, cov, Barnum's head .	400.00
Cov, 10"	750.00		
Cov, 12"	800.00		

KANSAS (Jewel with Dewdrop)

Non-flint originally produced by Co-Operative Flint Glass Co., Beaver Falls, PA. Later produced as part of the States pattern series by U. S. Glass Co. in 1901 and by Jenkins Glass Co, c1915–25. Also known with jewels stained in pink or gold. Mugs (smaller and inferior quality) have been reproduced in vaseline, amber, and blue.

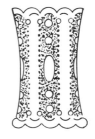

	Clear		Clear
Banana Stand.	90.00	Open, hs, 7"	35.00
Bowl		Open, hs, 8"	45.00
7", oval	35.00	Creamer.	40.00
8"	40.00	Goblet	55.00
Bread Plate, ODB	45.00	* Mug	
Butter, cov	65.00	Regular.	45.00
Cake Plate	45.00	Tall	25.00
Cake Stand		Pitcher	
7⅝"	45.00	Milk.	50.00
9"	75.00	Water	60.00
10"	85.00	Relish, 8½", oval.	20.00
Celery Vase	45.00	Salt Shaker.	50.00
Compote		Sauce, flat, 4"	12.00
Cov, hs, 5".	45.00	Sugar, cov	65.00
Cov, hs, 6".	50.00	Syrup.	125.00
Cov, hs, 7".	65.00	Toothpick	65.00
Cov, hs, 8".	85.00	Tumbler	45.00
Cov, ls, 5"	50.00	Whiskey	15.00
Open, hs, 5"	25.00	Wine	65.00
Open, hs, 6"	30.00		

KENTUCKY

Non-flint made by U. S. Glass Co. c1897 as part of the States pattern series. The goblet is found in ruby stained ($50.00). A footed, square sauce ($30.00) is known in cobalt blue with gold. A toothpick holder is also known in ruby stained ($150.00).

	Clear	Emerald Green		Clear	Emerald Green
Bowl, 8" d.	20.00	—	Plate, 7", sq	15.00	—
Butter, cov	50.00	—	Punch Cup	10.00	15.00
Cake Stand, 9½". . .	40.00	—	Salt Shaker, orig top	10.00	—
Creamer.	25.00	—	Sauce, ftd, sq	8.00	12.00
Cruet, os	45.00	—	Spooner	35.00	—
Cup	10.00	20.00	Sugar, cov	30.00	—
Goblet	20.00	50.00	Toothpick, sq	35.00	85.00
Nappy	10.00	15.00	Tumbler	20.00	30.00
Olive, handle	25.00	—	Wine	28.00	38.00
Pitcher, water	55.00	—			

KING'S CROWN (Ruby Thumbprint, X.L.C.R.)

Non-flint made by Adams & Co. Pittsburgh, PA., in the 1890s and later. Known as Ruby Thumbprint when pieces are ruby stained. Made in clear and with the thumbprints stained amethyst, gold, green, and yellow, and in clear with etching and trimmed in gold. It became very popular after 1891 as ruby stained souvenir ware. Approximately eighty-seven pieces documented. NOTE: Pattern has been copiously reproduced for the gift-trade market in milk glass, cobalt blue, and other colors. New pieces are easily distinguished: in the case of Ruby Thumbprint, the color is a very pale pinkish red. Available in amethyst stained in goblet ($30.00) and wine ($10.00) and in green stained in goblet ($25.00) and wine ($15.00). Add 30% for engraved pieces.

	Clear	Ruby Stained		Clear	Ruby Stained
Banana Stand, ftd . .	85.00	135.00	Honey Dish, cov, sq	100.00	175.00
Bowl			* Lamp, oil, 10"	135.00	—
9¼" d, pointed . . .	35.00	90.00	Mustard, cov, 4" h . .	35.00	75.00
10" d, scalloped . .	45.00	95.00	Olive Dish.	25.00	45.00
Butter, cov, 7½" d . .	50.00	90.00	Preserve, 10" l	35.00	50.00
* Cake Stand			Pickle, lobed	18.00	40.00
9" d.	68.00	125.00	Pitcher		
10" d.	75.00	125.00	Milk, tankard	75.00	100.00
Castor Bottle.	45.00	70.00	Water, bulbous. . .	95.00	225.00
Castor Set, glass			Water, tankard . . .	110.00	200.00
stand, 4 bottles . .	175.00	300.00	Plate, 7".	20.00	45.00
Celery Vase	40.00	60.00	Punch Bowl, ftd. . . .	275.00	300.00
* Champagne	25.00	35.00	Punch Cup	15.00	30.00
Claret.	35.00	50.00	Salt		
Compote			Ind, rect	15.00	35.00
Cov, hs, 8".	55.00	245.00	Master, sq	30.00	50.00
Cov, ls, 12"	90.00	225.00	Salt Shaker, 3⅛" h .	30.00	40.00
Open, hs, 8¼" . . .	75.00	95.00	* Sauce, 4"	15.00	20.00
Open, ls, 5¼" . . .	30.00	45.00	Spooner, 4¼" h . . .	45.00	50.00
* Cordial	45.00	—	* Sugar		
* Creamer, ah 3¼" h			Ind, open, 2¾" h .	25.00	45.00
Ind, tankard, ...	25.00	35.00	Table, cov, 6¾" h.	55.00	95.00
Table, 4⅞" h	50.00	65.00	Toothpick 2¾" h . . .	20.00	35.00
Cup and Saucer . . .	55.00	70.00	Tumbler, 3¾" h	20.00	35.00
Custard Cup	15.00	25.00	* Wine, 4⅜" h	25.00	40.00
* Goblet	30.00	45.00			

KING'S #500 (Bone Stem, Parrot, Swirl and Thumbprint)

Made by King, Son & Co. Pittsburgh, PA, in 1891. Continued by U. S. Glass Co. 1891–98, and made in a great number of pieces. It was made in clear, frosted, and a rich, deep blue, known as Dewey Blue, both trimmed in gold. A clear goblet with frosted stem ($50.00) is known. Also known in dark green and a ruby stained sugar is reported ($95.00).

	Clear w/ Gold	Dewey Blue w/ Gold		Clear w/ Gold	Dewey Blue w/ Gold
Bowl			Finger Bowl	15.00	35.00
7"	10.00	30.00	Lamp		
8"	12.00	35.00	Hand.	45.00	—
9"	14.00	45.00	Stand	65.00	—
Butter, cov	65.00	125.00	Pitcher, water	55.00	200.00
Cake Stand	40.00	60.00	Relish.	20.00	30.00
Castor Set, 3 bottles	75.00	200.00	Rose Bowl	20.00	45.00
Celery Vase	20.00	65.00	Salt Shaker.	15.00	40.00
Compote			Sauce	15.00	35.00
Cov, hs, 8".	50.00	75.00	Spooner	30.00	70.00
Open, hs, 10" . . .	25.00	40.00	Sugar, cov		
Creamer, bulbous, ah			Individual.	20.00	40.00
Individual.	20.00	35.00	Table	45.00	75.00
Table	30.00	50.00	Syrup.	55.00	225.00
Cruet	45.00	175.00	Tumbler	25.00	35.00
Cup	10.00	15.00			
Decanter, locking					
top	100.00	—			

KLONDIKE (Amberette, English Hobnail Cross, Frosted Amberette)

Non-flint attributed to A. J. Beatty and Co. c1885. It was also made by Hobbs, Brockunier & Co. and Dalzell, Gilmore and Leighton Co. c1880. Made in colors other than clear and amber stained, which are the original colors. Made to commemorate the Alaskan Gold Rush. The frosted panels depict snow; the amber bands, gold. Found clear and frosted, with or without scrolls, depending on the maker. Prices are listed for frosted; clear prices would be approximately 20% of those shown.

	Frosted Amber Stain		Frosted Amber Stain
Bowl, berry, 8"..........	200.00	Salt Shaker, single	100.00
Butter, cov	300.00	Sauce, flat	75.00
Cake Stand, 8", sq	450.00	Spooner	175.00
Celery Tray.............	200.00	* Sugar, cov	250.00
Celery Vase	225.00	Syrup, pewter lid........	650.00
Condiment Set, cruet and		Toothpick	350.00
shaker on tray	1,000.00	Tray, 5½", sq	200.00
Creamer...............	250.00	Tumbler	135.00
Cruet, os	450.00	Vase, trumpet shape	
Goblet	400.00	8"	225.00
Pitcher, water	650.00	10"	250.00
Punch Cup	100.00	Wine	400.00

KOKOMO (Bar and Diamond, R and H Swirl Band)

Non-flint made by Richards and Hartley, Tarentum, PA, c1885. Reissued by U. S. Glass Co., c1891 and Kokomo Glass Co., Kokomo, IN, c1901. Found in ruby stained and etched. Over fifty pieces manufactured.

	Clear	Ruby Stained		Clear	Ruby Stained
Bowl, 8½", ftd	24.00	—	Cruet	35.00	—
Bread Tray	30.00	45.00	Decanter, 9¾", wine	55.00	95.00
Butter, cov	35.00	—	Finger Bowl	25.00	35.00
Cake Stand	45.00	165.00	Goblet	25.00	45.00
Celery Vase	30.00	45.00	Lamp, hand, atypi-		
Compote			cal has no dia-		
Cov, hs, 7½"	35.00	165.00	monds.........	50.00	100.00
Open, hs, 5"	20.00	—	Pitcher, tankard....	55.00	100.00
Open, hs, 6"	25.00	—	Sauce, ftd, 5"	8.00	10.00
Open, hs, 7"	30.00	—	Spooner	25.00	45.00
Open, hs, 8"	35.00	—	Sugar, cov	45.00	65.00
Open, ls, 7½" ...	20.00	—	Sugar Shaker	35.00	75.00
Condiment Set, ob-			Syrup...........	45.00	130.00
long tray, shakers,			Tray, water	35.00	90.00
cruet..........	80.00	195.00	Tumbler	20.00	35.00
Creamer, ah	35.00	50.00	Wine	20.00	35.00

LEAF AND DART (Double Leaf and Dart, Pride)

Non-flint made by Richards and Hartley Flint Glass Co., Pittsburgh, PA, c1875. Reissued by U. S. Glass Co. c1891. Shards have been found at Boston and Sandwich Glass Co., Sandwich, MA, as well as Burlington Glass Works, Hamilton, Ontario, Canada.

	Clear		Clear
Bowl, 8¼", ftd	25.00	Salt, master, ftd	
Butter, cov	60.00	Cov.................	65.00
Celery Vase	30.00	Open	30.00
Creamer, ah	40.00	Sauce, 4", flat...........	8.50
Cruet, pedestal, ah	100.00	Spooner	30.00
Egg Cup...............	20.00	Sugar, cov	45.00
Goblet	28.00	Syrup................	90.00
Honey Dish.............	8.00	Tumbler, ftd	25.00
Pitcher, water, ah	80.00	Wine	30.00
Relish.................	15.00		

LEAF AND FLOWER

Made by Hobbs, Brockunier & Co., Wheeling, WV, c1890 and U. S. Glass Co., Pittsburgh, PA, c1891. It was made in clear and clear with amber stain. Acid etched (frosting) can be found in both clear and clear with amber stained pieces. A few pieces have been documented in clear with ruby stain.

	Clear	Clear w/ Amber Stain		Clear	Clear w/ Amber Stain
Bowl, scalloped			Finger Bowl,		
7", shallow	25.00	35.00	scalloped	55.00	85.00
8", deep	30.00	40.00	Pitcher, water,		
9", shallow	25.00	35.00	tankard	65.00	95.00
Butter, cov	60.00	90.00	Salt & Pepper Shak-		
Castor Set, mustard,			ers, pr	40.00	60.00
oil bottle, salt &			Sauce, flat		
pepper shakers,			4½"	15.00	30.00
leaf shaped tray	125.00	175.00	5"	25.00	30.00
Celery Basket, scal-			Spooner	25.00	40.00
loped, pressed			Sugar, cov	35.00	50.00
rope handle	35.00	65.00	Syrup, orig top	125.00	220.00
Celery Vase	35.00	75.00	Tumbler	20.00	35.00
Creamer	35.00	45.00			

LEAF AND STAR (Tobin)

Made by New Martinsville Glass Co., New Martinsville, WV, 1910–15. A toothpick (valued at $45.00) has been found in orange iridescent. Also found in ruby stained (add 100%).

	Clear w/ Gold		Clear w/ Gold
Bowl, berry	18.00	Hair Receiver, metal top	18.00
Butter, cov	35.00	Pitcher, water	50.00
Compote, jelly	18.00	Sauce, flat	8.50
Creamer	28.00	Spooner	25.00
Dresser Jar, metal top	18.00	Sugar, cov	30.00
Goblet	20.00	Tumbler	20.00

LEAF MEDALLION

Made by Northwood Glass Co., c1904. With gold trim, beading, and medallions.

	Clear	Green	Cobalt	Amethyst
Bowl, berry, ftd	12.00	25.00	50.00	50.00
Butter, cov	45.00	75.00	120.00	120.00
Cake Stand, 10"	35.00	70.00	140.00	140.00
Compote, open, jelly,				
5", 6"	30.00	55.00	65.00	75.00
Condiment Set, salt				
& pepper shakers				
cruet, tray	—	200.00	225.00	—
Creamer	30.00	60.00	85.00	90.00
Pitcher, water	50.00	100.00	225.00	225.00
Spooner	25.00	50.00	95.00	95.00
Sugar, cov	35.00	70.00	140.00	150.00
Tumbler	25.00	50.00	65.00	95.00

LENS AND STAR (Star and Oval)

Made by O'Hara Glass Co., Pittsburgh, PA, in 1880; in 1891 and after by U. S. Glass Co. It comes in clear with plain or frosted panels. Amber stained butter dish is known.

	Frosted		Frosted
Butter, cov	45.00	Spooner	20.00
Celery	30.00	Sugar, cov	45.00
Creamer	30.00	Syrup	45.00
Pitcher, water, barrel shape	50.00	Tumbler	25.00
Sauce	8.00	Waste Bowl.	20.00

LEVERNE (Star in Honeycomb)

Non-flint made by Bryce Bros., Pittsburgh, PA, in the late 1880s. Reissued by U. S. Glass Co. c1891. Wines found in amber and blue.

	Clear		Clear
Bowl, oval	20.00	Pitcher	
Butter, cov	40.00	Milk.	50.00
Cake Stand	35.00	Water	55.00
Celery Vase	35.00	Relish, 5¼ x 7¼"	15.00
Compote		Sauce, 4½"	
Cov, hs	60.00	Flat	8.00
Open, hs	35.00	Ftd	12.00
Creamer	35.00	Spooner	30.00
Cruet	50.00	Sugar, cov	35.00
Goblet	30.00	Tumbler	25.00
Pickle	15.00	Wine	20.00

LIBERTY (Cornucopia #2)

Non-flint pattern made by McKee & Brothers, Pittsburgh, PA, in 1892. Made in clear with some pieces found with engraving.

	Clear		Clear
Bowl, berry	10.00	Sauce, flat	10.00
Butter, cov	45.00	Spooner	25.00
Champagne	35.00	Sugar, cov	45.00
Creamer	30.00	Tumbler	30.00
Goblet	40.00	Water Tray	45.00
Pitcher, water, tankard	60.00	Wine	30.00

LIBERTY BELL (Centennial)

Made by Adams & Co., Pittsburgh, PA, for the Centennial Exposition, 1876. Some items also made in milk glass. Reproduced. Some reproductions bear the year "1976" and "200 Years" instead of the original inscriptions.

	Clear		Clear
Bowl, 8", ftd	100.00	Pickle	45.00
Bread Plate, 13⅜ x 9½"		Pitcher, water, ah	800.00
Clear, no signatures	85.00	Plate	
Milk Glass, sgd John Han-		6", dated	75.00
cock	300.00	8"	60.00
Butter, cov	145.00	10"	80.00
Children's Table Set	475.00	* Platter, 13 x 8", twig handles,	
Creamer		13 states	65.00
Applied Handle	95.00	Relish, oval	60.00
Reed Handle	100.00	Salt Dip, individual, oval	30.00
* Goblet	40.00	Salt Shaker	95.00
Mug		Sauce, ftd	20.00
Child's	200.00	Spooner	60.00
Snake Handle	400.00	Sugar, cov	90.00

LILY OF THE VALLEY

Non-flint possibly made by Boston and Sandwich Glass Co., Sandwich, MA, and King, Son & Co. in the 1870s. Shards have also been found at Burlington Glass Works, Hamilton, Ontario, Canada. Lily of the Valley on Legs is a name frequently

given to those pieces having three tall legs. Legged pieces include a covered butter, covered sugar, and creamer and spooner. Add 25% for this type.

	Clear		Clear
Butter, cov	70.00	Relish.	15.00
Buttermilk Goblet.	35.00	Salt, master	
Cake Stand	65.00	Cov.	125.00
Celery Tray.	40.00	Open	50.00
Celery Vase	55.00	Sauce, flat	12.00
Champagne	80.00	Spooner.	35.00
Compote		Sugar	
Cov, hs, 8½"	85.00	Cov.	75.00
Open, hs.	50.00	Open	35.00
Creamer, ah	65.00	Tumbler	
Cruet, os	110.00	Flat.	50.00
Egg Cup.	40.00	Footed	65.00
Goblet	55.00	Vegetable Dish, oval	30.00
Honey Dish.	10.00	Wine	100.00
Nappy, 4"	20.00		
Pickle, scoop shape	20.00		
Pitcher			
Milk.	125.00		
Water	135.00		

LINCOLN DRAPE WITH TASSEL

Flint made originally by Boston and Sandwich Glass Co., probably continued by other companies, c1865. Commemorative of Lincoln's death. Items without tassels are valued at 20% less. Some very rare pieces in cobalt blue are 200% more.

	Clear		Clear
Butter, cov	100.00	Honey Dish.	20.00
Celery Vase	90.00	Lamp, marble base	125.00
Compote		Pitcher, water, ah	350.00
Cov, hs, 8½"	150.00	Plate, 6"	80.00
Open, hs, 7½"	75.00	Salt, master, ftd.	125.00
Open, ls, 6"	65.00	Sauce, 4"	20.00
Creamer, ah	125.00	Spill	50.00
Egg Cup.	40.00	Spooner	75.00
Goblet		Sugar, cov	115.00
Lady's.	165.00	Syrup, ah	175.00
Water	120.00	Wine	135.00

LION (Frosted Lion)

Made by Gillinder and Sons, Philadelphia, PA, in 1876. Available in clear without frosting (20% less). Many reproductions.

	Frosted		Frosted
Bowl, oblong		Cordial	175.00
6½ x 4¼"	55.00	* Creamer.	75.00
8 x 5"	50.00	Cup and Saucer, child size .	45.00
Bread Plate, 12"	90.00	Egg Cup, 3½" h	65.00
Butter, cov		* Goblet	70.00
Lion's head finial	90.00	Marmalade Jar, rampant	
Rampant finial	125.00	finial	85.00
Cake Stand	85.00	Pitcher	
Celery Vase	85.00	Milk.	375.00
Champagne	175.00	Water	300.00
Cheese, cov, rampant lion		Relish, lion handles	38.00
finial	400.00	Salt, master, rect lid.	250.00
Children's Table Set	500.00	* Sauce, 4", ftd	25.00
Compote		* Spooner	75.00
Cov, hs, 7", rampant finial	150.00	Sugar, cov	
* Cov, hs, 9", rampant finial,		Lion head finial	90.00
oval, collared base	150.00	Rampant finial	110.00
Cov, 9", hs.	185.00	Syrup, orig top	350.00
Open, ls, 8"	75.00	Wine	200.00

LOCKET ON CHAIN (Stippled Beaded Shield)

Non-flint pattern made by A. H. Heisey Co., Newark, OH, c1896. Made in clear and clear with ruby stain. Rarely found in green, milk glass, or vaseline. Prices listed below are for plain clear pieces.

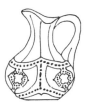

	Clear		Clear
Bowl, berry, 8" d	85.00	Salt Shaker	60.00
Butter Dish, cov	100.00	Sauce, flat, 4" d	35.00
Cake Stand, hs	125.00	Spooner	75.00
Compote, cov, hs, 8" d	175.00	Sugar, cov	100.00
Creamer, 4⅝" h	85.00	Tumbler	80.00
Goblet	85.00	Wine	70.00
Pitcher, water	185.00		

LOG CABIN

Non-flint made by Central Glass Co. Wheeling, WV, c1875. Also available in color, but rare. Creamer, spooner, and covered sugar reproduced in clear, chocolate, and cobalt blue.

	Clear		Clear
Bowl, cov, 8 x 5¼ x 3⅝"	400.00	Pitcher, water	300.00
Butter, cov	300.00	Sauce, flat	75.00
Compote, hs, 10½"	275.00	* Spooner	120.00
* Creamer	100.00	* Sugar, cov	275.00
Marmalade Jar, cov	275.00		

LOOP (Seneca Loop)

Flint, c1850s–60s; later in non flint. Made by several firms. Boston and Sandwich Glass Co. produced fiery opalescent pieces. Yuma Loop is a contemporary with comparable values.

	Flint	Non-Flint		Flint	Non-Flint
Bowl, 9"	50.00	25.00	Goblet	20.00	15.00
Butter, cov	60.00	40.00	Pitcher, water, ah	170.00	60.00
Cake Stand	95.00	50.00	Salt, master, ftd	25.00	18.00
Celery Vase	65.00	20.00	Spooner	30.00	24.00
Champagne	35.00	25.00	Sugar, cov	70.00	30.00
Compote			Syrup	95.00	—
Cov, hs, 9½"	135.00	60.00	Tumbler		
Open, hs, 9"	115.00	40.00	Footed	25.00	15.00
Cordial, 2¾" h	40.00	20.00	Water	40.00	20.00
Creamer, ah	70.00	35.00	Wine	30.00	12.00
Egg Cup	30.00	20.00			

LOOP AND DART

Clear and stippled non-flint of the late 1860s and early 1870s. Made by Boston and Sandwich Glass Co., Sandwich, MA, and Richards and Hartley, Tarentum, PA. Pattern related to Loop and Dart with Diamond Ornament, and Loop and Dart with Round Ornament, which was made by Portland Glass Co., Portland, ME. Flint add 25%.

	Clear		Clear
Bowl, 9", oval	25.00	Creamer	35.00
Butter, cov	45.00	Cruet, os	95.00
Cake Stand, 10"	40.00	Egg Cup	25.00
Celery Vase	35.00	Goblet	25.00
Compote		Lamp, oil	85.00
Cov, hs, 8"	85.00	Pitcher, water	75.00
Cov, ls, 8"	65.00	Plate, 6"	35.00

	Clear		Clear
Relish.	18.00	Tumbler	
Salt, master	50.00	Footed	30.00
Sauce	5.00	Water	25.00
Spooner	25.00	Wine	35.00
Sugar, cov	50.00		

LOOP AND DART WITH DIAMOND ORNAMENT

Clear and stippled non-flint of the late 1860s and early 1870s. Made by Boston and Sandwich Glass Co., and Richards and Hartley. Pattern related to Loop and Dart, and Loop and Dart with Round Ornament, which was made by Portland Glass Co., Portland, ME. Flint add 25%.

	Clear		Clear
Bowl, 9", oval	20.00	Sauce, flat	4.50
Butter, cov	45.00	Spooner	30.00
Celery Vase	35.00	Sugar, cov	40.00
Creamer	35.00	Tumbler	
Egg Cup	24.00	Footed	35.00
Goblet	32.00	Water	40.00
Relish.	15.00	Wine	35.00
Salt, master	18.00		

LOOP AND DART WITH ROUND ORNAMENT (Portland Loop and Jewel)

Clear and stippled non-flint of the late 1860s and early 1870s. Made by Portland Glass Co., Portland, ME. Pattern related to Loop and Dart, and Loop and Dart with Diamond Ornaments. Flint add 25%.

	Clear		Clear
Bowl, 9", oval	28.00	Pitcher, water	90.00
Butter, cov	80.00	Plate, 6"	35.00
Butter Pat	15.00	Relish.	15.00
Celery Vase	35.00	Salt, master	28.00
Champagne	85.00	Sauce, flat	8.00
Compote		Spooner	30.00
Cov, hs, 8"	85.00	Sugar, cov	50.00
Cov, ls, 8"	65.00	Tumbler	
Open, hs, 8"	45.00	Footed	30.00
Creamer	35.00	Water	35.00
Egg Cup	30.00	Wine	35.00
Goblet			
Buttermilk	20.00		
Water	32.00		

LOOP AND JEWEL (Jewel and Festoon, Queen's Necklace, Venus)

Non-flint made by Beatty Glass and National Glass Co. then continued by Indiana Glass Co. Made until 1915. About forty pieces known. A few rare pieces available in milk white, including salt shaker.

	Clear		Clear
Bowl, 8"	15.00	Relish, 8"	22.00
Butter, cov	55.00	Salt Shaker	15.00
Champagne	40.00	Sauce, flat, 4"	5.00
Compote, 6½"	20.00	Sherbet	45.00
Creamer	25.00	Spooner	30.00
Dish, 5" sq	15.00	Sugar, cov	40.00
Goblet	20.00	Syrup	55.00
Pickle, 8", rect	18.00	Vase, 8¾"	40.00
Pitcher, water	45.00	Wine	30.00
Plate, sq	15.00		

LOOP WITH DEWDROPS

Non-flint made by U. S. Glass Co., Pittsburgh, PA, 1892–98.

	Clear		Clear
Bowl, 8"	15.00	Cup and Saucer	25.00
Butter, cov	40.00	Goblet	25.00
Cake Stand. 10"	40.00	Pitcher, water	40.00
Celery	25.00	Salt & Pepper Shakers, pr	50.00
Compote, cov, 8", high		Spooner	20.00
standard	55.00	Sugar, cov	35.00
Condiment Set, tray	85.00	Tray, double handles	45.00
Creamer	30.00	Tumbler	20.00
Cruet	55.00	Wine	25.00

LORRAINE (Flat Diamond)

Non-flint pattern made by Fostoria Glass Co., Fostoria, OH, c1893.

	Clear	Ruby Stained		Clear	Ruby Stained
Bowl, berry	25.00	45.00	Spooner	25.00	40.00
Creamer	25.00	45.00	Sugar, cov	40.00	65.00
Pitcher, water	50.00	125.00	Tumbler	20.00	35.00
Salt Shaker	25.00	35.00			

LOUISIANA (Sharp Oval and Diamond, Granby)

Made by Bryce Bros., Pittsburgh, PA, in the 1870s. Reissued by U. S. Glass Co. c1898 as one of the States patterns. Also available with gold and also comes frosted.

	Clear		Clear
Bowl, 9", berry	20.00	Match Holder	35.00
Butter, cov	65.00	Mug, handled, gold top	25.00
Cake Stand	45.00	Nappy, 4", cov	30.00
Celery Vase	30.00	Pitcher, water	65.00
Compote		Relish	15.00
Cov, hs, 8"	75.00	Spooner	30.00
Open, hs, 5", jelly	40.00	Sugar, cov	45.00
Creamer	30.00	Tumbler	25.00
Goblet	30.00	Wine	35.00

MAGNET AND GRAPE (Magnet and Grape with Stippled Leaf)

Flint possibly made by Boston and Sandwich Glass Co. c1860. Later non-flint versions have grape leaf in either clear or stippled. Imperial Glass began producing reproductions from new molds for the Metropolitan Museum of Art, NY, in 1971. Each lead crystal piece was marked "M.M.A."

	Flint Frosted Leaf	Non-Flint Stippled or Clear Leaf		Flint Frosted Leaf	Non-Flint Stippled or Clear Leaf
Bowl, cov, 8"	175.00	75.00	* Creamer	175.00	40.00
Butter, cov	185.00	40.00	Decanter, os		
Celery Vase	150.00	25.00	Pint	150.00	75.00
Champagne	135.00	45.00	Quart	200.00	85.00
Compote			Egg Cup	75.00	20.00
Cov, hs, 4½"	125.00	—	* Goblet		
Open, hs, 7½"	110.00	65.00	Low Stem	75.00	—
Cordial, 4"	125.00	—	Regular stem	70.00	30.00

	Flint Frosted Leaf	Non-Flint Stippled or Clear Leaf		Flint Frosted Leaf	Non-Flint Stippled or Clear Leaf
Pitcher			Spooner	95.00	30.00
Milk, ah	—	75.00	* Sugar, cov	125.00	80.00
Water, ah	350.00	75.00	Syrup	125.00	55.00
Relish, oval	35.00	15.00	* Tumbler, water	110.00	30.00
Salt, ftd	50.00	25.00	Whiskey	140.00	25.00
Sauce, 4″	20.00	7.50	* Wine	90.00	50.00
Spill	65.00	—			

MAINE (Paneled Stippled Flower, Stippled Primrose)

Non-flint made by U. S. Glass Co., Pittsburgh, PA, c1899. Researchers dispute if goblet was made originally. Sometimes found with enamel trim or overall turquoise stain.

	Clear	Emerald Green		Clear	Emerald Green
Bowl, 8″	30.00	40.00	Mug	35.00	—
Bread Plate, oval, 10			Pitcher		
× 7¾″	30.00	—	Milk	65.00	85.00
Butter, cov	48.00	—	Water	50.00	125.00
Cake Stand	40.00	60.00	Relish	15.00	—
Compote			Salt Shaker, single	30.00	—
Cov, jelly	50.00	75.00	Sauce	15.00	—
Open, hs, 7″ . . .	20.00	45.00	Sugar, cov	45.00	75.00
Open, ls, 8″	38.00	55.00	Syrup	75.00	225.00
Open, ls, 9″	30.00	65.00	Toothpick	125.00	—
Creamer	30.00	—	Tumbler	30.00	45.00
Cruet, os	80.00	—	Wine	50.00	75.00

MANHATTAN

Non-flint with gold made by U. S. Glass Co. c1902. A depression glass pattern also has the "Manhattan" name. A table sized creamer and covered sugar are known in true ruby stained, and a goblet is known in old marigold carnival glass. Heavily reproduced by Anchor Hocking Glass Co. and Tiffin Glass Co.

	Clear	Rose Stained		Clear	Rose Stained
Biscuit Jar, cov	60.00	85.00	* Goblet	25.00	—
Bowl			Ice Bucket	—	65.00
6″	18.00	—	Olive, Gainsborough	30.00	—
8¼″, scalloped . . .	20.00	—	Pitcher, water, ½ gal		
* 9½″	20.00	—	Bulbous, ah	70.00	—
10″	22.00	—	Tankard, ah	60.00	125.00
12½″	25.00	—	Plate		
Butter, cov	55.00	—	5″	10.00	—
Cake Stand, 8″	45.00	55.00	6″	10.00	30.00
Carafe, water	40.00	65.00	8″	15.00	—
Celery Tray, 8″	20.00	—	10¾″	20.00	—
Celery Vase	25.00	—	Punch Bowl	125.00	—
Cheese, cov, 8⅜″ d	—	115.00	Punch Cup	10.00	—
Compote			Relish, 6″	12.00	—
Cov, hs, 9½″	60.00	—	Salt Shaker, single	20.00	35.00
Open, hs, 9½″ . . .	45.00	—	Sauce	14.00	20.00
Open, hs, 10½″ . .	50.00	—	* Spooner	20.00	—
* Creamer			Straw Holder, cov . .	95.00	—
Individual	20.00	—	* Sugar		
Table	30.00	60.00	Individual, open . .	15.00	—
Cruet			Table, cov	40.00	65.00
Large	65.00	115.00	Syrup	48.00	175.00
Small	50.00	—	* Toothpick	30.00	—

	Clear	Rose Stained		Clear	Rose Stained
Tumbler			Violet Bowl	20.00	—
Ice Tea	30.00	—	Water Bottle	40.00	—
Water	20.00	—	* Wine	20.00	—
Vase, 6"	18.00	—			

MAPLE LEAF (Leaf, Maple Leaf on Trunk)

Non-flint made by Gillinder and Sons, c1880. Heavily reproduced in clear and colors by L. G. Wright and others.

	Amber	Blue	Canary/ Vaseline	Clear	Frosted
Bowl					
5½", oval.	45.00	55.00	45.00	25.00	35.00
6", ftd	50.00	60.00	50.00	40.00	55.00
Bread Plate	70.00	85.00	75.00	75.00	85.00
* Butter, cov	75.00	80.00	75.00	65.00	70.00
* Cake Stand, 11" . . .	60.00	65.00	60.00	45.00	50.00
Celery	45.00	50.00	45.00	35.00	40.00
* Compote					
Cov, hs, 9".	65.00	90.00	65.00	85.00	100.00
Jelly	50.00	60.00	50.00	40.00	45.00
* Creamer.	65.00	65.00	68.00	50.00	55.00
* Goblet	85.00	100.00	95.00	65.00	90.00
* Pitcher					
Milk.	80.00	95.00	85.00	65.00	75.00
Water	85.00	100.00	90.00	75.00	80.00
Platter, 10½".	45.00	50.00	50.00	40.00	45.00
Sauce					
5"	15.00	20.00	20.00	10.00	15.00
6", ftd	28.00	30.00	28.00	15.00	20.00
* Spooner	60.00	75.00	60.00	40.00	45.00
* Sugar, cov	50.00	100.00	80.00	65.00	75.00
ª Tumbler	40.00	45.00	40.00	35.00	45.00

MARDI GRAS (Duncan and Miller #42, Paneled English Hobnail with Prisms)

Made by Duncan and Miller Glass Co. c1898. Available in gold trim and ruby stained.

	Clear	Ruby Stained		Clear	Ruby Stained
Bowl, 8", berry	18.00	—	Plate, 6"	10.00	—
Butter, cov	65.00	145.00	Punch Bowl	200.00	—
Cake Stand, 10" . . .	65.00	—	Punch Cup	10.00	—
Celery Tray, curled			Relish.	12.50	—
edges	25.00	—	Rose Bowl	25.00	50.00
Champagne, saucer	32.00	—	Sherry, flared or		
Children's Table Set	120.00	385.00	straight	35.00	—
Claret.	35.00	—	Spooner	25.00	—
Compote			Sugar, cov	35.00	65.00
Cov, hs	55.00	—	Syrup, metal lid. . . .	65.00	—
Open, jelly, 4½" . .	30.00	55.00	Toothpick	35.00	125.00
Cordial	35.00	—	Tumbler		
Creamer.	35.00	60.00	Bar	25.00	—
Finger Bowl	25.00	—	Champagne.	20.00	—
Goblet	35.00	—	Water	30.00	40.00
Lamp Shade.	35.00	—	Wine	30.00	65.00
Pitcher					
Milk.	50.00	—			
Water	75.00	200.00			

MARQUISETTE

Non-flint made by Co-Operative Glass Co., Beaver Falls, PA, c1880.

	Clear		Clear
Butter, cov	45.00	Goblet	30.00
Celery Vase	35.00	Pitcher, ah	75.00
Compote		Sauce	10.00
Cov, hs	60.00	Spooner	25.00
Open, hs, 7"	40.00	Sugar, cov	45.00
Open, ls	35.00	Wine	30.00
Creamer, ah	55.00		

MARSH FERN

Made by Riverside Glass Works, Wellsburg, WV, c1889. Some items are found with copper wheel engraving.

	Clear		Clear
Bowl, flat, 7½" d	30.00	Creamer	35.00
Butter, cov	40.00	Goblet	40.00
Cake Stand, hs, 9⅜"	50.00	Jelly Compote	30.00
Celery	45.00	Pitcher, water	80.00
Compote		Sauce, 4¼" d	10.00
Cov, hs, 7¼"	75.00	Spooner	35.00
Cov, ms, 6⅛"	70.00	Sugar, cov	35.00
Open, hs, 6⅛"	75.00		

MARSH PINK (Square Fuchsia)

Non-flint made in OH, c1880. Pieces are square shaped. Occasionally found in amber (prices 100% higher).

	Clear		Clear
Bowl, 9"	20.00	Pitcher, water	75.00
Butter, cov, handles	45.00	Plate, 10", sq	35.00
Cake Stand	45.00	Salt Shaker	20.00
Compote		Sauce	
Cov, hs, 7½"	50.00	Flat, handle	10.00
Cov, jelly, 5½"	30.00	Footed	15.00
Creamer	30.00	Spooner	25.00
Dish, 5", cov	30.00	Sugar, cov	35.00
Honey Dish, ftd, cov	50.00	Wine	20.00
Pickle Castor, sp frame	100.00		

MARYLAND (Inverted Loop and Fan, Loop and Diamond)

Made originally by Bryce Bros., Pittsburgh, PA. Continued by U. S. Glass Co. as one of its States patterns.

	Clear w/ Gold	Ruby Stained		Clear w/ Gold	Ruby Stained
Banana Dish	35.00	85.00	Pitcher		
Bowl, berry	15.00	35.00	Milk	42.50	135.00
Bread Plate	25.00	—	Water	50.00	100.00
Butter, cov	65.00	95.00	Plate, 7", round	25.00	—
Cake Stand, 8"	40.00	—	Relish, oval	15.00	55.00
Celery Tray	20.00	35.00	Salt Shaker, single	30.00	—
Celery Vase	28.00	65.00	Sauce, flat	10.00	15.00
Compote			Spooner	30.00	55.00
Cov, hs	65.00	100.00	Sugar, cov	45.00	60.00
Open, jelly	25.00	45.00	Toothpick	125.00	175.00
Creamer	25.00	55.00	Tumbler	25.00	50.00
Goblet	30.00	48.00	Wine	40.00	75.00
Olive, handled	15.00	—			

MASCOTTE (Dominion, Etched Fern and Waffle, Minor Block)

Non-flint made by Ripley and Co., Pittsburgh, PA, in the 1880s. Reissued by U. S. Glass Co. in 1891. The butter dish shown on Plate 77 of Ruth Webb Lee's *Victorian Glass* is said to go with this pattern. It has a horsehoe finial and was named for the famous "Maude S," "Queen of the Turf" trotting horse during the 1880s. Apothecary jar and pyramid jars made by Tiffin Glass Co. in the 1950s.

	Clear	Etched		Clear	Etched
Bowl			Open, hs, 9"	30.00	35.00
Cov, 5"	—	35.00	Open, ls, 8"	30.00	45.00
Cov, 6"	—	35.00	Creamer........	30.00	45.00
Cov, 7"	—	45.00	Goblet	40.00	45.00
Cov, 8"	—	50.00	Pitcher, water	55.00	65.00
Cov, 9"	—	55.00	Plate, turned in		
Open 9"	35.00	40.00	sides.........	40.00	45.00
Butter Pat.......	15.00	20.00	Pyramid Jar, 7" d,		
Butter, cov			one fits into other		
"Maude S"	100.00	100.00	and forms tall jar		
Regular........	50.00	65.00	type container with		
Cake Basket, handle	80.00	65.00	lid, three sizes		
Cake Stand	35.00	50.00	with flat sepa-		
Celery Vase	35.00	40.00	rators	50.00	55.00
Cheese, cov	70.00	80.00	Salt Dip	25.00	—
Compote			Salt Shaker, single	25.00	25.00
Cov, hs, 5".....	35.00	40.00	Sauce		
Cov, hs, 6".....	40.00	45.00	Flat..........	8.00	15.00
Cov, hs, 7".....	45.00	55.00	Footed	12.00	16.00
Cov, hs, 8".....	55.00	85.00	Spooner........	30.00	35.00
Cov, hs, 9".....	65.00	90.00	Sugar, cov	40.00	45.00
Open, hs, 5"	20.00	25.00	Tray, water	40.00	55.00
Open, hs, 6"	20.00	25.00	Tumbler	20.00	35.00
Open, hs, 7"	25.00	30.00	Wine	25.00	30.00
Open, hs, 8"	30.00	35.00			

MASONIC (Inverted Prism)

Non-flint made by McKee & Bros. Glass Co., Jeannette, PA, c1894–1920. Rare pieces are found in emerald green (add 50%) and in ruby stained (100%).

	Clear		Clear
Bowl, sq or round		Custard Cup............	15.00
4".................	20.00	Goblet	25.00
4½".................	20.00	Handle, salad fork........	20.00
5".................	20.00	Honey Dish, cov, flat, sq ...	40.00
6" (round only).........	20.00	Nappy, heart shape.......	30.00
7".................	25.00	Pitcher, water, tankard.....	60.00
8".................	30.00	Relish, serpentine shape ...	15.00
9", salad, silver frame....	45.00	Salt Dip	
Butter cov		Round..............	15.00
Flat.................	45.00	Square	15.00
Footed	60.00	Salt Shaker	
Cake Stand		Round..............	15.00
9".................	36.00	Square	25.00
10".................	40.00	Sardine Box, rect, flat	25.00
Celery	20.00	Spooner..............	25.00
Compote		Syrup, Jug	75.00
Cov, 8"	45.00	Sugar, cov	40.00
Open, 8½"............	35.00	Toothpick	30.00
Creamer................	25.00	Tumbler	15.00
Cruet	35.00	Wine	28.00

MASSACHUSETTS (Arched Diamond Points, Cane Variant, Geneva #2, M2-131, Star and Diamonds)

Made in the 1880s, unknown maker, reissued in 1898 by U. S. Glass Co. as one of the States series. The vase ($45.00) and wine ($45.00) are known in emerald green. Some pieces reported in cobalt blue and marigold carnival glass. Reproduced in clear and colors.

	Clear		Clear
Bar Bottle, metal shot glass		Pitcher, water	65.00
for cover	75.00	Plate, 8"	32.00
Basket, 4½", ah	50.00	Punch Cup	15.00
Bowl		Relish, 8½"	25.00
6", sq	17.50	Rum Jug	90.00
9", sq	20.00	Salt Shaker, tall	25.00
* Butter, cov	50.00	Sauce, sq, 4"	15.00
Celery Tray	30.00	Sherry	40.00
Champagne	35.00	Spooner	20.00
Cologne Bottle, os	37.50	Sugar, cov	40.00
Compote, open	35.00	Syrup	65.00
Cordial	55.00	Toothpick	40.00
Creamer	28.00	Tumbler	30.00
Cruet, os	45.00	Vase, trumpet	
Goblet	45.00	6½" h	25.00
Gravy Boat	30.00	7" h	25.00
Mug	20.00	9" h	35.00
Mustard Jar, cov	35.00	Whiskey	25.00
Olive	8.50	Wine	40.00

MEDALLION (Hearts and Spades, Spades)

Non-flint, c1880. Imperial Glass Co., Bellaire, OH, has reproduced the butter dish. These reproductions can be easily detected: often the design is reversed, new colors are harsh, and the "I.G." monogram can be found on the base.

	Amber and Canary	Apple Green and Blue	Clear
Bottle	65.00	55.00	40.00
* Butter, cov	40.00	50.00	35.00
Cake Stand, 9¼" . . .	45.00	55.00	25.00
Celery Vase	30.00	40.00	20.00
Compote, cov, hs . .	50.00	60.00	40.00
Creamer	40.00	45.00	30.00
Egg Cup	25.00	40.00	20.00
Goblet	35.00	45.00	20.00
Pickle	20.00	25.00	15.00
Pitcher, water	55.00	65.00	45.00
Sauce			
Flat	12.00	15.00	10.00
Footed	14.00	20.00	12.00
Spooner	28.00	40.00	20.00
Sugar, cov	40.00	50.00	25.00
Tumbler	25.00	35.00	15.00
Waste Bowl	32.00	45.00	20.00
Wine	30.00	40.00	20.00

MEDALLION SUNBURST

Made by J. B. Higbee Co. of Bridgeport, PA, c1905.

	Clear		Clear
Bowl		Goblet	24.00
8¼", sq	28.00	Mug, 3¼"	18.00
9¼", round	30.00	Pitcher	
Butter, cov	50.00	Milk	45.00
Butter Pat	5.00	Water	50.00
Cake Stand		Plate, 7¼"	25.00
9¼"	65.00	Punch Cup	15.00
10½"	70.00	Relish	12.00
Celery Vase	24.00	Salt Dip	10.00
Compote, open, hs, 8"	25.00	Salt & Pepper, pr.	35.00
Creamer	25.00	Sauce, flat	10.00
Cruet, os	20.00	Spooner	20.00

	Clear		Clear
Sugar, cov	30.00	Vase, 9½".	32.50
Toothpick	25.00	Wine	30.00
Tumbler	20.00		

MELROSE (Diamond Beaded Band)

Non-flint made by Greensburg Glass Co., Greensburg, PA, in 1887 in clear, etched, and ruby stained. Reissued by Brilliant Glass Co. 1887–88, McKee & Bros. c1901, J. B. Higbee Co. c1907, Dugan Glass Co. c1915, and New Martinsville Glass Co. in 1916. Add 20% for etching.

	Clear		Clear
Bowl, berry	20.00	Plate	
Butter, cov	45.00	7"	15.00
Cake Plate	30.00	8"	10.00
Cake Stand	32.00	Salt, individual	6.00
Celery Vase	25.00	Salt Shaker	15.00
Compote		Sauce, flat	8.00
Cov, hs, 8"	90.00	Spooner	30.00
Open, hs, 7"	25.00	Sugar, cov	38.00
Open, jelly	18.00	Tray, water 11½"	45.00
Creamer	30.00	Tumbler	15.00
Goblet	20.00	Waste Bowl	20.00
Pitcher, water, tankard	60.00	Wine	20.00

MICHIGAN (Loop and Pillar)

Non-flint made by U. S. Glass Co. c1902 as one of the States pattern series. The 10¼" bowl ($42.00) and punch cup ($12.00) are found with yellow or blue stain. Also found with painted carnations. Other colors include "Sunrise," gold, and ruby stained.

	Clear	Rose Stained		Clear	Rose Stained
Bowl			Olive, two handles	10.00	25.00
7½"	15.00	30.00	Pickle	12.00	20.00
9"	35.00	60.00	Pitcher		
10¼"	35.00	62.00	8"	50.00	—
Butter, cov			12", tankard	70.00	150.00
Large	60.00	125.00	Plate, 5½" d	15.00	—
Small	65.00	—	Punch Bowl, 8"	50.00	—
Celery Vase	40.00	85.00	Punch Cup	8.00	—
Compote			Relish	20.00	35.00
Jelly, 4½"	45.00	75.00	Salt Shaker, single, 3		
Open, hs, 9¼"	65.00	85.00	types	20.00	30.00
Creamer			Sauce	12.00	22.00
Ind, 6 oz, tankard	20.00	65.00	Sherbet cup, handled	15.00	20.00
Table	30.00	50.00	Spooner	50.00	72.00
Cruet, os	60.00	225.00	Sugar, cov	50.00	75.00
Crushed Fruit Bowl	75.00	—	Syrup	95.00	175.00
Custard Cup	15.00	—	* Toothpick	45.00	100.00
Finger Bowl	15.00	—	Tumbler	30.00	40.00
Goblet	35.00	65.00	Vase		
Honey Dish	10.00	—	Bud	35.00	40.00
Lemonade Mug	24.00	40.00	Ftd, large	45.00	—
Nappy, Gainsborough handle	35.00	—	Wine	35.00	50.00

MINERVA (Roman Medallion)

Non-flint made by Boston and Sandwich Glass Co., Sandwich, MA, c1870 as well as other American companies. Shards have been found at Burlington Glass Works, Hamilton, Ontario, Canada.

	Clear			Clear
Bowl		Cov, ls, 8″		125.00
Footed	40.00	Open, hs, 10½″, octagonal		
Rectangular		ftd		95.00
7″	25.00	Creamer		45.00
8 x 5″	30.00	Goblet		90.00
9″	45.00	Marmalade Jar, cov		150.00
Bread Plate	65.00	Pickle		25.00
Butter, cov	75.00	Pitcher, Water		185.00
Cake Stand		Plate		
8″	150.00	8″		55.00
9 x 6½″	100.00	10″, handled		60.00
10½″	120.00	Platter, oval, 13″		65.00
13″	145.00	Sauce		
Champagne	85.00	Flat		18.50
Compote		Footed, 4″		20.00
Cov, hs, 6″	85.00	Spooner		40.00
Cov, hs, 7″	110.00	Sugar, cov		65.00
Cov, ls, 7″	90.00	Waste Bowl		50.00
Cov, hs, 8″	150.00			

MINNESOTA

Non-flint made by U. S. Glass Co. in the late 1890s as one of the States patterns. A two-piece flower frog has been found in emerald green ($46.00).

	Clear	Ruby Stained		Clear	Ruby Stained
Banana Stand	65.00	—	Match Safe	25.00	—
Basket	65.00	—	Mug	25.00	—
Biscuit Jar, cov	55.00	150.00	Olive	15.00	25.00
Bonbon, 5″	15.00	—	Pitcher, water, tank-		
Bowl, 8½″, flared . . .	30.00	100.00	ard	85.00	200.00
Butter, cov	50.00	—	Plate		
Carafe	35.00	—	5″, turned up		
Celery Tray, 13″ . . .	25.00	—	edges	25.00	—
Compote			7⅜″ d	15.00	—
Open, hs, 10″,			Pomade Jar, cov . . .	35.00	—
flared	60.00	—	Relish	20.00	—
Open, ls, 9″, sq . .	55.00	—	Salt Shaker	25.00	—
Creamer			Sauce, boat shape	10.00	25.00
Individual	20.00	—	Spooner	25.00	—
Table	30.00	—	Sugar, cov	35.00	—
Cruet	35.00	—	Syrup	65.00	—
Cup	18.00	—	Toothpick, 3 handles	30.00	150.00
Goblet	35.00	50.00	Tray, 8″ l	15.00	—
Hair Receiver	30.00	—	Tumbler	20.00	—
Juice Glass	20.00	—	Wine	40.00	—

MISSOURI (Palm and Scroll)

Non-flint made by U. S. Glass Co. c1898 as one of the States pattern series. Also made in amethyst, blue, and canary.

	Clear	Emerald Green		Clear	Emerald Green
Bowl			Cov, hs, 7″	45.00	—
Cov, 6″ d	35.00	—	Cov, hs, 8″	50.00	—
Cov, 7″ d	45.00	—	Open, hs, 5″ . . .	25.00	—
Cov, 8″ d	50.00	—	Open, hs, 6″ . . .	30.00	—
Open, 6″ d	15.00	30.00	Open, hs, 7″ . . .	40.00	—
Open, 7″ d	15.00	35.00	Open, hs, 8″ . . .	45.00	—
Open, 8″ d	30.00	40.00	Open, hs, 9″ . . .	50.00	—
Butter, cov	45.00	65.00	Open, hs, 10″ . . .	60.00	—
Cake Stand, 9″	35.00	45.00	Cordial	35.00	60.00
Celery Vase	30.00	—	Creamer	25.00	40.00
Compote			Cruet	55.00	130.00
Cov, hs, 5″	35.00	—	Dish, cov 6″	65.00	65.00
Cov, hs, 6″	40.00	—	Doughnut Stand, 6″	40.00	55.00

	Clear	Emerald Green		Clear	Emerald Green
Goblet	50.00	60.00	Salt Shaker, single	35.00	45.00
Mug	35.00	45.00	Sauce, flat, 4"	10.00	16.00
Pickle, rect	15.00	25.00	Spooner	25.00	48.00
Pitcher			Sugar, cov	50.00	65.00
Milk	40.00	85.00	Syrup	85.00	175.00
Water	75.00	85.00	Tumbler	30.00	40.00
Relish	10.00	12.50	Wine	40.00	45.00

MITERED DIAMOND (Pyramid, Sunken Buttons)

Unknown maker, believed to be of Ohio origin. Made 1880–90.

	Amber	Apple Green	Blue	Clear	Vaseline
Bowl, 8", sq	20.00	—	—	—	—
Bread Plate	35.00	40.00	35.00	32.00	35.00
Butter, cov	60.00	60.00	70.00	55.00	65.00
Celery	25.00	30.00	30.00	20.00	30.00
Compote, ls, collared base					
Cov	60.00	65.00	60.00	55.00	60.00
Open	40.00	50.00	45.00	40.00	50.00
Creamer	30.00	40.00	35.00	30.00	35.00
Goblet	30.00	40.00	35.00	25.00	40.00
Pickle	20.00	25.00	25.00	15.00	25.00
Pitcher, water	55.00	60.00	60.00	50.00	60.00
Platter	35.00	40.00	35.00	32.00	35.00
Relish	20.00	25.00	25.00	15.00	25.00
Salt Shaker, orig top	20.00	30.00	25.00	15.00	25.00
Sauce, sq, flat	10.00	15.00	10.00	10.00	15.00
Spooner	30.00	30.00	30.00	25.00	30.00
Sugar, cov	45.00	50.00	50.00	45.00	50.00
Tumbler	—	—	25.00	—	—
Wine	45.00	35.00	35.00	30.00	35.00

MONKEY

Non-flint pattern attributed to George Duncan & Sons, Pittsburgh, PA, c1880. Made in clear and opalescent.

	Clear	Opalescent		Clear	Opalescent
Bowl, berry	125.00	175.00	Pitcher, water	250.00	850.00
Butter Dish, cov	195.00	300.00	Sauce, flat, 4" d	25.00	45.00
Celery Vase,			Spooner	95.00	125.00
scalloped	90.00	195.00	Sugar, cov	175.00	325.00
Creamer	125.00	250.00	Tumbler	100.00	195.00
Mug	85.00	150.00	Waste Bowl	100.00	145.00

MOON AND STAR (Palace)

Non-flint and frosted (add 30%). First made by Adams & Co., Pittsburgh, PA, in the 1880s and later by several manufacturers, including Pioneer Glass who probably decorated ruby stained examples. Also found with frosted highlights. Heavily reproduced in clear and color.

	Clear		Clear
Banana Stand	90.00	* Butter, cov	70.00
Bowl		Cake Stand, 10"	50.00
6" d	20.00	Carafe	40.00
8" d	25.00	Celery Vase	35.00
12½" d	45.00	Champagne	75.00
Bread Plate, rect	45.00	Claret	45.00

	Clear		Clear
* Compote		* Salt, individual	10.00
Cov, hs, 10"	68.00	* Salt & Pepper, pr.	70.00
Cov, ls, 6½"	55.00	Sauce	
Open, hs, 9"	35.00	Flat.	8.50
Open, ls, 7½"	25.00	Footed	12.00
* Creamer.	55.00	* Spooner	45.00
Cruet	125.00	* Sugar, cov	65.00
Egg Cup.	35.00	Syrup.	150.00
* Goblet	45.00	Tray, water	65.00
Lamp	140.00	Tumbler, ftd	50.00
Pickle, oval.	20.00	Waste Bowl.	65.00
Pitcher, water, ah	175.00	Wine	60.00
Relish.	20.00		

NAIL (Recessed Pillar-Red Top, Recessed Pillar-Thumbprint Band)

Non-flint pattern made by Ripley and Co., Pittsburgh, PA, c1892. Reissued by U. S. Glass Co., Pittsburgh, PA. Made in clear and clear with ruby stain. Pieces can be found plain or with copper wheel engraving.

	Clear	Ruby Stained		Clear	Ruby Stained
Bowl, berry	25.00	45.00	Pitcher, water	75.00	225.00
Butter Dish, cov . . .	45.00	95.00	Sauce, flat	15.00	30.00
Celery Vase	65.00	125.00	Spooner	25.00	30.00
Compote, cov, hs, 8"			Sugar, cov	40.00	80.00
d.	45.00	80.00	Tumbler	20.00	40.00
Creamer.	30.00	60.00	Wine	35.00	70.00
Goblet	35.00	65.00			

NAILHEAD (Gem)

Non-flint made by Bryce, Higbee and Co., Pittsburgh, PA, c1885. Shards have been found at Boston & Sandwich Glass Co. Also found in ruby stained (goblet at $30.00, pitcher at $65.00).

	Clear		Clear
Bowl, 6"	15.00	Cordial.	25.00
Bread Plate, 9" d.	20.00	Creamer.	25.00
Butter, cov	40.00	Goblet	25.00
Cake Stand, hs		Pitcher, water	35.00
9½".	30.00	Plate, sq, 7"	15.00
10½".	35.00	Relish, 5¼ × 8¾".	10.00
Celery Vase	30.00	Sauce, flat	10.00
Compote		Spooner.	24.00
Cov, 8", hs.	45.00	Sugar, cov	40.00
Cov, ls, 7"	45.00	Tumbler	25.00
Open, hs, 6½"	25.00	Wine	20.00
Open, 9½", hs	40.00		

NESTOR

Non-flint made by Northwood, Indiana, PA, 1903. Decorated with enamel.

	Clear	Green	Blue	Amethyst
Bowl, berry	25.00	30.00	45.00	45.00
Butter, cov	35.00	40.00	55.00	55.00
Cake Plate	35.00	40.00	55.00	55.00
Compote, open, jelly,				
5", 6"	40.00	45.00	60.00	60.00
Creamer.	35.00	60.00	45.00	55.00
Cruet, with stopper .	40.00	45.00	60.00	60.00
Pitcher, water	50.00	55.00	70.00	70.00
Salt Shakers, pair . .	50.00	55.00	70.00	70.00

	Clear	Green	Blue	Amethyst
Spooner	30.00	35.00	35.00	50.00
Sugar, cov	35.00	75.00	45.00	55.00
Toothpick	30.00	35.00	50.00	50.00
Tumbler	40.00	45.00	60.00	60.00

NEVADA

Non-flint made by U. S. Glass Co., Pittsburgh, PA, c1902 as a States pattern. Pieces are sometimes partly frosted and have enamel decoration. Add 20% for frosted.

	Clear		Clear
Biscuit Jar	45.00	Finger Bowl	25.00
Bowl		Jug	35.00
6" d, cov	35.00	Pickle, oval	10.00
7" d, open	20.00	Pitcher	
8" d, cov	45.00	Milk, tankard	45.00
Butter, cov	60.00	Water, bulbous	50.00
Cake Stand, 10"	35.00	Water, tankard	45.00
Celery Vase	25.00	Salt	
Compote		Individual	15.00
Cov, hs, 6"	40.00	Master	20.00
Cov, hs, 7"	45.00	Salt Shaker, table	15.00
Cov, hs, 8"	55.00	Sauce, 4" d	10.00
Open, hs, 6"	20.00	Spooner	35.00
Open, hs, 7"	30.00	Sugar, cov	35.00
Open, hs, 8"	35.00	Syrup, tin top	45.00
Creamer	30.00	Toothpick	40.00
Cruet	35.00	Tumbler	15.00
Cup, custard	12.00		

NEW ENGLAND PINEAPPLE (Loop and Jewel, Pineapple, Sawtooth)

Flint attributed to Boston and Sandwich Glass Co. or New England Glass Co. in the early 1860s. Rare in color. The goblet has been reproduced in clear, color, and milk glass with gilt trim.

	Flint	Non-Flint		Flint	Non-Flint
Bowl, 8", scalloped	85.00	—	Mug	95.00	—
Butter, cov	250.00	—	Pitcher		
Cake Stand	135.00	—	Milk	600.00	—
Castor Bottle	50.00	—	Water	350.00	—
Castor Set, 4 bottles,			Plate, 6"	90.00	—
complete	300.00	—	Salt		
Champagne	175.00	—	Individual	24.00	—
Compote			Master	45.00	40.00
Cov, hs, 5"	175.00	—	Sauce		
Cov, hs, 8"	225.00	—	Flat	15.00	10.00
Open, hs, 7"	90.00	—	Footed	25.00	—
Open, hs, 8½"	125.00	—	Spill Holder	60.00	—
* Cordial	175.00	—	Spooner	60.00	35.00
Creamer, ah	185.00	70.00	Sugar, cov	150.00	75.00
Cruet, os	175.00	—	Sweetmeat, cov	225.00	—
Decanter, qt, os	225.00	—	Tumbler		
Egg Cup	50.00	35.00	Bar	125.00	—
Goblet			Water	85.00	—
Lady's	100.00	—	Whiskey, ah	145.00	—
Regular	65.00	—	* Wine	150.00	—
Honey Dish, 3½" d	15.00	—			

NEW HAMPSHIRE (Bent Buckle, Modiste)

Non-flint made by U. S. Glass Co., Pittsburgh, PA, c1903 in the States pattern series.

	Clear w/ Gold	Rose Stained	Ruby Stained
Biscuit Jar, cov	75.00	—	—
Bowl			
Flared, 5½"	10.00	—	25.00
Flared, 8½"	15.00	25.00	—
Round, 8½"	18.00	30.00	—
Square, 8½"	25.00	35.00	—
Butter, cov	45.00	70.00	—
Cake Stand, 8¼". . .	30.00	—	—
Carafe	60.00	—	—
Celery Vase	35.00	50.00	—
Compote			
Cov, hs, 5".	50.00	—	—
Cov, hs, 6".	60.00	—	—
Cov, hs, 7".	65.00	—	—
Open	40.00	55.00	—
Creamer			
Individual.	20.00	30.00	—
Table	30.00	45.00	—
Cruet	55.00	135.00	—
Goblet	25.00	45.00	—
Mug, large	20.00	45.00	50.00
Pitcher, water			
Bulbous, ah.	90.00	—	—
Straight Sides,			
molded handle .	60.00	90.00	—
Relish.	18.00	—	—
Salt & Pepper, pr. . .	35.00	—	—
Sauce	10.00	—	—
Sugar			
Cov, table	45.00	60.00	—
Individual, open . .	20.00	25.00	—
Syrup.	75.00	—	50.00
Toothpick	25.00	40.00	40.00
Tumbler	20.00	35.00	40.00
Vase	35.00	50.00	—
Wine	25.00	50.00	—

NEW JERSEY (Loops and Drops)

Non-flint made by U. S. Glass Co., Pittsburgh, PA, c1900–08 in States pattern series. Items with perfect gold are worth more than those with worn gold. An emerald green 11" vase is known (value $75.00).

	Clear w/ Gold	Ruby Stained		Clear w/ Gold	Ruby Stained
Bowl			Goblet	40.00	65.00
8", flared	25.00	50.00	Molasses Can.	90.00	—
9", saucer	32.50	65.00	Olive	15.00	—
10", oval	30.00	75.00	Pickle, rect	15.00	—
Bread Plate	30.00	—	Pitcher		
Butter, cov			Milk, ah.	75.00	165.00
Flat.	75.00	100.00	Water		
Footed	125.00	—	Applied Handle	80.00	210.00
Cake Stand, 8"	65.00	—	Pressed Handle	50.00	185.00
Carafe	60.00	—	Plate, 8" d	30.00	45.00
Celery Tray, rect . . .	25.00	40.00	Salt & Pepper		
Compote			Hotel.	50.00	115.00
Cov, hs, 5", jelly . .	45.00	55.00	Small	35.00	55.00
Cov, hs, 8".	65.00	90.00	Sauce	10.00	30.00
Open, hs, 6¾" . . .	35.00	65.00	Spooner	27.00	75.00
Open, hs, 8"	60.00	75.00	Sugar, cov	60.00	80.00
Open, hs, 10½",			Sweetmeat, 8".	65.00	90.00
shallow	65.00	—	Syrup.	90.00	—
Creamer.	35.00	60.00	Toothpick	55.00	225.00
Cruet	50.00	—	Tumbler	30.00	50.00
Fruit Bowl, hs, 12½"			Water Bottle	45.00	90.00
d.	55.00	110.00	Wine	40.00	60.00

NORTHWOOD'S DRAPERY

Made by Harry Northwood Co., Wheeling, WV, c1905. Usually signed "N" in circle.

	White Opal	Blue Opal		White Opal	Blue Opal
Bowl, berry	80.00	100.00	Sauce	20.00	28.00
Butter, cov	145.00	165.00	Spoonor	45.00	55.00
Creamer	55.00	75.00	Sugar, cov	75.00	85.00
Pitcher, water	150.00	185.00	Tumbler	25.00	35.00

OAKEN BUCKET (Wooden Pail, Bucket Set)

Non-flint pattern made by Bryce, Higbee and Company, Pittsburgh, PA, c1880. Reissued by U. S. Glass Co., Pittsburgh, PA, after 1891 merger. Made in amber, amethyst, blue, canary yellow, and clear.

	Amber	Amethyst	Blue	Canary Yellow	Clear
Butter Dish, cov	90.00	225.00	110.00	100.00	65.00
Creamer	65.00	125.00	75.00	60.00	40.00
Pitcher, water	100.00	225.00	110.00	100.00	75.00
Spooner	60.00	100.00	65.00	55.00	35.00
Sugar, cov	70.00	150.00	80.00	70.00	45.00
Toothpick	40.00	85.00	45.00	40.00	25.00
Tumbler	30.00	60.00	35.00	30.00	20.00

O'HARA DIAMOND (Sawtooth and Star)

Non-flint made by O'Hara Glass Co. c1885. Reissued by U. S. Glass Co. 1891–1904.

	Clear	Ruby Stained		Clear	Ruby Stained
Bowl, berry			Pitcher, water,		
Individual	10.00	25.00	tankard	90.00	165.00
Master	25.00	75.00	Plate		
Butter, cov, ruffled			7"	20.00	—
base	45.00	125.00	8"	30.00	—
Compote			10"	40.00	—
Cov, hs	40.00	185.00	Salt, master	15.00	35.00
Open, hs, jelly	48.00	145.00	Salt Shaker	20.00	35.00
Condiment Set, pr			Spooner	20.00	55.00
salt & pepper,			Sugar, cov	35.00	90.00
sugar shaker, tray	125.00	250.00	Sugar Shaker	55.00	150.00
Creamer	30.00	60.00	Syrup	55.00	200.00
Cruet	55.00	150.00	Tray, water	30.00	45.00
Cup and Saucer	40.00	60.00	Tumbler	30.00	45.00
Goblet	25.00	50.00	Wine	25.00	35.00
Lamp, Oil	50.00	—			

ONE HUNDRED ONE (Beaded 101)

Non-flint made by Bellaire Goblet Co., Findlay, OH, in the late 1880s.

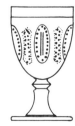

	Clear		Clear
Bread Plate, 101 border,		Creamer	45.00
Farm implement center,		* Goblet	50.00
11"	75.00	Lamp, hand, oil, 10"	80.00
Butter, cov	40.00	Pickle	20.00
Cake Stand, 9"	65.00	Pitcher, water, ah	125.00
Celery Vase	50.00	Plate	
Compote		6"	15.00
Cov, hs, 7"	60.00	7"	15.00
Cov, ls	60.00	8"	15.00

	Clear		Clear
Relish.	20.00	Spooner	25.00
Sauce		Sugar, cov	45.00
Flat	10.00	Wine	60.00
Footed	15.00		

OPEN ROSE (Moss Rose)

Non-flint attributed to Boston and Sandwich Glass Co., Sandwich, MA, c1870. Reproduced in clear and color.

	Clear		Clear
Bowl, oval, 9" x 6"	25.00	Goblet	
Butter, cov	55.00	Lady's	30.00
Cake Stand, hs	45.00	Regular	30.00
Celery Vase	30.00	Pitcher, water, ah	165.00
Compote		Relish	15.00
Cov, hs, 8"	75.00	Salt, master, ftd	30.00
Cov, hs, 9"	90.00	Sauce	10.00
Open, ls, 7½"	35.00	* Spooner	40.00
Creamer, ah	45.00	Sugar, cov	50.00
Egg Cup	25.00	Tumbler	50.00

PALM BEACH

Attributed to U. S. Glass Co., Pittsburgh, PA, c1905. Made in clear with fired-on colors, opalescent white, blue, and canary. Also made in carnival glass. Clear with color decoration is valued at 50% of blue opalescent prices. White opalescent is valued at 80% of blue opalescent prices. Carnival glass generally is higher than blue opalescent.

	Blue Opal	Canary Opal		Blue Opal	Canary Opal
Bowl, berry	90.00	100.00	Pitcher, water	200.00	215.00
Butter, cov	140.00	135.00	Sauce	25.00	25.00
Compote, jelly	60.00	60.00	Spooner	65.00	75.00
Creamer	50.00	50.00	Sugar, cov	90.00	95.00
Finger Bowl	45.00	45.00	Tumbler	45.00	50.00

PALMETTE (Hearts and Spades, Spades)

Non-flint, unknown maker, late 1870s. Shards have been found at Burlington Glass Works, Hamilton, Ontario, Canada. Syrup known in milk glass.

	Clear		Clear
Bowl		Egg Cup	40.00
8"	25.00	Goblet	35.00
9"	15.00	Lamp, 8½", all glass	95.00
Bread Plate, handled, 9" . . .	30.00	Pickle, scoop shape	20.00
Butter Dish, cov	60.00	Pitcher, bulbous, ah	
Butter Pat	35.00	Milk	135.00
Cake Plate, tab handles	35.00	Water	125.00
Cake Stand, hs	100.00	Relish	18.00
Castor Set, 5 bottles, sp		Salt, master, ftd	22.00
holder	125.00	Salt Shaker	55.00
Celery Vase	55.00	Sauce, flat, 6"	10.00
Champagne	75.00	Shaker, saloon, oversize . . .	80.00
Compote		Spooner	35.00
Cov, hs, 7"	65.00	Sugar, cov	55.00
Cov, hs, 8½"	75.00	Syrup, ah	125.00
Cov, hs, 9¾"	85.00	Tumbler	
Open, ls, 5½"	25.00	Bar	75.00
Open, ls, 7"	30.00	Water, ftd	40.00
Creamer, ah	65.00	Wine	110.00
Cup Plate	55.00		

PANAMA (Finecut Bar, Viking #2)

Made by U. S. Glass Co. c1891. A 1907 trade catalog shows fifty-six pieces.

	Clear		Clear
Bowl, berry	20.00	Pickle	15.00
Butter, cov	35.00	Pitcher	
Cake Stand	25.00	Milk	30.00
Celery Tray	20.00	Water	40.00
Creamer		Sugar, cov	35.00
individual	15.00	Spooner	20.00
Regular	20.00	Sweet Pea Bowl	15.00
Compote		Toothpick	35.00
Cov, hs	45.00	Tumbler	15.00
Cov, ls	30.00	Wine	20.00
Goblet	25.00		

PANELED DAISY (Brazil, Daisy and Panel)

Non-flint made by Bryce Bros., Pittsburgh, PA, in the late 1880s. Reissued by U S Glass Co. in 1891. Also found in amber (sugar shaker, $125.00) and blue (sugar shaker, $145.00). Milk glass pieces include 7" round plate ($40.00), 9" sq plate ($45.00), and sugar shaker ($80.00).

	Clear		Clear
Bowl		Creamer	48.00
5" x 7", oval	15.00	* Goblet	25.00
8", square	15.00	Mug	30.00
10½", sq	18.00	Pickle Jar	18.00
Butter, cov, 2 types	50.00	Pitcher, water	60.00
Cake Stand		Plate	
8"	30.00	Round, 7"	22.00
9"	40.00	Square, 9"	30.00
10¼"	45.00	Relish, 5 x 7", wider at one	
11"	50.00	end	22.00
Celery Vase	40.00	Salt Shaker	25.00
Compote		Sauce, flat, sq	8.00
Cov, hs, 5"	40.00	Spooner	25.00
Cov, hs, 6", jelly	45.00	Sugar, cov	40.00
Cov, hs, 7"	50.00	Sugar Shaker	45.00
Cov, hs, 8"	50.00	Syrup	70.00
Cov, hs, 10"	60.00	Tray, water	45.00
Open, hs, 7"	40.00	* Tumbler	25.00
Open, hs, 9"	40.00	Waste Bowl	15.00
Open, hs, 10"	40.00	Water Bottle	60.00
Open, hs, 11"	42.00		

PANELED FORGET-ME-NOT (Regal)

Non-flint, made by Bryce Bros., Pittsburgh, PA, c1880. Reissued by U. S. Glass Co. c1891. Shards have been found at Burlington Glass Works, Hamilton, Ontario, Canada. Made in clear, blue, and amber with limited production in amethyst and green.

	Amber	Blue	Clear
Bread Plate	35.00	45.00	30.00
Butter, cov	50.00	60.00	45.00
Cake Stand, 10"	70.00	90.00	45.00
Celery Vase	45.00	70.00	36.00
Compote			
Cov, hs, 7"	90.00	110.00	65.00
Cov, hs, 8"	80.00	100.00	68.00
Open, hs, 8½"	60.00	75.00	50.00
Open, hs, 10"	60.00	80.00	40.00
Creamer	45.00	60.00	35.00
Cruet, os	—	—	45.00
Goblet	50.00	65.00	32.00
Marmalade Jar, cov	60.00	80.00	50.00
Pickle, boat shape	25.00	35.00	15.00

	Amber	Blue	Clear
Pitcher			
Milk.	90.00	110.00	50.00
Water	90.00	110.00	75.00
Relish, scoop shape	55.00	55.00	65.00
Salt & Pepper, pr. . .	—	—	65.00
Sauce, ftd.	18.00	25.00	12.00
Spooner	40.00	50.00	25.00
Sugar, cov	60.00	80.00	40.00
Wine	55.00	70.00	60.00

PANELED "44" (Athenia, Reverse "44")

Non-flint made by U. S. Glass Co. c1912. Most pieces bear intertwined U. S. Glass Co. mark in base. Comes trimmed in gold and untarnishable platinum. Lemonade set (six-piece set, $150.00), goblet, and covered butter ($95.00) in rose or green staining. Some pieces in plain blue.

	Clear w/ Platinum		Clear w/ Platinum
Bonbon, trifid ftd, cov.	35.00	Olive, flat, handles.	30.00
Bowl, 8", flat	50.00	Pitcher, water	
Butter, cov, flat	55.00	Flat, bulbous, ½ gal	90.00
Candlestick, 7"	65.00	Footed, tankard	95.00
Cruet	65.00	Powdered Sugar, cov	55.00
Creamer		Salt & Pepper, pr.	75.00
Flat.	45.00	Sugar, cov, flat, handled. . . .	60.00
Footed	55.00	Toothpick	55.00
Finger Bowl	35.00	Tumbler, water	30.00
Goblet	45.00	Vase, loving cup shape	40.00
Lemonade Set, pitcher, 6 tumblers	200.00	Wine	50.00

PANELED GRAPE, LATE

Non-flint made by Kokomo Glass Manufacturing Co., Kokomo, IN, c1904. Original pattern has pink and green staining. Shards identified at Boston and Sandwich Glass Co., Sandwich, MA. Westmoreland Glass Co. made clear and milk glass reproductions for L. G. Wright Glass Co. c1960. The Summit Art Glass Co. has also made reproductions in clear and color. L. G. Wright has issued reproductions in many colors and clear.

	Clear		Clear
* Bowl, 8", cov.	35.00	* Spooner	20.00
* Butter, cov	40.00	* Sugar, cov	40.00
* Celery Vase	38.50	* Syrup, glass lid	40.00
* Compote, cov, 6½" d, 9" h . .	35.00	Toothpick	40.00
* Creamer.	25.00	Tumbler, water	35.00
* Goblet	30.00	Wine	40.00
* Pitcher			
Milk.	35.00		
Water	45.00		

PANELED HEATHER

Non-flint, unknown maker, c1890. Often found with gilt.

	Clear		Clear
Butter, cov	35.00	Goblet	25.00
Cake Stand	35.00	Spooner	30.00
Celery	25.00	Sugar, cov	35.00
Creamer.	20.00	Tumbler	15.00

PANELED HOLLY

Made by Harry Northwood Glass Co., Wheeling, WV, c1905. It was made in white and blue opalescent with gold trimmed holly leaves and enameling.

	Blue Opal	White Opal		Blue Opal	White Opal
Bowl, berry	50.00	40.00	Relish	150.00	35.00
Butter, cov	100.00	65.00	Sauce	15.00	10.00
Creamer	60.00	40.00	Spooner	50.00	35.00
Cruet	150.00	100.00	Sugar, cov	100.00	60.00
Pitcher, water	150.00	—	Tumbler	35.00	30.00

PANELED THISTLE (Canadian Thistle, Delta)

Non-flint made by J. P. Higbee Glass Co., Bridgeville, PA, c1910 20. Also made by Jefferson Glass Co., Toronto, Ontario, Canada. The Higbee Glass Co. often used a bee as a trademark. This pattern has been heavily reproduced with a similar mark. Occasionally found with gilt. Rare in ruby stained, with or without gilt.

	Clear		Clear
Basket, small size	65.00	* Plate	
* Bowl		7"	20.00
8", bee mark	25.00	10", bee mark	30.00
9", bee mark	30.00	Punch Cup, bee mark	20.00
Bread Plate	40.00	* Relish, bee mark	24.00
* Butter, cov	60.00	Rose Bowl, 5"	50.00
Cake Stand, 9"	35.00	* Salt, individual	20.00
Candy Dish, cov, ftd	30.00	* Salt Shaker	20.00
Celery Tray	20.00	* Sauce	
Celery Vase	40.00	Flared, bee mark	12.00
* Champagne, bee mark	40.00	Footed	20.00
* Compote		* Spooner	25.00
Open, hs, 8"	30.00	* Sugar, cov	45.00
Open, hs, 9"	35.00	* Toothpick, bee mark	45.00
Open, ls, 5", jelly	30.00	* Tumbler	25.00
* Creamer, bee mark	40.00	Vase	
Cruet, os	50.00	5"	25.00
Doughnut Stand, 6"	25.00	9¼"	25.00
* Goblet	35.00	* Wine, bee mark	30.00
* Honey Dish, cov, sq, bee mark	80.00		
* Pitcher			
Milk	60.00		
Water	70.00		

PAVONIA (Pineapple Stem)

Non-flint made by Ripley and Co. in 1885 and by U. S. Glass Co. in 1891. This pattern comes plain and etched.

	Clear	Ruby Stained		Clear	Ruby Stained
Bowl, 8"	25.00	55.00	Goblet	35.00	60.00
Butter, cov, flat	75.00	125.00	Mug	35.00	50.00
Cake Stand, hs, 9"	55.00	100.00	Pitcher		
Celery Vase, etched	45.00	75.00	Lemonade	95.00	135.00
Compote			Water	75.00	195.00
Cov, hs, 8"	75.00	85.00	Plate, 6½"	17.50	—
Open, jelly	35.00	—	Salt		
Creamer			Individual	15.00	50.00
Hotel	35.00	75.00	Master	28.00	50.00
Table	35.00	75.00	Salt Shaker	25.00	35.00
Cup and Saucer	35.00	45.00	Sauce, ftd, 3½" or		
Finger Bowl, ruffled			4"	15.00	20.00
underplate	48.00	110.00	Spooner, pedestal	45.00	50.00

	Clear	Ruby Stained		Clear	Ruby Stained
Sugar, cov			Tumbler	35.00	50.00
Hotel	45.00	75.00	Waste Bowl	60.00	55.00
Table	45.00	75.00	Wine	35.00	40.00
Tray, water, etched	75.00	85.00			

PEERLESS #1 (Lady Hamilton)

Made by Richards and Hartley Co., Pittsburgh, PA, in 1875 and continued for a number of years. Made in a great number of pieces, many size bowls, twenty-two compotes, five cake stands, and two types of goblets and creamers.

	Clear		Clear
Bowl, 7"	18.00	Goblet	
Bread Plate, oval	25.00	Angular Sided	25.00
Butter, covered	40.00	Rounded bowl	25.00
Cake Stand		Pickle	
Large	30.00	Flat Pointed Shape	15.00
Small	25.00	Round	12.00
Castor Set	75.00	Pickle Jar, cov.	40.00
Celery	25.00	Pitcher, water, ½ gal, ah	65.00
Champagne	20.00	Platter, oval	25.00
Compote		Salt	
Cov.	50.00	Cov.	35.00
Open	30.00	Open, individual	10.00
Creamer		Sauce	
Angular bowl	35.00	4"	8.00
Rounded bowl	25.00	5½"	8.00
Dish		Spooner	25.00
7"	10.00	Sugar, cov	40.00
8"	15.00	Tumbler	20.00
9"	20.00	Wine	25.00
Egg Cup, saucer base	20.00		

PENNSYLVANIA (Balder)

Non-flint issued by U. S. Glass Co. in 1898. Also known in ruby stained. A ruffled jelly compote documented in orange carnival.

	Clear w/ Gold	Emerald Green		Clear w/ Gold	Emerald Green
Biscuit Jar, cov	75.00	125.00	Goblet	24.00	—
Bowl			Juice Tumbler	10.00	20.00
4"	20.00	—	Molasses Can	75.00	—
8", berry	25.00	35.00	Pitcher, water	60.00	—
8", sq	20.00	40.00	Punch Bowl	175.00	—
Butter, cov	60.00	85.00	Punch Cup	10.00	—
Carafe	45.00	—	Salt Shaker	10.00	—
Celery Tray	30.00	—	Sauce	7.50	—
Celery Vase	45.00	—	* Spooner	24.00	35.00
Champagne	25.00	—	Sugar, cov	40.00	55.00
Cheese Dish, cov	65.00	—	Syrup	50.00	—
Children's Table Set	285.00	—	Toothpick	35.00	90.00
Compote, hs, jelly	50.00	—	Tumbler	28.00	40.00
Creamer	25.00	50.00	Whiskey	20.00	35.00
Cruet, os	45.00	—	Wine	15.00	40.00
Decanter, os	100.00	—			

PEQUOT

Shards have been found at Burlington Glass Works, Hamilton, Ontario, Canada. Some items are known in blue and amber. Add 100% for colors.

	Clear		Clear
Bowl, 6", pedestal	20.00	Celery Vase	45.00
Butter, cov	48.00	Champagne	45.00

	Clear		Clear
Compote		Pitcher, water, applied hollow	
Cov, hs, 7½"	55.00	reeded handle	150.00
Open, hs, 7½"	35.00	Spooner	40.00
Creamer	48.00	Sugar, cov	55.00
Goblet	45.00	Wine	35.00
Marmalade Jar	50.00		

PICKET (London, Picket Fence)

Non-flint made by the King, Son & Co., Pittsburgh, PA, c1890. Toothpick holders are known in apple green, vaseline, and purple slag.

	Clear		Clear
Bowl, 9½", sq	30.00	Goblet	30.00
Bread Plate	70.00	Pitcher, water	75.00
Butter, cov	45.00	Salt	
Celery Vase	40.00	Individual	10.00
Compote		Master	35.00
Cov, hs, 6"	65.00	Sauce	
Cov, hs, 8"	85.00	Flat	15.00
Cov, ls, 8"	95.00	Footed	20.00
Open, hs, 6"	30.00	Spooner	30.00
Open, hs, 7", sq	35.00	Sugar, cov	45.00
Open, hs, 8"	35.00	Toothpick	35.00
Open, hs, 10", sq	70.00	Tray, water	65.00
Open, ls, 7"	50.00	Waste Bowl	40.00
Creamer	48.00	Wine	85.00

PINEAPPLE AND FAN #1 (Heisey's #1255)

Made by A. H. Heisey and Co., Newark, OH, c1897 before the Heisey trademark was used. Came in about seventy pieces. Pieces often trimmed in gold. Also known in custard and ruby stained (toothpick $125.00).

	Clear	Emerald Green		Clear	Emerald Green
Banana Stand	50.00	—	Goblet	15.00	25.00
Biscuit Jar, cov	65.00	150.00	Mug	30.00	45.00
Bowl, 5½"	15.00	30.00	Pitcher, water	80.00	225.00
Butter, cov	50.00	175.00	Rose Bowl	35.00	75.00
Cake Stand	45.00	75.00	Salt, individual	25.00	—
Celery Tray, flat....	25.00	45.00	Salt Shaker	20.00	65.00
Compote			Spooner	30.00	65.00
Open, hs, 8"	50.00	225.00	Sugar, cov		
Open, jelly, 5" ...	35.00	—	Individual	25.00	50.00
Creamer			Table	45.00	125.00
Individual	25.00	50.00	Syrup	60.00	250.00
Table	35.00	95.00	Toothpick	75.00	150.00
Cruet	60.00	295.00	Tumbler	25.00	60.00
Custard Cup	15.00	30.00	Vase, 10", trumpet..	25.00	45.00

PINEAPPLE AND FAN #2 (Cube with Fan, Holbrook)

Non-flint made by Adams & Co., Pittsburgh, PA. Later made by U. S. Glass Co. in 1891. Also found in emerald green, ruby stained, and white milk glass trimmed in gold.

	Clear		Clear
Bowl, 8"	25.00	Finger Bowl	25.00
Butter, cov	40.00	Goblet	25.00
Cake Stand, 9"	35.00	Pitcher, water, tankard	45.00
Cologne	15.00	Plate, 6½"	15.00
Creamer	25.00	Punch Bowl, 12"	60.00
Cruet, os	55.00	Rose Bowl	20.00
Decanter	40.00	Salt, individual	20.00

	Clear		Clear
Spooner	25.00	Tumbler	15.00
Sugar, cov	30.00	Waste Bowl	15.00
Syrup	50.00	Whiskey	15.00
Tray, ice cream	25.00	Wine	20.00

PLEAT AND PANEL (Derby)

Non-flint made by Bryce Bros., Pittsburgh, PA, in the 1880s and by U. S. Glass Co. in 1891. Found in square and rectangular forms. Rare in blue, canary, amber, and amethyst. Colored items valued at 50% to 75% higher. Do not confuse with the Depression era Heisey pattern of the same name.

	Clear		Clear
Bowl, 8", cov	55.00	Lamp, 6½"	65.00
Bread Plate	40.00	Marmalade Jar, cov	50.00
Butter, cov, handles	75.00	Pitcher, water	50.00
Butter Pat	40.00	* Plate	
Cake Stand		6"	20.00
8"	30.00	8"	24.00
10"	40.00	Relish, 8½"	18.00
Celery Vase	35.00	Salt, master	20.00
Compote		Salt Shaker, 3¼" h	35.00
Cov, hs, 8"	50.00	Sauce, 5", sq, ftd	20.00
Cov, ls, 7", sq	45.00	Spooner	30.00
Open, hs, 8"	35.00	Sugar, cov	40.00
Open, ls, 6", sq	20.00	Tray, water, 14 x 9¼"	50.00
Creamer	35.00	Wine	50.00
* Goblet, 6"	30.00		

PLUME

Non-flint made by Adams & Co., Pittsburgh, PA, c1890 and by U. S. Glass Co. in 1891. Has both horizontal and vertical plumes. Early goblets have plume motif at base of stem. Also found etched. Pattern contains forty-six pieces. Some items are frosted. L. G. Wright has been reproducing goblets since 1960.

	Clear	Ruby Stained		Clear	Ruby Stained
Bowl			* Goblet	35.00	55.00
8", scalloped rim	25.00	60.00	Pickle	20.00	35.00
8", sq	45.00	75.00	Pitcher, ah		
Butter, cov	50.00	165.00	Bulbous	65.00	200.00
Cake Stand, 10"	50.00	125.00	Tankard	60.00	200.00
Celery Vase	30.00	65.00	Sauce, flat, 4"	15.00	—
Compote			Spooner	25.00	40.00
Cov, hs, 6" d	45.00	125.00	Sugar, cov	45.00	60.00
Open, hs, 7"	45.00	75.00	Syrup	65.00	—
Open, hs, 8"	50.00	80.00	Tray, 12½" d	40.00	—
Creamer	35.00	50.00	Tumbler	25.00	35.00

PLUTEC

Made by McKee & Bros. Glass Co., Pittsburgh, PA, c1900. Some pieces trademarked "PRES-CUT."

	Clear		Clear
Bowl	12.00	Plate	
Butter, cov	25.00	10¾"	25.00
Cake Stand	25.00	11"	25.00
Celery Vase	20.00	Sauce, flat	8.00
Compote, open, hs	25.00	Spooner	20.00
Creamer	25.00	Sugar, cov	25.00
Decanter	45.00	Toothpick	20.00
Goblet	15.00	Tray, wine	30.00
Pickle	15.00	Tumbler	15.00
Pitcher, water	45.00	Wine	15.00

POGO STICK (Crown)

Made by Lancaster Glass Co., Lancaster, OH, in 1910.

	Clear		Clear
Bowl, berry	15.00	Plate, 7″	10.00
Butter, cov	40.00	Relish	15.00
Cake Stand	35.00	Sauce, flat	6.00
Celery Vase	20.00	Spooner	20.00
Compote, open	20.00	Syrup Jug, metal top	45.00
Creamer	25.00	Sugar, cov	35.00
Cruet	25.00	Tumbler	15.00
Pitcher, water	35.00		

POINTED JEWEL (Spear Point)

Made by Columbia Glass Co., Findlay, OH, c1888 and by U. S. Glass Co., Pittsburgh, PA, 1892–98. Made in clear, although some pieces have been found with ruby stained decoration.

	Clear		Clear
Bowl, berry	20.00	Cup and Saucer	45.00
Butter, cov	60.00	Dish, flat, 7½″	20.00
Cake Stand	35.00	Goblet	20.00
Celery	20.00	Honey Dish, cov, rect	45.00
Children's Table Set	140.00	Pitcher, water	45.00
Cologne Bottle, os	50.00	Sauce	8.00
Compote		Spooner	25.00
Cov, hs	45.00	Sugar, cov	35.00
Jelly	20.00	Tray, sq	45.00
Open, ls	30.00	Tumbler	20.00
Creamer	30.00	Wine	15.00

POLAR BEAR (Alaska, Arctic, Frosted Polar Bear, Ice Berg, North Pole, Polar Bear and Seal)

Non-flint made by Crystal Glass Co., Bridgeport, OH, c1883. Made in clear and frosted.

	Clear	Frosted		Clear	Frosted
Bread Plate	95.00	150.00	Pitcher, water	250.00	275.00
Creamer	125.00	155.00	Sauce, flat	30.00	35.00
Goblet	100.00	115.00	Sugar, cov	175.00	200.00
Ice Bowl	85.00	100.00	Tray, water	175.00	200.00
Pickle Dish	50.00	65.00	Waste Bowl	85.00	100.00

POPCORN

Non-flint attributed to Boston and Sandwich Glass Co. in the late 1860s. Pieces were made with handles resembling an ear of corn, a flat oval which was filled with lines. Pieces with an outstanding ear known as "with ear" and the others "lined ear."

	Clear		Clear
Butter, cov	65.00	Pitcher, water	
Cake Stand		Applied Handle	65.00
8″	50.00	Applied Strap Handle	100.00
11″	75.00	Sauce	10.00
Cordial	75.00	Spooner	35.00
Creamer, 4⅞″ h.	40.00	Sugar, cov	45.00
Goblet		Wine, with ear	65.00
Lined ear	30.00		
With ear	50.00		

PORTLAND

Non-flint made by several companies c1880–1900. An oval pintray in ruby souvenir ($20.00) is known and a flat sauce ($25.00).

	Clear w/ Gold		Clear w/ Gold
Basket, ah	85.00	Jam Jar, SP cov	35.00
Biscuit Jar, cov	90.00	Pitcher, water, straight sides	55.00
Bowl, berry, 7" d	20.00	Pomade Jar, SP top	30.00
Butter, cov	50.00	Puff Box, glass lid	35.00
Cake Stand, 10½"	45.00	Punch Bowl, 13⅝", ftd	150.00
* Candlestick		Punch Cup	10.00
7" h, flared	85.00	Relish	15.00
9" h	55.00	Ring Tree	85.00
Carafe, water	45.00	Salt Shaker	15.00
Celery Tray	25.00	Sauce	8.00
Compote		Spooner	30.00
Cov, hs, 6"	60.00	Sugar	
Open, hs, 8¼"	40.00	Breakfast, open	35.00
Open, hs, 9½"	45.00	Table, cov	45.00
Open, ls, 7"	45.00	Sugar Shaker	40.00
Creamer		Syrup	50.00
Breakfast	20.00	Toothpick	25.00
Table	30.00	Tumbler	25.00
Tankard	30.00	Vase, 9" h	30.00
Cruet, os	55.00	Water Bottle	40.00
Decanter, qt, handled	50.00	Wine	30.00
Goblet	35.00		

POWDER AND SHOT (Horn of Plenty, Powder Horn and Shot)

Flint; shards have been found at Boston and Sandwich Glass Co., Sandwich, MA, c1870, and also at Portland Glass Co., Portland, ME. Finial of covered pieces resembles a flattened upright fan or plume.

	Clear		Clear
Butter, cov	95.00	Egg Cup	50.00
Castor Bottle	40.00	Goblet	65.00
Celery Vase	95.00	Pitcher, water	150.00
Compote		Salt, master, ftd	45.00
Cov, hs	100.00	Sauce	20.00
Open, ls	50.00	Spooner	55.00
Creamer, ah	75.00	Sugar, cov	80.00

PRESSED DIAMOND (Block and Diamond, Zephyr)

Made by Central Glass Co., Wheeling, WV, in the 1880s. Comes in clear, amber, blue, and light straw colored (yellow, not vaseline).

	Amber	Blue	Clear	Yellow
Bowl, berry	15.00	20.00	12.00	20.00
Butter, cov	50.00	60.00	40.00	90.00
Cake Stand	30.00	50.00	—	—
Celery	25.00	45.00	22.00	40.00
Creamer	45.00	50.00	30.00	50.00
Cup, custard or sherbet, (rare)	15.00	20.00	12.00	20.00
Finger, bowl	16.00	20.00	14.00	20.00
Goblet	35.00	45.00	30.00	40.00
Pitcher, water	60.00	65.00	45.00	65.00
Salt Shaker	20.00	35.00	12.00	40.00
Spooner	45.00	60.00	25.00	45.00
Sugar, cov	55.00	75.00	35.00	65.00
Wine	25.00	35.00	20.00	40.00

PRIMROSE

Non-flint made by Canton Glass Co., Canton, OH, c1885. Also made in milk glass. Apple green is scarce.

	Amber and Yellow	Blue and Green	Clear
Bowl, 8"	30.00	35.00	25.00
Butter, cov	50.00	60.00	35.00
Cake Stand, 10" . . .	50.00	65.00	40.00
Celery Vase	35.00	40.00	25.00
Compote, cov, ls, 6"	40.00	45.00	30.00
Creamer.	35.00	48.00	30.00
Egg Cup.	30.00	35.00	20.00
Goblet			
Knob Stem	40.00	45.00	30.00
Plain Stem	35.00	40.00	25.00
Lamp, finger	—	—	195.00
Pickle.	18.00	20.00	14.00
Pitcher			
Milk	45.00	55.00	35.00
Water	55.00	50.00	48.00
Plate			
4½".	15.00	20.00	12.00
9", handled	30.00	35.00	20.00
Platter, 12 x 8"	35.00	45.00	30.00
Relish.	18.00	20.00	14.00
Sauce, ftd.	18.00	25.00	15.00
Spooner	25.00	30.00	20.00
Sugar, cov	40.00	55.00	35.00
Tray, water	50.00	60.00	35.00
Waste Bowl.	30.00	35.00	30.00
Wine	40.00	45.00	30.00

PRINCESS FEATHER (Lacy Medallion, Rochelle)

Flint and non-flint made by Bakewell, Pears and Co. in the 1860s and 1870s. Later made by U. S. Glass Co. after 1891. Shards have been identified at Boston and Sandwich Glass Co. and several Canadian factory sites. Also made in milk glass. A rare blue opaque tumbler has been reported.

	Clear		Clear
Bowl		Goblet	45.00
7", cov, pedestal	45.00	Pitcher, water	75.00
7", oval	20.00	Plate	
8", oval	25.00	6"	30.00
9", oval	30.00	7"	35.00
Butter, cov	50.00	8"	40.00
Cake Plate, handled	35.00	9"	45.00
Celery Vase	40.00	Relish.	20.00
Compote		Sauce	8.00
Cov, hs, 7".	50.00	Spooner	30.00
Cov, hs, 8".	50.00	Sugar	
Open, ls, 8"	35.00	Cov.	55.00
Creamer, ah	55.00	Open	25.00
Dish, oval.	20.00	Wine	45.00
Egg Cup.	40.00		

PRISCILLA #1 (Alexis, Findlay)

Non-flint made by Dalzell, Gilmore and Leighton, Findlay, OH, in the late 1890s and continued by National Glass Co. Fenton reproduced pattern in clear, colors, and opalescent in 1951. Also introduced many forms different from the original such as 12½" plate, goblet, wine, 6" handled bonbon, and sugar and creamer.

	Clear		Clear
Banana Stand	80.00	* Goblet	40.00
Biscuit Jar	145.00	Mug	20.00
Bowl		Pickle Dish	15.00
7½" d	15.00	Pitcher, water, ah	
9¼" w, sq	25.00	Bulbous	90.00
10¼" d, straight sides	50.00	Tankard	85.00
Butter, cov	65.00	* Plate	25.00
Cake Stand, 9½", hs	60.00	Relish	15.00
Celery Vase	55.00	* Rose Bowl	30.00
* Compote		* Sauce	8.00
Cov, hs, 9"	75.00	Saucer	8.00
Open, hs, 7"	45.00	Spooner	30.00
Open, hs, 10", scalloped	60.00	* Sugar, cov	
* Creamer		Individual	30.00
Individual, 3" h	10.00	Table	60.00
Table	25.00	Syrup	90.00
Cruet, os	65.00	* Toothpick	40.00
Cup	10.00	Tumbler	25.00
Doughnut Stand	60.00	* Wine	35.00

PRISCILLA #2 (Fostoria's 676)

Made by Fostoria Glass Co., Moundsville, WV, in 1898. Also made in custard with green or gold trim and white milk glass.

	Clear	Emerald Green		Clear	Emerald Green
Bowl, 8½", berry	15.00	35.00	Pickle	15.00	25.00
Butter, cov	65.00	95.00	Pitcher, water	30.00	65.00
Cake Stand	35.00	70.00	Salt Shaker		
Carafe, water	40.00	65.00	Large	12.00	30.00
Celery Vase	35.00	60.00	Small	12.00	30.00
Compote			Sauce, flat, 4½"	10.00	15.00
Cov	55.00	75.00	Sherbet	8.00	15.00
Open	40.00	55.00	Spooner	30.00	50.00
Creamer	35.00	70.00	Sugar, cov	45.00	80.00
Cruet, os	65.00	250.00	Syrup, nickel top	55.00	150.00
Egg Cup	20.00	35.00	Toothpick, 4½"	35.00	65.00
Finger Bowl	15.00	20.00	Tumbler	25.00	35.00
Marmalade Jar, cov	45.00	115.00	Water Bottle	45.00	95.00

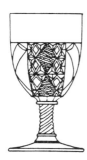

PRISM ARC (Cross Log)

Unknown maker.

	Clear		Clear
Bowl, berry, 8"	18.00	Pitcher, water	45.00
Butter, cov	35.00	Plate	10.00
Cake Stand	30.00	Sauce	6.00
Celery	20.00	Spooner	25.00
Creamer	25.00	Sugar, cov	30.00
Cruet, os	50.00	Tumbler	30.00
Goblet	20.00	Wine	20.00
Mug	15.00		

PRISM WITH DIAMOND POINTS

Flint made by Bryce Bros., Pittsburgh, PA, c1880. Reissued by U. S. Glass Co. c1891. Shards have been found at Boston and Sandwich Glass Co. A flint milk glass spooner is known.

	Clear		Clear
Bowl	30.00	Celery Vase	35.00
Butter, cov	65.00	Compote, cov, hs, 6"	90.00

	Clear		Clear
Creamer	75.00	Salt, master, cov	30.00
Egg Cup		Spooner	45.00
Double	55.00	Sugar, cov	50.00
Single	25.00	Tumbler	40.00
Goblet	45.00	Wine	50.00
Pitcher, water	100.00		

PSYCHE AND CUPID

Non-flint, unknown maker, c1870.

	Clear		Clear
Butter, cov	60.00	Pitcher	
Celery Vase	40.00	Milk	60.00
Compote, cov		Water	75.00
hs	75.00	Sauce, ftd, 4½"	15.00
ls	55.00	Spooner	45.00
Creamer, 7"	50.00	Sugar, cov	55.00
Goblet	40.00	Wine	45.00
Marmalade Jar, cov	85.00		

QUARTERED BLOCK (Duncan and Miller #24)

Made by Duncan & Miller Co., Washington, PA, c1903.

	Clear	Ruby Stained		Clear	Ruby Stained
Bowl	25.00	60.00	Orange Bowl	30.00	65.00
Butter, cov	45.00	125.00	Pitcher, water	45.00	150.00
Cake Stand, 9"	50.00	—	Sauce	7.50	—
Celery Vase	30.00	—	Spooner	20.00	45.00
Compote			Sugar, cov	40.00	45.00
Cov, hs	50.00	—	Syrup	50.00	—
Open, hs	35.00	—	Toothpick	30.00	85.00
Creamer	30.00	55.00	Tumbler	20.00	40.00
Custard Cup	10.00	15.00	Vase	18.00	—
Goblet	35.00	—	Water Bottle	35.00	—
Lamp	75.00	—	Wine	30.00	—

QUEEN (Daisy and Button with Pointed Panels, Daisy with Depressed Button, Paneled Daisy and Button, Pointed Panel Daisy and Button, Sunk Daisy and Button)

Non-flint pattern made by McKee Glass Co., Jeannette, PA, c1894. Shards have been made at Burlington Glass Works site, Hamilton, Ontario, Canada. Original production included amber, apple green, blue, canary yellow, and clear.

	Amber	Apple Green	Blue	Canary Yellow	Clear
Bowl, berry, 8½" d	45.00	45.00	50.00	45.00	30.00
Butter Dish, cov	85.00	85.00	95.00	80.00	55.00
Cake Stand, hs, 6½" d	60.00	60.00	65.00	50.00	30.00
Compote, cov, hs	75.00	75.00	90.00	70.00	45.00
Creamer	35.00	35.00	40.00	35.00	30.00
Goblet	30.00	30.00	35.00	30.00	25.00
Pitcher, water	75.00	75.00	80.00	75.00	55.00
Sauce, flat, 4" d	15.00	15.00	20.00	15.00	10.00
Spooner	30.00	30.00	35.00	30.00	25.00
Sugar, cov	50.00	55.00	55.00	50.00	50.00
Tumbler	30.00	35.00	35.00	30.00	25.00

QUEEN ANNE (Bearded Man)

Non-flint made by LaBelle Glass Co., Bridgeport, OH, c1879. Finials are Maltese cross. At least twenty-eight pieces are documented. A table set and water pitcher are known in amber.

	Clear		Clear
Bowl, cov		Pitcher	
8", oval	45.00	Milk	75.00
9", oval	55.00	Water	85.00
Bread Plate	50.00	Salt Shaker	40.00
Butter, cov	65.00	Sauce	15.00
Celery Vase	35.00	Spooner	40.00
Compote, cov, ls, 9"	75.00	Sugar, cov	55.00
Creamer	40.00	Syrup	100.00
Egg Cup	45.00		

QUESTION MARK (Oval Loop)

Made by Richards and Hartley Glass Co. in 1888 and later by U. S. Glass Co. in 1892. An 1888 catalog lists thirty-two pieces. Scarce in ruby stained.

	Clear		Clear
Bowl		Cordial	20.00
4", round, ftd	15.00	Creamer	30.00
7", oblong	18.00	Goblet	25.00
7", round, ftd	20.00	Nappy, ftd	20.00
8", oblong	25.00	Pickle Jar, cov	45.00
8", round, ftd	25.00	Pitcher	
9", oblong	30.00	Milk, bulbous, 1 qt	40.00
10", oblong	25.00	Milk, tankard, 1 qt	45.00
Bread Tray	30.00	Water, bulbous, ½ gal.	50.00
Butter, cov	30.00	Water, tankard, ½ gal.	55.00
Candlestick, chamber, finger		Salt Shaker	15.00
loop	45.00	Sauce, 4", collared	10.00
Celery Vase	28.00	Spooner	20.00
Compote		Sugar Shaker	35.00
Cov, hs, 7"	50.00	Sugar, cov	25.00
Cov, hs, 8"	65.00	Tumbler	20.00
Open, hs, 7"	25.00	Wine	20.00
Open, ls	15.00		

RAINDROP

Non-flint made by Doyle and Co., Pittsburgh, PA, c1885. Reissued by U. S. Glass Co., Pittsburgh, PA, in 1891. An apple green hat ($75.00) and opaque blue milk glass pitcher are known. Also may have been made in white and blue milk glass.

	Amber and Canary	Blue	Clear
ABC Plate	40.00	45.00	30.00
Butter Dish, cov	48.00	60.00	40.00
Cake Plate	40.00	50.00	30.00
Compote			
Cov			
hs	55.00	65.00	45.00
ls	45.00	55.00	35.00
Open			
hs	40.00	50.00	30.00
ls	35.00	45.00	25.00
Creamer	35.00	45.00	20.00
Cup and Saucer	40.00	50.00	25.00
Egg Cup, double	35.00	45.00	25.00
Finger Bowl	25.00	35.00	15.00
Lamp, miniature	85.00	—	—
Pickle	25.00	35.00	20.00
Pitcher, water	45.00	55.00	35.00
Relish	20.00	30.00	10.00

	Amber and Canary	Blue	Clear
Sauce			
Flat..........	12.00	14.00	10.00
Footed	15.00	18.00	12.00
Syrup..........	50.00	60.00	35.00
Tray, water.......	45.00	55.00	35.00
Tumbler........	25.00	35.00	18.00
Wine	25.00	35.00	20.00

RED BLOCK (Late Block)

Non-flint with red stain made by Doyle and Co., Pittsburgh, PA. Later made by five companies, plus U. S. Glass Co. in 1892. Prices for clear 50% less.

	Ruby Stained		Ruby Stained
Banana Boat.	75.00	Mustard, cov...........	55.00
Bowl, 8"...............	75.00	Pitcher, water, 8" h	175.00
Butter, cov	110.00	Relish Tray............	25.00
Celery Vase, 6½"	85.00	Rose Bowl	75.00
Cheese Dish, cov	125.00	Salt Dip, individual.......	50.00
Creamer		Salt Shaker............	75.00
Individual............	45.00	Sauce, flat, 4½"	20.00
Table	70.00	Spooner..............	45.00
Decanter, 12", os, variant...	175.00	Sugar, cov	90.00
*Goblet	35.00	Tumbler	40.00
Mug..................	50.00	*Wine	40.00

REVERSE TORPEDO (Bull's Eye Band, Bull's Eye with Diamond Point #2, Pointed Bull's Eye)

Non-flint made by Dalzell, Gilmore and Leighton Glass Co., Findlay, OH, c1888–90. Also attributed to Canadian factories. Sometimes found with copper wheel etching.

	Clear		Clear
Banana Stand, 9¾".......	100.00	Open, hs, 7"	65.00
Basket	175.00	Open, hs, 8⅜" d	45.00
Biscuit Jar, cov	135.00	Open, hs, jelly	50.00
Bowl		Open, ls, 9¼", ruffled	85.00
8½", shallow	30.00	Doughnut Tray	90.00
9", fruit, pie crust rim	70.00	Goblet	85.00
10½", pie crust rim......	75.00	Honey Dish, sq, cov	145.00
Butter, cov, 7½" d	75.00	Jam Jar, cov...........	85.00
Cake Stand, hs..........	85.00	Pitcher, tankard, 10¼".....	160.00
Celery Vase	55.00	Sauce, flat, 3¾"	10.00
Compote		Spooner..............	30.00
Cov, hs, 7"...........	80.00	Sugar, cov	85.00
Cov, hs, 10"..........	125.00	Syrup................	165.00
Cov, hs, 6"..........	80.00	Tumbler	30.00
Open, hs, 10½" d, V shape			
bowl	90.00		

RIBBED GRAPE (Raisin)

Flint pattern attributed to Boston & Sandwich Glass Co., Sandwich, MA, c1850. Original production included clear, deep blue, peacock green, milk white, and sapphire blue. Color pieces are rare.

	Clear		Clear
Butter Dish, cov	125.00	Sauce, flat	20.00
Celery Vase	65.00	Spooner..............	35.00
Compote, cov, hs, 6" d	175.00	Sugar, cov	100.00
Creamer...............	150.00	Wine	60.00
Goblet	60.00		

RIBBED IVY

Flint attributed to Boston and Sandwich Glass Co., Sandwich, MA, c1850.

	Clear		Clear
Bowl, 6"	15.00	Salt, master	
Butter, cov	100.00	Cov.	125.00
Castor Bottle.	35.00	Open, scalloped rim	40.00
Celery Vase	300.00	Sauce	12.00
Champagne	100.00	Spooner	40.00
Compote		Sugar, cov	80.00
Cov, hs, 6", jelly	125.00	Sweetmeat, cov, on stand . .	165.00
Open, hs, 9", scalloped		Tumbler	
edge	100.00	Bar	75.00
Creamer	125.00	Water	70.00
Decanter, quart, os	150.00	Whiskey	
Egg Cup.	30.00	Handled	100.00
Goblet	45.00	Plain.	70.00
Hat.	350.00	Wine	100.00
Pitcher, water, ah	250.00		

RIBBON (Frosted Ribbon, Rebecca at the Well, Simple Frosted Ribbon)

Non-flint, usually frosted, made by Bakewell, Pears and Co., Pittsburgh, PA, in the late 1870s. It has been erroneously called "Frosted Ribbon" at times, which can be confusing. Other Ribbon patterns are Clear Ribbon, Frosted Ribbon, Double Ribbon, Fluted Ribbon, and Grated Ribbon. Compotes have been reproduced in clear and color by Fostoria for the Henry Ford Museum gift shop, and are usually marked "HFM." L. G. Wright Co., New Martinsville, WV, reproduced the goblet. It is unmarked, but can usually be identified by its rough textured frosting.

	Frosted		Frosted
Bowl, berry	55.00	Pickle Jar, cov	95.00
Butter, cov	70.00	Pitcher	
Cake Stand, 8½"	50.00	Milk, 1 qt	65.00
Celery Vase	40.00	Water, ½" gal	75.00
Champagne	75.00	Platter, 9" x 13", oblong, cut	
Cheese, cov	95.00	corners	62.50
Cologne Bottle, os.	65.00	Salt Shaker.	40.00
* Compote		Sauce	
Cov, hs, 8"	75.00	Footed	18.00
Cov, ls, 7"	45.00	Tab-handled	18.00
Open, hs, 10½", SP, Dol-		Spooner	35.00
phin stand	250.00	Sugar, cov	65.00
Open, ls, 7"	35.00	Tray, water, 15"	100.00
Creamer.	30.00	Waste Bowl.	45.00
* Goblet	35.00	Wine	125.00

RIBBON CANDY (Bryce)

Non-flint made by Bryce Bros., Pittsburgh, PA, in the 1880s. Reissued by U. S. Glass Co. in the 1890s. Bowls come in a variety of sizes: open or with lids; flat or with a low collared foot. Also known in emerald green.

	Clear		Clear
Bowl		Compote	
3½", round	10.00	Cov, ls, 5"	30.00
4", round	10.00	Cov, ls, 6"	30.00
8", oval	25.00	Cov, ls, 7"	40.00
8", round	25.00	Cov, ls, 8"	40.00
Butter, cov		Open, hs, 5"	20.00
Flat	50.00	Open, hs, 6"	25.00
Footed	55.00	Open, hs, 7"	30.00
Cake Stand		Open, hs, 8"	35.00
8"	30.00	Open, ls, 3"	12.00
10½"	45.00	Open, ls, 4"	12.00
Claret.	65.00	Open, ls, 5"	12.00

	Clear		Clear
Open, ls, 6"	15.00	8"	25.00
Open, ls, 7"	20.00	9½"	30.00
Open, ls, 8"	25.00	11"	35.00
Cordial	55.00	Relish	10.00
Creamer	25.00	Salt Shaker	35.00
Cruet, os	65.00	Sauce	
Cup and Saucer	40.00	Flat, 4"	10.00
Goblet	65.00	Footed, 4"	12.00
Honey Dish, cov, sq	75.00	Spooner	30.00
Lamp, oil	75.00	Sugar, cov	40.00
Pitcher		Syrup	90.00
Milk	45.00	Tumbler	25.00
Water	75.00	Wine	55.00
Plate			
6"	18.00		

ROANOKE

Non-flint made by Ripley Glass Co., Pittsburgh, PA, c1885. Reissued by U. S. Glass Co., Pittsburgh, PA, after the 1891 merger. Found in clear, emerald green, canary-yellow, and ruby stained.

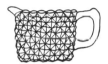

	Clear	Ruby Stained		Clear	Ruby Stained
Bowl			Creamer		
Deep, rounded			Flat, 3½" h	35.00	50.00
sides	25.00	45.00	Ftd	40.00	60.00
Shallow, pinched			Goblet	25.00	40.00
sides	25.00	45.00	Pitcher, water, ½ gal		
Butter, cov, ftd	55.00	75.00	Jug	45.00	90.00
Cake Stand, hs,			Tankard, ah	45.00	90.00
curled scalloped			Relish Tray	25.00	—
rim			Rose Bowl	30.00	—
8" d	75.00	—	Salt, open		
9" d	75.00	—	Individual	10.00	30.00
10" d	75.00	—	Master	18.00	50.00
Compote			Sauce, flat	10.00	20.00
Cov, hs, 6" d	45.00	90.00	Spooner, ftd	20.00	40.00
Open, deep bowl,			Sugar, cov	40.00	60.00
5" d	25.00	40.00	Tumbler	20.00	35.00
Open, saucer			Wine	30.00	45.00
bowl, 9" d	45.00	80.00			

ROBIN HOOD

Made by Fostoria Glass Co., Moundsville, WV, in 1898. Pieces have been reported in clear and emerald green. A creamer ($50.00), molasses can ($65.00), and pickle ($30.00) can be found in milk white. Some of the larger items have two rows of the large eyes of the pattern.

	Clear	Emerald Green		Clear	Emerald Green
Bowl, berry	20.00	35.00	Molasses Can, Brit-		
Butter, cov	50.00	48.00	tania lid	40.00	50.00
Cake Stand	35.00	48.00	Nappy, 4½"	8.00	—
Celery	20.00	30.00	Pitcher, water	45.00	65.00
Compote, hs			Pickle	15.00	20.00
Cov	40.00	65.00	Salt Shaker	18.00	25.00
Open	30.00	50.00	Spooner	20.00	—
Creamer	25.00	35.00	Sugar, cov	30.00	35.00
Cruet, os	45.00	60.00	Tumbler	25.00	35.00
Mug	15.00	25.00			

ROMAN KEY (Frosted Roman Key)

Flint glass of the 1860s made by Union Glass Co. and by others in several variants. Available in clear but not as popular. Sometimes erroneously called "Greek Key."

	Frosted		Frosted
Bowl		Decanter, os	150.00
8"	45.00	Egg Cup	45.00
10"	50.00	Goblet	50.00
Butter, cov	80.00	Mustard Jar, cov	45.00
Castor Set, SP holder	125.00	Pitcher, water	225.00
Celery Vase, ftd	80.00	Plate, 6"	35.00
Champagne	85.00	Relish	20.00
Compote		Salt, ftd	45.00
Open, hs, 8", cable rim	60.00	Sauce, 4"	18.00
Open, ls, 7"	95.00	Spooner	45.00
Cordial	75.00	* Sugar, cov	85.00
* Creamer, ah	115.00	Tumbler, bar	45.00
Custard Cup	30.00	Wine	85.00

ROMAN ROSETTE

Non-flint made by Bryce, Walker and Co., Pittsburgh, PA, c1890. Reissued by U. S. Glass Co. in 1892 and 1898. Attributed to Portland Glass Co. Also seen with English registry mark and known in amber stained.

	Clear	Ruby Stained		Clear	Ruby Stained
Bowl			Mug	35.00	—
6"	12.00	—	Pitcher		
8½"	15.00	50.00	Milk	45.00	150.00
Bread Plate	30.00	75.00	Water	50.00	140.00
Butter, cov	50.00	125.00	Plate, 7½"	35.00	65.00
Cake Stand, 9"	45.00	—	Relish, oval, 9"	20.00	40.00
Celery Vase	30.00	95.00	Salt & Pepper, glass		
Compote			tray	40.00	100.00
Cov, hs, 4½", jelly	50.00	—	Sauce	15.00	20.00
Cov, hs, 6"	65.00	—	Spooner	25.00	45.00
Creamer	32.00	45.00	Sugar, cov	40.00	80.00
Cordial	50.00	—	Syrup	85.00	125.00
*Goblet	40.00	—	Wine	45.00	65.00

ROBE BANDS (Argent, Clear Panels with Cord Band)

Made by Bryce Bros., Pittsburgh, PA, c1870s. Later made by U. S. Glass Co. after 1891.

	Clear		Clear
Bowl	15.00	Pitcher, water	40.00
Bread Plate, medallion		Plate, medallion center	
center	30.00	6"	15.00
Butter, cov	40.00	7"	20.00
Cake Stand	35.00	Relish	15.00
Celery Vase	20.00	Sauce, ftd	10.00
Compote, double knob stem		Spooner	20.00
Cov	35.00	Sugar, cov	30.00
Open	20.00	Tumbler	20.00
Creamer	25.00	Wine	25.00
Goblet, double knob stem	25.00		

ROSE-IN-SNOW (Rose)

Non-flint made by Bryce Bros., Pittsburgh, PA, in the square form c1880. Also made in the more common round form by Ohio Flint Glass Co. and after 1891 by U. S. Glass Co. Both styles reissued by Indiana Glass Co., Dunkirk, IN. Reproductions made by several companies, including Imperial Glass Co., as early as 1930 and continuing through the 1970s.

	Amber and Canary	Blue	Clear
Bowl, 8" sq	40.00	50.00	30.00
Butter, cov			
Round	50.00	125.00	45.00
Square	60.00	150.00	50.00
Cake Stand, 9"	85.00	175.00	90.00
Compote			
Cov, hs, 8"	125.00	175.00	80.00
Cov, ls, 7"	100.00	150.00	75.00
Open, ls, 5¾" . . .	40.00	120.00	35.00
Creamer			
Round	60.00	100.00	45.00
Square	65.00	120.00	45.00
* Goblet	40.00	55.00	35.00
Marmalade Jar, cov .	70.00	125.00	60.00
* Mug, "In Fond			
Remembrance" . .	45.00	110.00	32.00
* Pickle Dish			
Double, 8½" x 7"	45.00	110.00	100.00
Single, oval, han-			
dles at end	25.00	95.00	20.00
Pitcher, water, ah . .	175.00	200.00	125.00
Plate			
5"	40.00	40.00	35.00
6"	30.00	80.00	18.00
7"	30.00	82.00	20.00
* 9"	30.00	85.00	20.00
Platter, oval	—	—	125.00
Sauce			
Flat	15.00	20.00	12.00
Footed	8.00	48.00	18.00
Spooner			
Round	30.00	80.00	25.00
Square	38.50	100.00	35.00
Sugar, cov			
Round	55.00	120.00	50.00
* Square	50.00	140.00	45.00
Sweetmeat, cov, 5¾"			
d	80.00	155.00	65.00
Toddy Jar, cov,			
underplate	150.00	155.00	125.00
Tumbler	60.00	100.00	50.00

ROSE POINT BAND (Water Lily # 2)

Made by Indiana Glass Co., Dunkirk, IN, c1900 in clear glass only. Sometimes found with floral decorations in color with gold trim.

	Clear	Color Flashed		Clear	Color Flashed
Bowl, Berry	15.00	22.00	Goblet	20.00	—
Butter, cov	40.00	60.00	Pitcher, water	40.00	—
Cake Plate, flat in sil-			Plate, flat, serving . .	20.00	—
ver holder, 10" . . .	45.00	—	Punch Cup	8.00	—
Compote			Sauce, footed	9.00	—
Jelly	25.00	—	Spooner	15.00	—
7½" open, ruffled			Sugar		
edge	35.00	—	Individual, open . .	20.00	—
Creamer			Table	25.00	—
Individual, ftd	20.00	25.00	Wine	20.00	32.00
Table	20.00	25.00	Water Tray	30.00	50.00

ROSE SPRIG

Non-flint made by Campbell, Jones and Co., Pittsburgh, PA, 1886. Complete table line produced in amber, blue, canary-yellow, and clear.

	Amber and Canary	Blue	Clear
Biscuit Jar, dome lid	200.00	250.00	100.00
Cake Stand, 9"	75.00	90.00	70.00
Celery Vase	50.00	60.00	40.00
Compote			
Cov, hs.	125.00	125.00	75.00
Open, hs, 7"	70.00	70.00	60.00
Open, hs, 8", oval	72.00	75.00	60.00
Creamer.	65.00	55.00	45.00
* Goblet	55.00	70.00	40.00
Mug	55.00	55.00	40.00
Nappy, 6"	30.00	35.00	25.00
Pitcher			
Milk.	65.00	70.00	50.00
Water	65.00	70.00	50.00
Plate, 8"	38.00	45.00	30.00
Relish, boat shape .	30.00	35.00	25.00
* Salt			
Patent Date 1888.	65.00	75.00	50.00
Sleigh	30.00	40.00	25.00
Sauce, ftd.	25.00	35.00	20.00
Spooner	30.00	35.00	25.00
Sugar, cov	55.00	70.00	45.00
Tray, water	55.00	70.00	45.00
Tumbler	40.00	45.00	35.00
Wine	55.00	75.00	50.00

ROSETTE (Magic)

Non-flint made by Bryce Bros., Pittsburgh, PA, in the late 1880s. Continued by U. S. Glass Co. after the 1891 merger. Later made in OH in 1898.

	Clear		Clear
Bowl, 7¼", cov	30.00	Pickle.	12.00
Bread Plate, 9", handles . . .	25.00	Pitcher	
Butter, cov	35.00	Milk, qt	50.00
Cake Stand		Water, ½ gal	65.00
7"	24.00	Plate, 7"	12.00
10"	26.00	Relish, fish shape	15.00
11"	35.00	Salt Shaker.	25.00
Celery Vase, 8"	20.00	Sauce, flat, handled.	8.00
Compote		Spooner	25.00
Cov, hs, 6"	40.00	Sugar, cov	35.00
Cov, hs, 8".	70.00	Sugar Shaker	35.00
Cov, hs, 11½"	50.00	Tray, 10¼"	35.00
Open, hs, 7"	30.00	Tumbler, 5".	18.50
Open, hs, 4½", jelly	25.00	Vegetable, open	25.00
Creamer.	25.00	Waste Bowl.	25.00
Goblet	25.00	Wine	25.00
Mug	20.00		

ROSETTES AND PALMS

Non-flint made by J. B. Higbee Co. c1910.

	Clear		Clear
Banana Stand.	40.00	Pickle Dish	20.00
Biscuit Jar, cov	50.00	Pitcher, water	45.00
Butter, cov	45.00	Plate, 10"	25.00
Cake Stand, 9½".	35.00	Sauce, flat	18.00
Celery Vase, flat	18.00	Spooner	25.00
Compote, open, hs	25.00	Sugar, cov	35.00
Creamer.	35.00	Wine	24.00
Goblet	30.00		

ROYAL CRYSTAL

Non-flint pattern made by Tarentum Glass Co., Tarentum, PA, c1894. Made in clear and clear with ruby stain.

	Clear	Ruby Stained		Clear	Ruby Stained
Bowl, 6" d, flared . . .	20.00	30.00	Pitcher, water,		
Butter Dish, cov . . .	45.00	90.00	tankard	65.00	120.00
Cake Stand, hs, 10"			Sauce, ftd, 4" d	10.00	20.00
d.	45.00	90.00	Spooner	30.00	50.00
Celery Vase, 6½" h .	30.00	60.00	Sugar, cov, 7½" h . .	40.00	75.00
Compote, cov, hs, 7"			Toothpick	30.00	60.00
d.	60.00	120.00	Tumbler	20.00	35.00
Creamer, 5¼" h. . . .	35.00	65.00	Wine	25.00	45.00
Goblet, 6½" h	25.00	45.00			

ROYAL IVY (New Jewel)

Non-flint made by Northwood Glass Co. in 1889. Made in cased spatter, clear and frosted rainbow cracquelle, clear with amber, stained ivy, and clambroth opaline. These last mentioned were experimental pieces, not made in sets.

	Clear Frosted	Rubena Clear	Rubena Frosted
Bowl, berry, master .	40.00	75.00	125.00
Butter, cov	100.00	175.00	275.00
Creamer, ah	60.00	150.00	200.00
Cruet	90.00	225.00	325.00
Finger Bowl	25.00	50.00	65.00
Marmalade Jar, SP cov	125.00	—	—
Miniature Lamp	—	—	350.00
Pickle Castor, SP frame	125.00	—	375.00
Pitcher, water, ah . .	110.00	175.00	275.00
Rose Bowl	55.00	70.00	85.00
Salt Shaker, orig top	25.00	30.00	40.00
Sauce	20.00	25.00	35.00
Spooner	45.00	70.00	95.00
Sugar, cov	150.00	165.00	180.00
Sugar Shaker	65.00	135.00	150.00
Syrup	120.00	225.00	300.00
Toothpick	50.00	90.00	125.00
Tumbler	35.00	50.00	75.00

ROYAL LADY (Belmont's Royal, Royal)

Made by Belmont Glass Co., Bellaire, OH, c1881. Some pieces have ball feet. A light amber bread plate ($75.00) is known.

	Clear		Clear
Bread Plate, crying child in center	55.00	Creamer	95.00
Butter, cov, 6 sided skirted		Dish, cov, oval	110.00
base	140.00	Salt, master, 6 sided skirted	
Celery Vase	80.00	base	20.00
Cheese Dish, cov, base has		Spooner	95.00
portrait center, large dome		Sugar, cov	95.00
lid	150.00	Tray, ice cream	120.00
Compote, cov, hs, 9", mkd			
"Fox" in lid design	150.00		

ROYAL OAK (Acorn)

Non-flint made by Northwood Glass Co., Martins Ferry, Ohio, c1890. In the early 1900s, it was made in opaque, white with colored tops and colored acorns and leaves. Milk-white pieces are rare.

	Clear Frosted	Rubena Clear	Rubena Frosted
Butter, cov	150.00	175.00	185.00
Creamer, ah	75.00	125.00	150.00
Cruet, os	150.00	425.00	480.00
Mustard Jar, cov . . .	90.00	—	—
Pickle Castor	100.00	150.00	225.00
Pitcher, water	100.00	350.00	350.00
Salt Shaker, orig top	40.00	45.00	65.00
Sauce	15.00	20.00	25.00
Spooner	50.00	90.00	100.00
Sugar, cov, acorn finial	85.00	150.00	180.00
Sugar Shaker	75.00	135.00	165.00
Syrup	135.00	200.00	275.00
Toothpick	45.00	85.00	125.00
Tumbler	40.00	60.00	80.00

SAINT BERNAND

Non-flint pattern made by Fostoria Glass Co., Fostoria, OH, c1894.

	Clear		Clear
Bowl, berry, 8″ d	35.00	Goblet	35.00
Butter Dish, cov	75.00	Pitcher, water, bulbous.	55.00
Cake Stand, hs	40.00	Salt Shaker.	20.00
Celery Vase	35.00	Sugar, cov	75.00
Compote, cov, hs, 8″ d.	60.00	Tumbler	20.00
Creamer.	35.00		

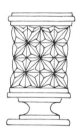

SANDWICH STAR

Flint pattern attributed to Boston & Sandwich Glass Co., Sandwich, MA, c1850. Made in amethyst, clambroth, clear, electric blue, jade green, opaque blue, and opaque lavender. Colors are rare.

	Clear		Clear
Butter Dish, cov	350.00	Goblet	400.00
Champagne	350.00	Pitcher, water	500.00
Compote, open, hs, scalloped rim.	350.00	Spooner.	100.00
Creamer.	375.00	Sugar.	425.00
		Wine	350.00

SAWTOOTH (Mitre Diamond)

An early clear flint made in the late 1850s by the New England Glass Co., Boston and Sandwich Glass Co., and others. Later made in non-flint by Bryce Bros. and U. S. Glass Co. Also known in milk glass, clear deep blue, and canary yellow.

	Flint	Non-Flint		Flint	Non-Flint
Butter, cov	75.00	45.00	Goblet	50.00	20.00
Cake Stand, 10″ . . .	85.00	55.00	Pitcher, water		
Celery Vase, 10″ . . .	60.00	30.00	Applied handle. . .	150.00	95.00
Champagne	65.00	30.00	Pressed handle . .	—	55.00
Compote			Plate, 6½″.	45.00	30.00
Cov, hs, 9½″	85.00	48.00	Pomade Jar, cov . . .	50.00	35.00
Open, ls, 8″, sawtooth edge	50.00	30.00	Salt		
			Cov, ftd	65.00	40.00
Cordial	50.00	30.00	Open, smooth edge	25.00	20.00
Creamer					
Applied handle. . .	75.00	40.00	Spooner	70.00	30.00
Pressed handle . .	—	30.00	Sugar, cov	65.00	35.00
Cruet, acorn stopper	100.00	—	Tumbler, bar.	50.00	25.00
Egg Cup.	45.00	25.00	Wine, knob stem . . .	35.00	20.00

SAWTOOTHED HONEYCOMB (Serrated Block and Loop, Union's Radiant)

Non-flint made by Steimer Glass Co., Buckhannon, WV, c1906. The molds were sold to Union Stopper Co., Morgantown, WV, c1908.

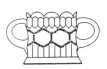

	Clear	Ruby Stained		Clear	Ruby Stained
Bonbon	25.00	35.00	Salt Shaker, orig top	20.00	35.00
Bowl, 9" d	15.00	45.00	Sauce, 4" d		
Butter, cov	40.00	100.00	Flat	10.00	20.00
Celery Vase	25.00	80.00	Ftd	12.00	25.00
Compote, open, hs	35.00	50.00	Spooner	30.00	45.00
Creamer, 4" h, ph	25.00	40.00	Sugar		
Cruet, os	50.00	125.00	Cov	45.00	75.00
Goblet	25.00	60.00	Open	35.00	45.00
Orange Bowl, 14½"			Syrup, orig top	60.00	175.00
d	65.00	125.00	Toothpick	25.00	150.00
Pitcher, water, 10" h,			Tumbler, 3¾" h	20.00	40.00
ph	50.00	145.00			

SAXON

Non-flint pattern made by Adams & Co., Pittsburgh, PA, c1888. Reissued by U. S. Glass Co., Pittsburgh, PA, after 1892. Made in clear. Several items can be found in ruby stained and often with souvenir inscriptions. Prices listed below are for plain clear pieces.

	Clear		Clear
Bowl, 8" d, belled, scalloped rim	15.00	Goblet	30.00
Bread Plate	30.00	Pitcher, water	45.00
Butter Dish, cov	35.00	Sauce, flat, 4" d	10.00
Cake Stand, hs, 9" d	40.00	Spooner	25.00
Celery Vase	25.00	Sugar, cov	35.00
Compote, cov, hs, 6" d	25.00	Tumbler	20.00
Creamer, 7" h	25.00	Wine	35.00

SCALLOPED DIAMOND POINT (Late Diamond Point Band, Panel with Diamond Point, Diamond Point with Flute)

Non-flint not to be confused with early flint Diamond Point. Made by Central Glass Co., Wheeling, WV. Also made by U. S. Glass Co. after 1891. A wine ($75.00) is known in electric blue and in amber ($50.00).

	Clear		Clear
Bowl, oval, 9"	20.00	Goblet	30.00
Butter Dish, cov	55.00	Mustard Jar, cov	30.00
Cake Stand		Pickle Dish, oval	20.00
8"	30.00	Pickle Jar, cov	45.00
12"	45.00	Plate	
Cheese Dish, cov, 8"	50.00	5"	12.00
Compote		9"	20.00
Cov, hs, 8"	75.00	Sauce, ftd, 4"	10.00
Open, hs, 7" d	40.00	Spooner	25.00
Cov, 5", jelly	35.00	Sugar, cov	40.00
Creamer	50.00	Wine	35.00

SCALLOPED SIX POINTS

Non-flint pattern made by George Duncan & Sons, Washington, PA, c1897 to 1912.

	Clear		Clear
Bowl, 9" sq	30.00	Cake Stand, hs	40.00
Butter Dish, cov	45.00	Celery Tray	25.00

	Clear		Clear
Compote, open, ls........	30.00	Spooner...............	30.00
Creamer...............	35.00	Sugar, cov	45.00
Goblet	40.00	Tumbler	25.00
Pitcher, water, tankard.....	50.00	Wine	25.00

SCALLOPED SWIRL (York Herringbone)

Non-flint made by unknown American maker in the late 1880s and by U.S. Glass Co. after 1891. Often found with souvenir etching.

	Clear	Ruby Stained		Clear	Ruby Stained
Bowl, berry.......	25.00	60.00	Goblet	25.00	40.00
Butter, cov	50.00	75.00	Pitcher, water	55.00	90.00
Cake Plate, 10"....	30.00	60.00	Spooner	20.00	45.00
Celery	20.00	50.00	Sugar, cov	35.00	65.00
Compote, cov, 7"...	45.00	75.00	Toothpick	—	45.00
Creamer.........	25.00	55.00	Tumbler	25.00	45.00

SCALLOPED TAPE (Jewel Band)

Non-flint, c1880, unknown maker. Occasionally found in amber, blue, canary, and light green.

	Clear		Clear
Bread Plate, oval, "Bread Is The Staff of Life".......	45.00	Pitcher Milk.................	35.00
Butter, cov	35.00	Water	55.00
Cake Stand	35.00	Plate, 6"...............	15.00
Celery Vase	30.00	Relish................	10.00
Compote		Sauce	
Cov, hs, 8".............	55.00	Flat, 4"	8.50
Open, hs.............	40.00	Ftd	12.00
Creamer...............	25.00	Spooner	20.00
Dish, rect, cov, 8"	45.00	Sugar, cov	35.00
Egg Cup...............	25.00	Tray, 6 x 7"............	25.00
Goblet	25.00	Wine	20.00

SCROLL (Stippled Scroll)

Non-flint made by George Duncan & Sons Co., Pittsburgh, PA, c1870. Also made in milk glass and light blue opaque.

	Clear		Clear
Butter, cov	50.00	Sauce	10.00
Celery	30.00	Spooner..............	30.00
Compote		Sugar	
Cov, hs.............	65.00	Cov.............	45.00
Open, hs.............	35.00	Open	25.00
Creamer, ah	40.00	Tumbler, ftd	25.00
Goblet	35.00	Wine	30.00
Pitcher, water, ah	75.00		
Salt, ftd			
Individual.............	20.00		
Master	25.00		

SCROLL WITH ACANTHUS

Made by Northwood Glass Co., Wheeling, WV, after 1903. There is sometimes enameled decoration on the transparent pieces. Transparent colors are 20% less; purple slag, 50% higher.

	Blue Opal	Canary Opal	White Opal
Bowl, berry	60.00	65.00	35.00
Butter, cov, ftd.	125.00	110.00	50.00
Compote, jelly, 5" . .	50.00	45.00	30.00
Creamer.	100.00	85.00	40.00
Pitcher, water	285.00	255.00	100.00
Sauce	25.00	25.00	20.00
Spooner	45.00	50.00	30.00
Sugar, cov	110.00	125.00	45.00
Tumbler	40.00	35.00	25.00

SCROLL WITH FLOWERS

Non-flint attributed to Central Glass Co. in the 1870s and Canton Glass Co., Canton, OH, c1880. Occasionally found in amber, apple green, and blue.

	Clear		Clear
Butter, cov	40.00	Mustard Jar, cov	50.00
Cake Plate, 10½", handled. .	25.00	Pickle, handled	18.00
Celery	36.00	Pitcher, water	45.00
Compote, cov	45.00	Plate, double-handled, 10½"	40.00
Cordial	35.00	Sauce, double-handled	10.00
Creamer.	40.00	Spooner	28.50
Egg Cup, handled	20.00	Sugar, cov	45.00
Goblet	25.00	Wine	30.00

SEASHELL

Non-flint pattern whose maker has not been identified, c1870.

	Clear		Clear
Butter Dish, cov	85.00	Pitcher, water	60.00
Cake Stand, hs	35.00	Sauce, ftd	15.00
Celery Vase	30.00	Spooner	25.00
Compote, cov, hs	70.00	Sugar, cov	60.00
Creamer.	25.00	Wine	25.00
Goblet	30.00		

SEDAN (Paneled Star and Button)

Clear non-flint made in the 1870s.

	Clear		Clear
Bowl.	20.00	Pitcher, water	35.00
Butter, cov	30.00	Relish.	10.00
Celery Tray.	15.00	Salt Shaker.	20.00
Celery Vase	25.00	Sauce, flat	8.00
Compote		Spooner	15.00
Cov, hs, 8½"	35.00	Sugar, cov	35.00
Open, hs	20.00	Tumbler	20.00
Creamer.	20.00	Wine	15.00
Goblet	15.00		

SHELL AND JEWEL (Jewel and Shell, Victor, Nugget, Late Nugget)

Non-flint made by Westmoreland Glass Co. c1893. Made by Fostoria Glass Co. in 1898. Attributed to Sydenham Glass Co., Wallaceburg, Ontario, Canada, c1895 and Jefferson Glass Co., Toronto, Ontario, Canada, c1920. American-made items have more rounded shell decorations. Canadian-made items have pointed shells sometimes with row of balls between fans. Limited production in amber, cobalt blue, green, and carnival.

	Amber	Blue	Clear
Banana Stand, 10" .	—	—	65.00
Bowl, 8"	35.00	—	20.00
Butter, cov	—	—	60.00
Cake Stand, 10" . . .	—	—	50.00
Compote, open, hs, 7"	—	—	35.00
Creamer	—	—	40.00
Honey Dish, cov . . .	—	—	25.00
Orange Bowl	—	—	65.00
Pitcher, water	50.00	60.00	45.00
Sauce	—	—	12.00
Spooner	—	—	20.00
Sugar, cov	—	—	50.00
Tray, water	—	—	50.00
Tumbler	35.00	40.00	25.00
Water Set, 8 pcs . . .	300.00	350.00	200.00

SHELL AND TASSEL (Shell and Spike)

Non-flint made by George A. Duncan and Sons, Pittsburgh, PA, in the 1880s. It was patented by Augustus Heisey on July 26, 1881. Two forms were issued: square with shell shaped finials, and later, round with frosted dog finials. Also made in azure blue, amber, and canary, but are rare.

	Round	Square		Round	Square
Bowl, 12", oval	85.00	—	Ice Cream Tray. . . .	65.00	—
Bread Plate	55.00	65.00	Nappy	20.00	25.00
Butter, cov, dog finial	125.00	125.00	Oyster Plate	225.00	—
			Pitcher, water	85.00	85.00
Butter Pat, shell shaped	25.00	—	Salt Shaker.	50.00	—
Cake Stand, 12" . . .	60.00	90.00	Sauce		
Celery Vase	55.00	55.00	Flat	10.00	10.00
Compote			Ftd	10.00	15.00
Open, hs, 10" . . .	75.00	65.00	Spooner	38.00	40.00
Open, jelly, 4½" . .	—	45.00	Sugar, cov, dog finial	100.00	85.00
Creamer.	40.00	55.00	Vase, 7½", scalloped rim	100.00	—
* Goblet	40.00	—			

SHERATON (Ida)

Non-flint made by Bryce, Higbee and Co., Pittsburgh, PA, c1885. Also attributed to Burlington Glass Works, Hamilton, Ontario, Canada.

	Amber	Blue	Clear
Bowl, 8"	35.00	40.00	15.00
Bread Plate	45.00	50.00	25.00
Butter, cov	40.00	50.00	25.00
Celery Vase	30.00	35.00	28.50
Compote, open, ls, 7"	25.00	30.00	20.00
Creamer.	35.00	45.00	30.00
Goblet	40.00	50.00	35.00
Pitcher			
Milk.	40.00	50.00	30.00
Water	45.00	55.00	35.00
Relish, handled. . . .	25.00	30.00	15.00
Sauce, flat	15.00	18.00	10.00
Spooner	24.00	30.00	18.00
Sugar, cov	40.00	55.00	30.00
Tumbler	35.00	40.00	30.00
Wine	35.00	40.00	30.00

SHOSONE (Blazing Pinwheels, Floral Diamond, Victor)

Non-flint made by U. S. Glass Co., Pittsburgh, PA, c1895–96. Made in clear, emerald green, and amber or ruby stained. Westmoreland Glass Co. copied the pattern and sold it through its Sterling line.

	Amber Stained	Clear	Green	Ruby Stained
Banana Stand, hs . .	85.00	65.00	55.00	85.00
Bowl				
5" d, flared	40.00	25.00	35.00	40.00
6" d, straight sides	40.00	25.00	35.00	40.00
7" d, belled	45.00	30.00	40.00	45.00
8" d, straight sides	45.00	30.00	40.00	45.00
Butter, domed cov . .	75.00	45.00	65.00	85.00
Cake Stand, hs, 10" d.	—	40.00	55.00	—
Celery Vase	85.00	35.00	65.00	85.00
Compote				
Cov, hs, 6".	—	45.00	—	—
Cov, hs, 7".	—	50.00	—	—
Cov, ls, 7"	—	50.00	—	—
Cov, ls, 8"	—	55.00	—	—
Open, ls, 4½" . . .	—	35.00	—	—
Open, ls, 7"	—	45.00	—	—
Open, ls, 9".	—	50.00	—	—
Open, ls, 10"	—	55.00	—	—
Creamer				
Individual.	35.00	25.00	30.00	35.00
Table, 5" h	45.00	25.00	45.00	45.00
Goblet, 6½" h	55.00	30.00	—	60.00
Horseradish, cov . . .	—	30.00	40.00	—
Ice Tub, tab handles	75.00	35.00	65.00	75.00
Jelly Dish, 5½" w, double handles . .	25.00	15.00	25.00	25.00
Olive Tray, 7¾" l . . .	25.00	20.00	25.00	25.00
Pickle Tray	25.00	20.00	25.00	25.00
Pitcher, water, ah, ½ gal				
Bulbous.	175.00	50.00	150.00	175.00
Tankard	175.00	50.00	150.00	175.00
Plate, 7" d, sq	—	30.00	35.00	—
Salt, master	55.00	25.00	—	65.00
Salt Shaker, orig top	45.00	20.00	40.00	45.00
Sauce, flat, 4" d . . .	20.00	20.00	10.00	20.00
Spooner	40.00	25.00	35.00	55.00
Sugar, cov				
Individual.	55.00	35.00	55.00	65.00
Table	65.00	40.00	65.00	75.00
Toothpick, 2¾" h . . .	225.00	40.00	85.00	225.00
Tumbler, 2¾" h	45.00	35.00	40.00	45.00
Wine, 4½" h	35.00	30.00	35.00	45.00

SHRINE (Jewel with Moon and Star)

Non-flint made by Beatty & Indiana Glass Co., Dunkirk, IN, around the late 1880s.

	Clear		Clear
Bowl		Platter	40.00
4"	15.00	Relish.	15.00
6½".	25.00	Salt Shaker.	30.00
9½".	30.00	Sauce	15.00
Butter, cov	50.00	Spooner	30.00
Cake Stand, 8½"	40.00	Sugar, cov	50.00
Celery	45.00	Tumbler	
Creamer.	40.00	Lemonade.	40.00
Goblet	45.00	Water	35.00
Mug	25.00		
Pickle	20.00		
Pitcher, water			
Normal Size	50.00		
Jumbo Size	100.00		

SHUTTLE (Hearts of Loch Haven)

Non-flint made by Indiana Tumbler and Goblet Co., Greentown, IN, c1896 and Indiana Glass Co., Dunkirk, IN, c1898.

	Clear		Clear
Bowl, berry	25.00	Mug	25.00
Butter, cov	50.00	Pitcher, water	50.00
Cake Stand	115.00	Salt Shaker, orig top	45.00
Celery Vase	30.00	Spooner	20.00
Cordial	32.00	Sugar, cov	40.00
Creamer	30.00	Tumbler	25.00
Custard Cup	10.00	Wine	20.00
Goblet	60.00		

SKILTON (Early Oregon)

Made by Richards and Hartley of Tarentum, PA, in 1888 and by U. S. Glass Co. after 1891. This is not one of the U. S. Glass States pattern series and should not be confused with Beaded Loop, which is Oregon #1, named by U. S. Glass Co. It is better known as Skilton (named by Millard) to avoid confusion with Beaded Loop.

	Clear	Ruby Stained		Clear	Ruby Stained
Bowl			Creamer	30.00	55.00
4", round	10.00	—	Dish, oblong, sq . . .	25.00	—
5", round	15.00	—	Goblet	35.00	50.00
6", round	20.00	—	Olive, handled	20.00	—
7", rect	20.00	—	Pickle	15.00	—
8", rect	25.00	—	Pitcher		
9", rect	30.00	—	Milk	45.00	125.00
Butter, cov	45.00	110.00	Water	50.00	125.00
Cake Stand	35.00	—	Salt & Pepper, pr. . .	45.00	—
Celery Vase	35.00	95.00	Sauce, ftd	12.00	20.00
Compote			Spooner, flat	25.00	55.00
Cov, hs, 7"	45.00	—	Sugar, cov	35.00	85.00
Cov, hs, 8"	45.00	—	Tray, water	45.00	—
Open, ls, 4"	10.00	—	Tumbler	25.00	40.00
Open, ls, 7"	25.00	—	Wine	35.00	50.00
Open, ls, 8"	30.00	75.00			

SMOCKING

Flint made c1850. Shards have been found at Boston and Sandwich Glass Co., Sandwich, MA. Some variants. Rare in color.

	Clear		Clear
Bar Bottle, blob top	100.00	Spill Holder	75.00
Bowl, 9"	75.00	Spooner	40.00
Compote, cov, ls, 7"	90.00	Sugar	
Creamer	90.00	Cov	85.00
Egg Cup	50.00	Open	50.00
Goblet	85.00	Vase, 10"	65.00
Lamp, oil, 9" h	145.00	Whiskey	75.00
Pitcher, water	115.00	Wine	45.00

SNAIL (Compact, Double Snail, Small Comet)

Non-flint made by George Duncan and Sons, Pittsburgh, PA, c1880, and by U. S. Glass Co. after the 1891 merger. U. S. Glass Co. Production expanded this clear pattern by the addition of ruby staining. Add 30% for copper wheel engraved pieces.

	Clear	Ruby Stained		Clear	Ruby Stained
Banana Stand	150.00	225.00	Bowl		
Basket, cake			4"	20.00	90.00
9"	85.00	—	4½"	20.00	—
10"	95.00	—	7", cov	60.00	45.00

	Clear	Ruby Stained		Clear	Ruby Stained
7", oval	28.00	45.00	Pitcher		
7", round	28.00	45.00	Milk, tankard	100.00	250.00
8", cov	60.00	45.00	Water, bulbous	126.00	—
8", oval	28.00	45.00	Water, tankard	135.00	250.00
8", round	28.00	45.00	Plate		
9", oval	30.00	—	5"	35.00	—
9", round	30.00	—	6"	35.00	—
10"	35.00	45.00	7"	40.00	—
Butter, cov	75.00	160.00	Punch Cup	30.00	—
Cake Stand			Relish, 7", oval	25.00	—
9"	85.00	—	Rose Bowl		
10"	95.00	—	3"	50.00	—
Celery Tray	35.00	—	5"	45.00	—
Celery Vase	40.00	85.00	6"	45.00	—
Cheese, cov	95.00	—	7"	50.00	—
Compote			Salt		
Cov, hs, 6"	50.00	—	Individual	35.00	40.00
Cov, hs, 7"	50.00	100.00	Master	35.00	75.00
Cov, hs, 8"	80.00	135.00	Salt Shaker		
Cov, hs, 10"	125.00	—	Bulbous	65.00	90.00
Open, hs, 6"	30.00	—	Straight sides	60.00	90.00
Open, hs, 7"	45.00	—	Sauce	25.00	45.00
Open, hs, 8"	35.00	—	Spooner	45.00	75.00
Open, hs, 9", twist-ed stem, scal-loped	75.00	—	Sugar		
			Individual, cov	50.00	—
Cracker Jar, cov	85.00	—	Regular, cov	60.00	100.00
Creamer	65.00	75.00	Sugar Shaker	85.00	200.00
Cruet, os	100.00	275.00	Syrup	125.00	225.00
Custard Cup	30.00	—	Tumbler	55.00	65.00
Finger Bowl	50.00	—	Vase	50.00	90.00
Goblet	65.00	95.00	Violet Bowl, 3"	50.00	—
Marmalade, cov	90.00	125.00	Wine	65.00	—

SNOW BAND (Puffed Bands)

Unknown maker, c1885.

	Clear	Amber	Blue
Bowl	18.00	22.00	25.00
Butter, cov	40.00	45.00	50.00
Cake Stand	25.00	25.00	30.00
Creamer	25.00	30.00	35.00
Goblet	20.00	25.00	45.00
Pickle	15.00	18.00	20.00
Pitcher, water	45.00	50.00	55.00
Sugar, cov	35.00	40.00	45.00
Spooner	20.00	25.00	30.00
Tumbler	25.00	30.00	35.00
Wine	18.00	20.00	25.00

SOUTHERN IVY

Non-flint, c1880s.

	Clear		Clear
Bowl, 8"	15.00	Sauce, flat	10.00
Butter, cov	25.00	Spooner	15.00
Creamer	20.00	Sugar	
Cruet, os	30.00	Cov	25.00
Pitcher, water	30.00	Open	15.00

SPANISH-AMERICAN

Made in the late 1890s in commemoration of Admiral Dewey and the Spanish-American War. Two pitchers were made by the Beatty-Brady Glass Co., Dunkirk, IN. The only known matching pieces are listed below.

	Clear	Green		Clear	Green
Water Pitcher, Admiral Dewey, Flagship Olympia, flags, cannon balls around base	70.00	—	Water Pitcher, Captain Gridley, "You may fire when ready", bullets around base	85.00	250.00
Tumbler, portrait of Dewey, matches pitcher.........	50.00	—	Tumbler to match ..	80.00	—

SPIREA BAND (Earl, Nailhead Variant, Spirea, Squared Dot)

Non-flint made by Bryce, Higbee and Co., Pittsburgh, PA, c1885.

	Amber	Blue	Clear	Vaseline
Bowl, 8"	25.00	40.00	20.00	30.00
Butter, cov	50.00	55.00	35.00	45.00
Cake Stand, 11" ...	45.00	55.00	40.00	45.00
Celery Vase	40.00	50.00	25.00	40.00
Compote, cov, hs, 7"	44.00	65.00	40.00	44.00
Cordial	38.00	42.00	20.00	38.00
Creamer.........	32.50	44.00	35.00	35.00
Goblet	30.00	35.00	25.00	35.00
Pitcher, water	65.00	80.00	35.00	60.00
Platter, 10½"......	32.00	42.00	20.00	32.00
Relish.	30.00	35.00	18.00	30.00
Sauce				
Flat..........	10.00	12.00	5.00	9.00
Ftd	15.00	18.00	8.00	14.00
Spooner	30.00	35.00	20.00	35.00
Sugar, open	32.00	40.00	25.00	32.00
Tumbler	24.00	35.00	20.00	30.00
Wine	30.00	35.00	20.00	30.00

SPRIG (Ribbed Palm)

Non-flint made by Bryce, Higbee and Co., Pittsburgh, PA, c1880.

	Clear		Clear
Bowl, 10", scalloped	35.00	Pitcher, water	50.00
Bread Plate	40.00	Relish.	15.00
Butter, cov	65.00	Salt	
Cake Stand, 8"	35.00	Individual............	35.00
Celery Vase	40.00	Master	50.00
Compote		Sauce	
Cov, hs	60.00	Flat................	10.00
Open, hs.............	45.00	Ftd	15.00
Creamer..............	30.00	Spooner	25.00
Goblet	30.00	Sugar, cov	40.00
Pickle Dish	15.00	Tumbler	25.00
Pickle Jar	65.00	Wine	40.00

SQUAT PINEAPPLE (Lone Star)

Made by McKee & Bros. Glass Co. in 1898. Available in many pieces.

	Clear	Emerald Green		Clear	Emerald Green
Butter, cov	45.00	55.00	Creamer.........	25.00	35.00
Cake Stand	30.00	45.00	Cruet, os	55.00	65.00
Celery Tray.......	20.00	30.00	Dish............	20.00	25.00
Compote			Goblet	30.00	35.00
Cov...........	60.00	75.00	Pickle...........	15.00	22.00
Open	35.00	55.00	Pitcher, water	45.00	55.00

	Clear	Emerald Green		Clear	Emerald Green
Relish, handle.....	18.00	25.00	Syrup, metal top ...	55.00	65.00
Salt & Pepper Shak-			Tray, water.......	50.00	65.00
ers, pr.........	45.00	55.00	Tumbler	25.00	30.00
Spooner.........	20.00	25.00	Wine	20.00	25.00
Sugar, covered	35.00	45.00			

STAR IN BULL'S EYE

Non-flint made by U. S. Glass Co., Pittsburgh, PA, c1905. Made in clear, with or without gilt trim, and sometimes found with rose stain (add 50%).

	Clear w/ Gold		Clear w/ Gold
Bowl, berry.............	25.00	Goblet	25.00
Butter, cov	35.00	Pitcher, water	45.00
Cake Stand	40.00	Spooner	25.00
Compote, cov	45.00	Sugar, cov	35.00
Creamer...............	25.00	Tumbler	20.00
Cruet	30.00	Wine	20.00

STAR ROSETTED

Non-flint made by McKee & Bros. Glass Co., Pittsburgh, PA, c1875. Reproduced in color.

	Clear		Clear
Bread Plate	50.00	Goblet	25.00
Butter, cov	48.00	Pickle................	14.00
Compote		Pitcher, water	50.00
Cov, hs, 8½"	60.00	Plate, 7"...............	15.00
Cov, jelly	55.00	Relish, 9"	14.00
Cov, sweetmeat........	55.00	Sauce	
Open, hs, 6½"	18.00	Flat................	8.50
Open, hs, 7½"	20.00	Footed	12.00
Open, hs, 8½"	35.00	Spooner..............	25.00
Creamer...............	35.00	Sugar, cov	48.00

STARS AND STRIPES (Brilliant)

Non-flint made by Jenkins Glass Co., Kokomo, IN, in 1899. Also made by Federal Glass Co., Columbus, OH, c1914. Appeared in 1899 Montgomery Ward catalog as "Brilliant."

	Clear		Clear
Bowl, berry.............	15.00	Pitcher, water	35.00
Butter, cov	30.00	Salt Shaker.............	15.00
Celery Vase	15.00	Sauce	6.00
Cordial................	15.00	Spooner..............	15.00
Creamer...............	18.00	Sugar, cov	20.00
Cruet Set	35.00	Tumbler	15.00
Cup, sherbert, handled	12.00	Vase	10.00
Goblet	20.00	Wine	15.00

STATES, THE (Cane and Star Medallion)

Non-flint made by U. S. Glass Co. Pittsburgh, PA, in 1905. Also found in emerald green (add 50%). Prices given for clear with good gold trim.

	Clear		Clear
Bowl		Butter, cov	65.00
7", round, 3 handles.....	25.00	Celery Tray.............	20.00
9¼", round	30.00	Celery Vase	20.00

	Clear		Clear
Cocktail	25.00	Relish, diamond shape	35.00
Compote		Salt & Pepper	40.00
Open, hs, 7"	30.00	Sauce, flat, 4", tub shape	15.00
Open, hs, 9"	40.00	Spooner	25.00
Creamer		Sugar	
Individual, oval	18.00	Individual, open	15.00
Regular, round	30.00	Regular, cov	40.00
Goblet	35.00	Syrup	65.00
Pickle Tray	15.00	Toothpick, flat, rectangular,	
Pitcher, water	45.00	curled lip	45.00
Plate, 10"	25.00	Tray, 7¼" l, 5½" w	18.00
Punch Bowl, 13" d	75.00	Tumbler	22.00
Punch Cup	8.00	Wine	30.00

STIPPLED CHAIN

Clear non-flint made by Gillinder and Sons, Philadelphia, PA, c1880.

	Clear		Clear
Bowl	15.00	Pitcher, water	65.00
Butter, cov	50.00	Relish	10.00
Cake Stand	45.00	Salt, ftd	20.00
Celery Vase	40.00	Sauce, flat	10.00
Creamer	35.00	Spooner	25.00
Egg Cup	20.00	Sugar, cov	40.00
Goblet	20.00	Tumbler	20.00
Pickle	15.00		

STIPPLED DOUBLE LOOP

Clear and stippled non-flint of the 1870s.

	Clear		Clear
Butter, cov	50.00	Pitcher, water	55.00
Cake Stand	40.00	Salt Shaker	20.00
Celery Vase	40.00	Spooner	20.00
Creamer	30.00	Sugar, cov	25.00
Goblet	60.00	Tumbler	30.00

STIPPLED FORGET-ME-NOT

Non-flint made by Findlay Glass Co. Findlay, OH, in the 1880s. Also found in amber, blue, and white.

	Clear		Clear
Bowl, 7"	45.00	Plate	
Bread Plate, kittens, tab		7", Baby in Tub reaching	
handles	75.00	for ball	55.00
Butter, cov	50.00	7", Star center	30.00
Cake Stand		9", Kitten center, handles	55.00
9"	35.00	9", Star center	35.00
10"	75.00	Relish, oval	15.00
12"	80.00	Salt, master, oval	35.00
Celery Vase, 8" h	35.00	Sauce, ftd	15.00
Compote		Saucer	10.00
Cov, hs, 8"	50.00	Spooner	25.00
Cov, ls, 6"	45.00	Sugar, cov	35.00
Open, hs	45.00	Toothpick, hat shaped	100.00
Cordial	75.00	Tray, water	
Creamer	30.00	Aquatic Scene	50.00
Cup	20.00	Herons	75.00
* Goblet	45.00	Storks	75.00
Mug	30.00	Tumbler	30.00
Pitcher, water	50.00	Wine	35.00

STIPPLED GRAPE AND FESTOON

Non-flint made by Doyle and Co, Pittsburgh, PA, c1870. Reissued by U. S. Glass Co. c1891. Shards have also been found at Boston and Sandwich Glass Co., Sandwich, MA. Pieces have applied handles and acorn finials.

	Clear		Clear
Bowl, 6″	25.00	Goblet	32.50
Butter, cov		Pickle	30.00
Flange	60.00	Pitcher	
Regular	45.00	Milk	75.00
Celery Tray	35.00	Water	90.00
Celery Vase	45.00	Plate, 6″	35.00
Compote		Relish	30.00
Cov, hs, 8″	45.00	Sauce, flat	12.00
Cov, ls, 8″	35.00	Spooner	30.00
Cov, ls, 9″	55.00	Sugar	
Open, ls	35.00	Cov	60.00
Cordial	30.00	Open	40.00
Creamer	50.00	Wine	45.00
Egg Cup	35.00		

STIPPLED PEPPERS

Non-flint attributed to Boston and Sandwich Glass Co. Sandwich, MA, in the 1870s.

	Clear		Clear
Creamer, ah	35.00	Sauce	6.00
Egg Cup	20.00	Spooner	25.00
Goblet	30.00	Sugar, cov	35.00
Pitcher, water, ah	75.00	Tumbler, ftd	20.00
Salt, ftd	15.00		

STIPPLED STAR

Non-flint made by Gillinder and Sons, Philadelphia, PA, in the 1870s. Originally produced in clear with limited production in blue. L. G. Wright Glass Co. reproduced items in color, plus added salts to the line with new molds.

	Clear		Clear
Bread Plate, Mother	40.00	* Goblet	30.00
Butter, cov	50.00	Pitcher, water	75.00
Celery Vase	40.00	Sauce	
Compote		Flat	6.00
* Cov, hs, 12″	65.00	Footed	10.00
Open, hs, 8″	45.00	Spooner	25.00
* Creamer, applied handle	40.00	* Sugar, cov	45.00
Egg Cup	35.00	* Wine	35.00

STRAWBERRY (Fairfax)

Non-flint, made by Bryce, Walker & Co., Pittsburgh, PA, c1870. Designed and patented by John Bryce in 1870. Shards have been found at Boston and Sandwich Glass Co., Sandwich MA, and Burlington Glass Works, Hamilton, Ontario, Canada.

	Clear	Milk		Clear	Milk
Bowl, oval, 9¼″ x 6″	30.00	—			
Butter, cov	55.00	50.00	Pickle Tray	20.00	—
Celery Vase	45.00	—	Pitcher, water, ah	125.00	135.00
Compote			Relish Tray	20.00	—
Cov, hs, 8″	75.00	—	Sauce, flat	14.00	—
Cov, ls, 8″	65.00	—	Spooner	40.00	40.00
Creamer, ah	65.00	75.00	Sugar, cov	50.00	75.00
* Egg Cup	37.50	32.00	Syrup, ah	95.00	—
* Goblet	40.00	60.00	Tumbler, bar	45.00	—
Honey Dish	20.00	—	Wine	65.00	—

STRAWBERRY AND CURRANT (Multiple Fruits)

One of a non-flint series of fruit patterns which has become known as Multiple Fruits (Cherry and Fig, Loganberry and Grape, Blackberry and Grape, and Cornucopia with Sprig of Cherries). They were made by Dalzell, Gilmore, and Leighton, Findlay, OH. A Loganberry and Grape jelly goblet, with "U" shaped bowl is of inferior quality and not part of the pattern.

There are matching pieces in all forms, although whether or not all forms were made in all four patterns is not known. Reproduction goblets and other items are found in clear, opalescent, and colors. L. G. Wright Glass Co. has also added some additional forms through its reproduction line, including compotes with crimped and ruffled rims.

	Clear		Clear
Butter, cov	50.00	Pitcher	
Celery Vase	35.00	Milk	40.00
Cheese, cov	50.00	Water	50.00
Compote		Sauce, ftd	10.00
Cov, hs, 8″ d	70.00	Spooner	35.00
Open, hs	35.00	Sugar, cov	40.00
Creamer	40.00	Syrup	80.00
* Goblet	35.00	Tumbler	25.00
Mug	35.00		

STRIGIL

Non-flint made in the 1880s by Tarentum Glass Co, Tarentum, PA. May be gilded.

	Clear		Clear
Bowl, 8″	20.00	Punch Cup	10.00
Butter, cov	35.00	Sauce, flat	5.00
Celery Tray	15.00	Spooner	18.00
Celery Vase	25.00	Sugar, cov	32.00
Creamer	15.00	Table Set, 5 pcs	90.00
Cruet, os	25.00	Tumbler	18.00
Egg Cup	20.00	Wine	25.00
Goblet	40.00		
Pitcher			
Milk	30.00		
Water	35.00		

SUNBURST (Flattened Diamond and Sunburst)

Non-flint made by Burlington Glass Works, Hamilton, Ontario, Canada. Made in clear with pieces occasionally found in amber or blue.

	Clear		Clear
Bread Plate, 11″ d,		Goblet	25.00
GUTDODB	25.00	Plate, 7″ d	15.00
Cake Stand	30.00	Relish	12.00
Creamer	25.00	Sauce	6.00
Egg Cup	18.00	Wine	20.00

SUNFLOWER (Lily)

Non-flint made by Atterbury & Co., Pittsburgh, PA, c1880. Shards have been found at Burlington Glass Works, Hamilton, Ontario, Canada. Made in clear, amber, and milk glass.

	Amber	Clear	Milk Glass
Bowl	35.00	25.00	45.00
Butter, cov	80.00	55.00	110.00
Creamer	60.00	40.00	80.00
Pitcher, water	75.00	60.00	115.00
Spooner	42.00	30.00	48.00

	Amber	Clear	Milk Glass
Sugar			
Cov.	55.00	50.00	75.00
Open	35.00	28.00	40.00

SWAG WITH BRACKETS

Made by Jefferson Glass Co., Steubenville, OH, c1904. Also found in non-opalescent, gold trimmed, amethyst, blue, and vaseline.

	Blue and Canary Opal	Green Opal	White Opal
Butter, cov	175.00	150.00	100.00
Compote, jelly.	45.00	55.00	30.00
Creamer.	80.00	75.00	55.00
Cruet, os	150.00	110.00	—
Pitcher, water	185.00	200.00	130.00
Salt Shaker.	50.00	40.00	35.00
Spooner	72.00	65.00	40.00
Sugar, cov	135.00	85.00	50.00
* Toothpick	125.00	85.00	40.00
Tumbler	65.00	50.00	35.00

SWAN (Plain Swan, Swan with Mesh)

Non-flint pattern attributed to the Canton Glass Co., Canton, OH, c1882. Original production in amber, blue, canary yellow, and clear. Rarely found in color.

	Clear		Clear
Butter Dish, cov	125.00	Sauce, flat, 4" d	20.00
Compote, cov, hs	125.00	Spooner, double handles . . .	95.00
Creamer.	75.00	Sugar, cov, double handles .	175.00
Goblet	80.00	Wine	90.00
Pitcher, water	350.00		

TACOMA (Jeweled Diamond and Fan, Triple X)

Non-flint pattern made by Greensburg Glass Co., Greensburg, PA, c1804. Production continued by National Glass, c1900.

	Clear	Ruby Stained		Clear	Ruby Stained
Banana Dish.	25.00	55.00	Goblet	25.00	50.00
Bowl, oval, 10" l . . .	30.00	60.00	Pitcher, water,		
Butter Dish, cov . . .	45.00	100.00	bulbous.	40.00	150.00
Cake Stand, hs, 9"			Sauce, flat, 4" d . . .	10.00	20.00
d.	40.00	120.00	Spooner	25.00	55.00
Celery Tray.	25.00	55.00	Sugar, cov	45.00	95.00
Compote, open, hs,			Tumbler	20.00	40.00
7" d.	50.00	165.00	Wine	20.00	45.00
Creamer.	35.00	65.00			

TEARDROP AND TASSEL (Sampson)

Non-flint made by the Indiana Tumbler and Goblet Co., Greentown, IN, c1895.

	Clear	Cobalt Blue	Emerald Green	Nile Green Opaque
Bowl, 7½".	40.00	55.00	50.00	75.00
Butter, cov	55.00	95.00	155.00	325.00

	Clear	Cobalt Blue	Emerald Green	Nile Green Opaque
Celery Vase	40.00	—	—	—
Compote				
Cov, hs, 7".	75.00	90.00	80.00	125.00
Cov, jelly	65.00	—	—	—
Open, ls, 5".	20.00	—	—	—
Open, ls, 8".	30.00	45.00	35.00	65.00
Creamer.	45.00	100.00	45.00	90.00
Goblet	110.00	125.00	175.00	95.00
Pickle.	20.00	55.00	40.00	55.00
Pitcher, water	50.00	150.00	150.00	900.00
Salt Shaker.	50.00	75.00	60.00	70.00
Sauce	15.00	20.00	20.00	—
Spooner	30.00	45.00	35.00	65.00
Sugar, cov	60.00	135.00	70.00	90.00
Tumbler	40.00	50.00	45.00	65.00
Wine	65.00	80.00	70.00	110.00

TENNESSEE (Jewel and Crescent, Jeweled Rosette)

Non-flint made by King, Son & Co., Pittsburgh, PA, and continued by U. S. Glass Co. in 1899 as part of the States series.

	Clear	Colored Jewels		Clear	Colored Jewels
Bowl			Open, hs, 8"	40.00	—
Cov, 6"	35.00	—	Open, hs, 9"	50.00	—
Cov, 7"	40.00	—	Open, hs, 10" . . .	65.00	—
Cov, 8"	50.00	—	Open, ls, 7"	35.00	—
Open, 8"	35.00	40.00	Creamer.	30.00	—
Bread Plate	40.00	75.00	Cruet	65.00	—
Butter, cov	55.00	—	Goblet	40.00	—
Cake Stand			Mug	40.00	—
8"	35.00	—	Pitcher		
9½".	38.00	—	Milk.	55.00	—
10½".	45.00	—	Water	65.00	—
Celery Vase	35.00	—	Relish.	20.00	—
Compote			Salt Shaker.	30.00	—
Cov, hs, 5".	40.00	55.00	Spooner	35.00	—
Cov, hs, 6".	45.00	—	Sugar, cov	45.00	—
Cov, hs, 7".	50.00	—	Syrup	90.00	—
Cov, hs, 8".	60.00	—	Toothpick	75.00	85.00
Open, hs, 5"	25.00	—	Tumbler	35.00	—
Open, hs, 6"	30.00	—	Wine	65.00	85.00
Open, hs, 7"	35.00	—			

TEUTONIC (I. H. C., Pittsburgh Fan)

Made by McKee & Bros., Glass Co., Pittsburgh, PA, in 1897. Originally made in clear; reported in emerald green and with blocks stained in colors of pink, blue, amber, and ruby.

	Clear	Blocks Color Stained	Emerald Green	Ruby Stained
Bowl.	18.00	—	—	—
Butter, cov	45.00	—	—	—
Cake Stand	25.00	—	—	—
Celery vase	18.00	—	—	—
Creamer.	25.00	—	35.00	—
Cup, custard or				
punch	10.00	—	15.00	—
Finger Bowl,				
underplate.	35.00	45.00	—	—
Goblet	20.00	—	—	35.00
Pickle, handled	18.00	—	20.00	—
Plate	12.00	—	15.00	—
Salt Shaker.	12.00	—	—	—

	Clear	Blocks Color Stained	Emerald Green	Ruby Stained
Spooner	18.00	—	20.00	—
Sugar				
Individual, open	15.00	—	—	—
Regular, open	20.00	—	—	—
Tumbler	15.00	—	—	30.00
Water Bottle	40.00	—	—	—

TEXAS (Loop with Stippled Panels)

Non-flint made by U. S. Glass Co., Pittsburgh, PA, c1900, in the States pattern series. Occasionally pieces are found in ruby stained. Reproduced in solid colors by Crystal Art Glass Co. and Boyd Glass Co., Cambridge, OH.

	Clear w/ Gold	Rose Stained		Clear w/ Gold	Rose Stained
Bowl			Pickle, 8½"	25.00	50.00
7"	20.00	40.00	Pitcher, water	125.00	400.00
9", scalloped	35.00	50.00	Plate, 9"	35.00	60.00
Butter, cov	75.00	125.00	Salt Shaker	25.00	—
Cake Stand, 9½",			Sauce		
hs	65.00	125.00	Flat	10.00	20.00
Celery Tray	30.00	50.00	Footed	20.00	25.00
Celery Vase	40.00	85.00	Spooner	35.00	80.00
Compote			Sugar		
Cov, hs, 6"	60.00	125.00	* Individual, cov	45.00	—
Cov, hs, 7"	70.00	150.00	Table, cov	75.00	125.00
Cov, hs, 8"	75.00	175.00	Syrup	75.00	175.00
Open, hs, 5"	45.00	75.00	Toothpick	25.00	95.00
* Creamer			Tumbler	40.00	100.00
Individual	20.00	45.00	Vase		
Table	45.00	85.00	6½"	25.00	—
Cruet, os	60.00	165.00	9"	35.00	—
Goblet	95.00	110.00	Wine	75.00	140.00
Horseradish, cov	50.00	—			

TEXAS BULL'S EYE (Bryce's Fllley, Bull's Eye Variant)

Originated by Bryce Bros., Pittsburgh, PA, c1875, A. J. Beatty & Sons, Steubenville, OH, c1888, and U. S. Glass Co., Pittsburgh, PA, after 1891. Canadian makers include Diamond Glass Co., Montreal, Quebec, c1902, and Burlington Glass Works, Hamilton, Ontario, where shards have been found. Originally made in semi-flint (no bell tone, but some lead content).

	Clear		Clear
Butter, cov	55.00	Lamp, oil, 5½"	85.00
Castor Bottle	65.00	Pitcher, water	55.00
Celery Vase	35.00	Sauce, flat	5.00
Champagne, 5" h	40.00	Spooner	25.00
Cordial	35.00	Sugar, cov	45.00
Creamer	35.00	Tumbler, 3¾" h	50.00
Egg Cup	30.00	Wine, 3⁹⁄₁₆" h	25.00
Goblet	30.00		

TEXAS STAR (Swirl and Star, Snowflake Base)

Non-flint made by Steimer Glass Co., Buckhannon, WV, c1903–08. Body of pieces are paneled. Pattern appears on the base, which is frosted around the design.

	Clear		Clear
Bowl, 9½"	45.00	Cruet	50.00
Butter, cov	55.00	Pitcher, water, tankard, ah	60.00
Cake Plate, 11"	40.00	Punch Bowl	125.00
Celery Tray	20.00	Punch Cup	12.00

	Clear		Clear
Salt & Pepper Shakers, pr . .	55.00	Toothpick	35.00
Syrup	50.00	Tumbler	20.00
Sugar Shaker	40.00		

THISTLE (Early Thistle, Scotch Thistle)

Non-flint made by Bryce, Walker & Co. in 1872. Shards have been found at Burlington Glass Works, Hamilton, Ontario, Canada.

	Clear		Clear
Bowl, 8″	30.00	Relish.	25.00
Butter, cov	55.00	Salt, master, ftd.	35.00
Cake Stand, large	75.00	Sauce, flat, 4″	12.00
Compote		Spooner	35.00
Cov, hs	85.00	Sugar	
Cov, ls	75.00	Cov.	65.00
Cordial	60.00	Open, buttermilk type	40.00
Creamer, ah	65.00	Syrup	100.00
Egg Cup.	40.00	Tumbler	40.00
Goblet	45.00	Wine	50.00
Pickle.	25.00		
Pitcher, ah			
Milk, 1 qt.	125.00		
Water, ½ gal	100.00		

THOUSAND EYE

The original pattern was non-flint made by Adams & Co., Tarentum, PA, in 1875 and by Richards and Hartley in 1888. (Pattern No. 103). It was made in two forms: Adams with a three knob stem finial, and Richards and Hartley with a plain stem with a scalloped bottom. Several glass companies made variations of the original pattern and reproductions were made as late as 1981. Crystal Opalescent was produced by Richards and Hartley only in the original pattern. (Opalescent celery vase $70.00; open compote, 8″, $115.00; 6″ creamer, $85.00; ¼ gallon water pitcher, $140.00; ½ gallon water pitcher, $180.00; 4″ footed sauce, $40.00; spooner, $60.00; and 5″ covered sugar, $80.00). Covered compotes are rare and would command 40% more than open compotes. A 2″ mug in blue is known.

	Amber	Apple Green	Blue	Clear	Vaseline
ABC Plate, 6″, clock center	55.00	60.00	55.00	45.00	55.00
Bowl, large, carriage shape	85.00	—	85.00	—	85.00
Butter, cov					
6¼″.	65.00	75.00	70.00	45.00	90.00
7½″.	65.00	75.00	70.00	45.00	90.00
Cake Stand					
10″	50.00	80.00	55.00	30.00	85.00
11″	50.00	80.00	55.00	30.00	85.00
Celery, hat shape . .	50.00	65.00	60.00	35.00	55.00
Celery Vase, 7″. . . .	50.00	60.00	52.00	45.00	55.00
Christmas Light. . . .	30.00	45.00	35.00	25.00	40.00
Cologne Bottle	25.00	45.00	35.00	20.00	45.00
Compote, cov, ls, 8″, sq.	—	100.00	100.00	—	—
Compote, open					
6″	35.00	40.00	40.00	25.00	40.00
7″	45.00	50.00	45.00	35.00	45.00
8″, round	40.00	50.00	45.00	35.00	50.00
8″, sq, hs.	40.00	50.00	50.00	40.00	55.00
9″	50.00	60.00	55.00	40.00	55.00
10″	55.00	65.00	60.00	45.00	60.00
Cordial	35.00	55.00	40.00	25.00	60.00
Creamer					
4″	35.00	40.00	40.00	25.00	40.00
6″	40.00	75.00	55.00	35.00	75.00
Creamer and Sugar Set	—	150.00	—	100.00	—

	Amber	Apple Green	Blue	Clear	Vaseline
*Cruet, 6"..........	40.00	60.00	50.00	35.00	60.00
Egg Cup..........	65.00	85.00	70.00	45.00	90.00
*Goblet	40.00	45.00	40.00	35.00	45.00
Honey Dish, cov,					
6 × 7¼"........	85.00	95.00	90.00	70.00	95.00
Inkwell, 2" sq	45.00	—	75.00	35.00	80.00
Jelly Glass	25.00	30.00	25.00	15.00	25.00
Lamp, kerosene					
hs, 12"	120.00	150.00	130.00	100.00	140.00
hs, 15"	125.00	155.00	135.00	110.00	150.00
ls, handled	110.00	115.00	110.00	90.00	120.00
Mug					
2½"..........	25.00	30.00	25.00	20.00	35.00
3½"..........	25.00	30.00	25.00	20.00	35.00
Nappy					
5"...........	35.00	—	40.00	30.00	45.00
6"...........	40.00	—	45.00	35.00	55.00
8"...........	45.00	—	50.00	45.00	60.00
Pickle..........	25.00	30.00	30.00	20.00	30.00
Pitcher					
Milk, cov, 7".....	85.00	110.00	115.00	70.00	105.00
Water, ¼ gal	70.00	85.00	80.00	55.00	80.00
Water, ½ gal	80.00	95.00	85.00	65.00	85.00
Water, 1 gal.....	90.00	100.00	95.00	85.00	95.00
*Plate, sq, folded corners					
6"...........	25.00	30.00	30.00	25.00	30.00
8"...........	30.00	30.00	30.00	25.00	30.00
10"..........	35.00	50.00	40.00	25.00	35.00
Platter					
8 × 11", oblong..	40.00	50.00	45.00	40.00	45.00
11", oval	75.00	80.00	55.00	40.00	75.00
Salt Shaker, pr					
Banded........	60.00	70.00	65.00	60.00	65.00
Plain..........	50.00	60.00	55.00	40.00	60.00
Salt, ind	80.00	95.00	90.00	50.00	90.00
Salt, open, carriage shape	65.00	85.00	75.00	50.00	75.00
Sauce					
Flat, 4"	10.00	20.00	15.00	8.00	15.00
Footed, 4"....	15.00	25.00	16.00	10.00	20.00
Spooner.........	35.00	50.00	40.00	30.00	45.00
*String Holder	35.00	60.00	45.00	30.00	45.00
Sugar, cov, 5"	55.00	75.00	60.00	50.00	60.00
Syrup, pewter top ..	80.00	100.00	70.00	55.00	70.00
Toothpick					
Hat..........	35.00	55.00	60.00	30.00	45.00
Plain..........	35.00	50.00	55.00	25.00	40.00
Thimble........	55.00	—	—	—	—
Tray, water					
12½", round	65.00	80.00	65.00	55.00	60.00
14", oval	65.00	80.00	75.00	60.00	75.00
*Tumbler	30.00	65.00	35.00	25.00	30.00
*Wine	35.00	50.00	40.00	20.00	40.00

THREE-FACE

Non-flint made by George A. Duncan & Son, Pittsburgh, PA, c1878. Designed by John E. Miller, a designer with Duncan, who later became a member of the firm. It has been heavily reproduced by L. G. Wright Glass Co. and other companies as early as the 1930s. Imperial Glass Co. was commissioned by the Metropolitan Museum of Art, NY. These pieces bear the "M.M.A." monogram.

	Clear		Clear
Biscuit Jar, cov	300.00	11".................	165.00
*Butter, cov	140.00	12½"...............	225.00
*Cake Stand		Celery Vase	
9"..................	150.00	Plain................	95.00
10".................	160.00	Scalloped	95.00

	Clear		Clear
* Champagne		Open, ls, 6"	75.00
Hollow stem	250.00	Open, jelly, paneled	
Saucer type	150.00	"Huber" top	85.00
* Claret	100.00	* Creamer	135.00
* Compote		* Goblet	85.00
Cov, hs, 7"	165.00	* Lamp, oil	150.00
Cov, hs, 8"	175.00	Marmalade Jar	200.00
Cov, hs, 9"	190.00	Pitcher, water	375.00
Cov, hs, 10"	225.00	* Salt Dip	35.00
Cov, ls, 6"	160.00	* Salt & Pepper	75.00
Cov, ls, 4"	150.00	* Sauce, ftd	25.00
Open, hs, 7"	75.00	* Spooner	80.00
Open, hs, 8"	85.00	* Sugar, cov	125.00
Open, hs, 9"	135.00	* Wine	150.00

THREE PANEL

Non-flint made by Richards and Hartley Co., Tarentum, PA, c1888, and by U. S. Glass Co. in 1891. Shards have been found at Burlington Glass Works, Hamilton, Ontario, Canada.

	Amber	Blue	Clear	Vaseline
Bowl				
7"	25.00	40.00	20.00	45.00
8½"	25.00	40.00	20.00	45.00
10"	40.00	50.00	35.00	48.00
Butter, cov	45.00	50.00	40.00	50.00
Celery Vase, ruffled				
top	55.00	65.00	35.00	55.00
Compote, open, ls,				
7"	35.00	55.00	25.00	40.00
Creamer	40.00	45.00	25.00	40.00
Cruet	250.00	—	—	—
* Goblet	30.00	40.00	25.00	35.00
Mug	35.00	45.00	25.00	35.00
Pitcher, water	100.00	125.00	40.00	110.00
Sauce, ftd	15.00	15.00	10.00	15.00
Spooner	42.50	45.00	30.00	40.00
Sugar, cov	55.00	60.00	45.00	70.00
Tumbler	35.00	40.00	20.00	30.00

THUMBPRINT, EARLY (Argus, Giant Baby Thumbprint)

Flint originally produced by Bakewell, Pears and Co., Pittsburgh, PA, c1850–60. Made by several factories in various forms. Reproduced in color by Fenton.

	Clear		Clear
Ale Glass	40.00	Creamer	60.00
Banana Boat	150.00	Decanter, qt, os	
Berry Set, 7 pcs	195.00	Pattern base	125.00
Bitters Bottle	140.00	Plain base	85.00
Bowl, 6"	35.00	Egg Cup	40.00
Cake Stand	50.00	Goblet	50.00
Celery Vase		Honey Dish	10.00
Patterned base	100.00	Plate, 8"	50.00
Plain base	90.00	Salt, master, ftd	35.00
Champagne	100.00	Spooner	45.00
Claret	70.00	Sugar, cov	65.00
Compote		Tumbler	45.00
* Cov, 4"	80.00	Wine	75.00
* Cov, ls, 7"	100.00		
Open, 8", scalloped top,			
flared	125.00		

TOKYO

Made by Jefferson Glass Co., Steubenville, OH, c1905. Also found in clear, blue, and apple green—all with gold trim. Some reproductions made by and signed Fenton.

	Blue Opal	Green Opal	White Opal
Bowl, berry	55.00	45.00	35.00
Butter, cov	135.00	100.00	70.00
Compote, jelly	40.00	45.00	35.00
Creamer	80.00	60.00	50.00
Cruet	185.00	140.00	90.00
Dish, 6½"	40.00	45.00	40.00
Pitcher, water	185.00	150.00	100.00
Salt Shaker	50.00	40.00	30.00
Sauce	30.00	25.00	20.00
Spooner	45.00	40.00	30.00
Sugar, cov	95.00	75.00	60.00
Toothpick	110.00	80.00	50.00
Tumbler	50.00	45.00	35.00
Vase	60.00	60.00	45.00

TORPEDO (Pigmy)

Non-flint made by Thompson Glass Co., Uniontown, PA, c1889. A black amethyst master salt ($150.00) is also known.

	Clear	Ruby Stained		Clear	Ruby Stained
Banana Stand	75.00	—	8", plain base, pattern on bowl . . .	85.00	—
Bowl			Marmalade Jar, cov	85.00	—
Cov, 7" d, 7¼" h. .	65.00	—	Pickle Castor, sp		
Cov, 8"	40.00	—	holder	125.00	—
Open, 4"	—	20.00	Pitcher		
Open, 7"	18.00	—	Milk, 8½"	75.00	150.00
Open, 8"	20.00	—	Water, 10½"	85.00	175.00
Open, 9"	20.00	45.00	Punch Cup	25.00	—
Open, 9½", flared			Salt		
rim	38.00	—	Individual	20.00	—
Butter, cov	85.00	—	Master	35.00	—
Cake Stand, 10" . . .	85.00	—	Salt Shaker, single, 2		
Celery Vase, scal-			types	50.00	—
loped top	40.00	—	Sauce, 4½", collared		
Compote			base	15.00	—
Cov, hs, 13¾" . . .	165.00	—	Spooner, scalloped		
Cov, hs, 4", jelly . .	65.00	—	top	45.00	—
Open, jelly	48.00	—	Sugar, cov	65.00	—
Creamer	50.00	—	Syrup	95.00	175.00
Cruet, os, ah	80.00	—	Tray, water		
Cup and Saucer . . .	60.00	—	10", round	85.00	—
Decanter, os, 8" . . .	85.00	—	11¾", clover		
Finger Bowl	55.00	—	shaped	75.00	—
Goblet	45.00	85.00	Tumbler	45.00	60.00
Lamp			Wine	90.00	—
3", handled	75.00				

TREE OF LIFE (Portland's)

Flint and non-flint made by Portland Glass Co., Portland, ME, c1870. Originally made in green, purple, yellow, amber, and light and dark blue. Color is rare today. A blue finger bowl in a SP holder is valued at $175.00. Prices shown for non-flints.

	Clear		Clear
Bowl, berry, oval	30.00	Champagne	55.00
Butter, cov	55.00	Compote	
Celery Vase, SP frame	55.00	Open, hs, 8½"	125.00
Cologne Bottle, facetted		Open, hs, 10"	110.00
stopper	48.00	Open, ls, 10"	50.00

	Clear			Clear
Creamer		Water		
Applied handle	70.00	Applied handle		95.00
Molded handle	50.00	Molded handle		65.00
Silverplated holder	75.00	Plate, 6"		25.00
Egg Cup	30.00	* Sauce		
Epergne, sgd "P.G. Co.		3¾"		12.00
Patd"	125.00	Leaf shape		15.00
Finger Bowl, underplate	60.00	Spooner		35.00
Fruit Dish, SP holder	90.00	Sugar		
* Goblet		* Covered		70.00
Clear shield on side	50.00	Silverplated holder		75.00
Plain	35.00	Tray, water		90.00
Regular, sgd, "P.G. Flint"	65.00	Tumbler, ftd		40.00
Ice Cream Tray	50.00	Vase		50.00
Lemonade	25.00	* Wine		55.00
Pitcher				
Milk				
Applied handle	95.00			
Molded handle	65.00			

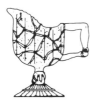

TREE OF LIFE WITH HAND (Pittsburgh Tree of Life)

Non-flint, made by Hobbs, Brockunier & Co., Wheeling, WV, c1875–80.

	Clear		Clear
Biscuit Jar	—	Goblet, signed	40.00
Bowl, oval		Ice Cream Tray	40.00
8"	25.00	Pitcher, water	150.00
10"	35.00	Plate, 6"	35.00
Butter, cov	75.00	Punch Cup	15.00
Cake Stand, 10"	100.00	Sauce, shell shape	
Celery Vase	40.00	Flat	20.00
Compote, cov, 6", high		Ftd	25.00
standard	65.00	Spooner	35.00
Compotes, open		Sugar, cov	65.00
5", low standard	65.00	Tumbler	30.00
10½", high standard	80.00	Wine	35.00
Creamer, signed	65.00		

TRIPLE TRIANGLE

Made by Doyle and Co., Pittsburgh, PA, in 1890. Continued by U. S. Glass Co. after 1891.

	Clear	Ruby Stained		Clear	Ruby Stained
Bowl			Cup	15.00	30.00
6", round	15.00	30.00	* Goblet	25.00	45.00
8", rect	20.00	40.00	Mug	10.00	35.00
9", round	20.00	40.00	Pitcher, water	65.00	135.00
10", rect	25.00	45.00	Sauce, flat	10.00	20.00
Bread Plate	38.50	90.00	Spooner, handled	20.00	55.00
Butter, cov, handled	40.00	80.00	Sugar, handled, cov	40.00	75.00
Celery Tray	30.00	45.00	Tumbler	20.00	38.50
Creamer	35.00	55.00	* Wine	20.00	45.00

TRUNCATED CUBE (Thompson's #77)

Non-flint made by Thompson Glass Co., Uniontown, PA, c1894. Also found with copper wheel engraving.

	Clear	Ruby Stained		Clear	Ruby Stained
Bowl			Celery Vase	40.00	55.00
4", berry	—	15.00	Creamer		
8"	—	40.00	Individual	20.00	30.00
Butter, cov	50.00	90.00	Regular	35.00	65.00

	Clear	Ruby Stained		Clear	Ruby Stained
Cruet, os, ph	35.00	90.00	Sugar, cov		
Decanter, os, 12" h	60.00	150.00	Individual	20.00	35.00
Goblet	30.00	50.00	Regular	30.00	65.00
Pitcher, ah			Syrup	40.00	100.00
Milk, 1 qt	50.00	100.00	Toothpick	30.00	45.00
Water, ½ gal	60.00	115.00	Tray, water	20.00	40.00
Salt Shaker, single	15.00	30.00	Tumbler	22.50	35.00
Sauce, 4"	30.00	50.00	Wine	25.00	40.00
Spooner	30.00	50.00			

TULIP WITH SAWTOOTH

Originally made in flint by Bryce Bros., Pittsburgh, PA, c1854. Later made in non-flint by U. S. Glass Co. c1891. Shards have been found at Burlington Glass Works, Hamilton, Ontario, Canada.

	Flint	Non-Flint		Flint	Non-Flint
Bottle, bar	75.00	80.00	Egg Cup	40.00	—
Butter, cov	125.00	80.00	* Goblet	65.00	35.00
Celery Vase	85.00	25.00	Mug	80.00	—
Champagne	75.00	35.00	Pitcher, water	150.00	—
Compote			Plate, 6"	60.00	—
Cov, hs, 6"	90.00	—	Pomade Jar	65.00	—
Cov, hs, 8½"	95.00	—	Salt, master, plain		
Cov, ls, 8½"	85.00	—	edge	28.00	15.00
Open, hs, 8"	—	60.00	Spooner	35.00	20.00
Open, ls, 9"	60.00	—	Sugar, cov	95.00	—
Creamer	85.00	—	Tumbler		
Cruet, os			Bar	85.00	25.00
Applied handle	60.00	—	Footed	50.00	—
Pressed handle	—	40.00	* Wine	45.00	25.00
Decanter, os					
Handle	150.00				
No handle	150.00	55.00			

TWO PANEL

Non-flint in oval forms made by Richards and Hartley Glass Co., Tarentum, PA, 1880, and by U. S. Glass Co. in 1891.

	Amber	Apple Green	Blue	Clear	Vaseline
Bowl					
5½"	35.00	40.00	40.00	15.00	25.00
8"	35.00	40.00	40.00	20.00	35.00
10 x 8½ x 3"	35.00	50.00	40.00	25.00	30.00
Butter, cov	50.00	55.00	55.00	30.00	40.00
Celery Vase	45.00	50.00	50.00	25.00	40.00
Compote, cov hs,					
6½", oval	55.00	85.00	85.00	35.00	75.00
7⅜ x 9 x 12¾"	—	100.00	—	—	—
8"	85.00	85.00	95.00	35.00	95.00
10 x 8½ x 3"	—	100.00	—	—	—
Creamer, 6"	60.00	65.00	65.00	35.00	45.00
* Goblet	30.00	35.00	45.00	28.00	40.00
Lamp, high standard	85.00	125.00	100.00	45.00	115.00
Marmalade Jar, cov.	75.00	95.00	100.00	45.00	100.00
Mug	30.00	35.00	40.00	20.00	30.00
Pitcher, water	60.00	60.00	65.00	35.00	50.00
Platter	25.00	30.00	30.00	20.00	30.00
Salt					
Individual	15.00	18.00	15.00	5.00	15.00
Master	20.00	25.00	20.00	10.00	12.00
Salt Shaker	40.00	45.00	40.00	25.00	30.00
Sauce					
Flat, oval	10.00	10.00	10.00	8.00	10.00
Footed	12.00	14.00	15.00	10.00	12.00

	Amber	Apple Green	Blue	Clear	Vaseline
Spooner	45.00	50.00	45.00	25.00	35.00
Sugar, cov	65.00	70.00	72.00	40.00	60.00
Tray, water	50.00	55.00	55.00	45.00	50.00
Tumbler	35.00	42.50	35.00	15.00	40.00
Waste Bowl.	40.00	45.00	40.00	20.00	30.00
*Wine	40.00	45.00	40.00	20.00	30.00

U. S. COIN

Non-flint frosted, clear, and gilted pattern made by U. S. Glass Co., Pittsburgh, PA, in 1892 for three or four months. Production was stopped by the U. S. Treasury because real coins, dated as early as 1878, were used in the molds. The 1892 coin date is the most common. Lamps with coins on font and stem would be 50% more.

	Clear	Frosted		Clear	Frosted
Ale Glass	250.00	350.00	Epergne	—	1,000.00
Bowl			Goblet	300.00	450.00
6"	170.00	220.00	Goblet, dimes	—	550.00
9"	215.00	325.00	Lamp		
* Bread Plate	175.00	325.00	Round font	275.00	450.00
Butter, cov, dollars			Square font	300.00	—
and halves	250.00	450.00	Mug, handled	200.00	300.00
Cake Stand, 10" . . .	225.00	400.00	Pickle	200.00	—
Celery Tray.	200.00	—	Pitcher		
Celery Vase,			Milk.	600.00	600.00
quarters	135.00	350.00	Water	400.00	800.00
Champagne	—	400.00	Sauce, ftd, 4", quar-		
Compote			ters.	100.00	185.00
Cov, hs, 7".	300.00	500.00	* Spooner, quarters . .	225.00	325.00
Cov, hs, 8", quar-			* Sugar, cov	225.00	400.00
ters and dimes	—	415.00	Syrup, dated pewter		
Open, hs, 7", quar-			lid	—	525.00
ters and dimes .	200.00	300.00	* Toothpick	180.00	275.00
Open, hs, 7", quar-			Tray, water, 8",		
ters and halves	225.00	350.00	round	275.00	—
Open, 8⅜" d,			* Tumbler	135.00	235.00
6½" h.	—	240.00	Waste Bowl.	225.00	250.00
* Creamer.	350.00	600.00	Wine	225.00	375.00
Cruet, os	375.00	500.00			

U. S. REGAL

Made by U. S. Glass Co., Pittsburgh, PA, c1906. One of the many imitation-cut patterns that were so popular. The bowls are slightly squared in shape.

	Clear		Clear
Basket, wide handle	35.00	Sugar, cov	30.00
Butter, cov	35.00	Spooner.	25.00
Creamer.	25.00	Tumbler	20.00
Goblet	20.00		

U. S. SHERATON (Greek Key)

Made by U. S. Glass Co., Pittsburgh, PA, in 1912. This pattern was made only in clear, but can be found trimmed with gold or platinum. Some pieces are marked with the intertwined U. S. Glass trademark.

	Clear		Clear
Bonbon, 6", ftd	15.00	8", flat.	12.00
Bowl		8", ftd, sq	14.00
6", ftd, sq	15.00	Bureau Tray	30.00

	Clear		Clear
Butter, cov	35.00	Pomade Jar	14.00
Celery Tray	30.00	Puff Box	14.00
Compote		Punch Bowl, cov, 14"	90.00
Open, 4", jelly	12.00	Ring Tree	25.00
Open, 6"	14.00	Salt Shaker	
Creamer		Squat	12.00
After dinner, tall, sq ft	12.00	Tall	15.00
Berry, bulbous, sq ft	15.00	Salt, individual	17.00
Large	18.00	Sardine Box	35.00
Cruet, os	25.00	Spooner	
Finger Bowl, underplate	24.00	Handled	15.00
Goblet	18.00	Tray	12.00
Lamp, miniature	50.00	Sugar, cov	
Marmalade Jar	35.00	Individual	15.00
Mug	15.00	Regular	20.00
Mustard Jar, cov	30.00	Sundae Dish	10.00
Pickle	10.00	Syrup, glass lid	35.00
Pin Tray	12.00	Toothpick Holder, lay down	35.00
Pitcher, water		Tumbler	
One half gallon	30.00	Iced Tea	15.00
Squat, medium	30.00	Water	12.00
Tankard	35.00		
Plate, sq			
4½"	8.00		
9"	12.00		

UTAH (Frost Flower, Twinkle Star)

Non-flint made by U. S. Glass Co., Pittsburgh, PA, and Gas City, IN, in 1901 in the States Pattern series. Add 25% for frosting.

	Clear		Clear
Bowl		Open, hs, 7½"	25.00
Cov, 6"	20.00	Open, hs, 8"	30.00
Open, 8"	18.00	Open, hs, 9"	35.00
Butter, cov	35.00	Open, hs, 10"	40.00
Cake Plate, 9"	20.00	Condiment Set, salt & pepper	
Cake Stand		shakers, holder	45.00
7"	35.00	Creamer	30.00
8"	20.00	Cruet	40.00
10"	30.00	Goblet	25.00
Castor Set, 2 bottles	40.00	Pickle	12.00
Celery Vase	20.00	Pitcher, water	45.00
Compote		Salt Shaker, orig top	20.00
Cov, hs, 5"	40.00	Sauce, 4"	8.50
Cov, hs, 6"	45.00	Spooner	15.00
Cov, hs, 7"	50.00	Sugar, cov	35.00
Cov, hs, 8"	60.00	Syrup	50.00
Open, hs, 6"	20.00	Tumbler	15.00
Open, hs, 7"	25.00	Wine	25.00

VALENCIA WAFFLE (Block and Star #1)

Made by Adams & Co., Pittsburgh, PA, c1885. Reissued by U. S. Glass after 1891.

	Amber	Apple Green	Blue	Clear	Vaseline
Bowl, berry	15.00	25.00	20.00	12.00	15.00
Bread Plate	30.00	35.00	30.00	25.00	35.00
Butter, cov	55.00	65.00	45.00	40.00	42.50
Cake Stand, 10"	60.00	40.00	45.00	38.00	40.00
Celery Vase	30.00	38.00	42.50	28.00	32.00
Castor set, complete	60.00	75.00	65.00	50.00	60.00
Compote					
Cov, hs, 7" d	60.00	75.00	75.00	50.00	70.00
Cov, ls	40.00	50.00	65.00	30.00	40.00
Creamer	35.00	—	45.00	30.00	32.50
Dish	20.00	—	25.00	10.00	20.00

	Amber	Apple Green	Blue	Clear	Vaseline
Goblet	40.00	—	40.00	30.00	35.00
Pitcher					
Milk.	50.00	60.00	55.00	40.00	50.00
Water	65.00	60.00	55.00	40.00	50.00
Relish or Pickle. . . .	20.00	20.00	25.00	15.00	20.00
Salt Dip	35.00	—	—	—	—
Salt Shaker.	20.00	30.00	35.00	15.00	35.00
Sauce, ftd, 4″, sq. . .	12.00	—	18.00	10.00	15.00
Spooner	30.00	—	35.00	20.00	35.00
Sugar, cov	40.00	—	50.00	35.00	45.00
Syrup	100.00	125.00	125.00	60.00	—
Tray, 10½ x 8″	—	35.00	—	—	—
Tumbler	25.00	—	30.00	18.00	25.00

VALENTINE

Non-flint pattern made by U. S. Glass Co., Pittsburgh, PA, 1891–95.

	Clear		Clear
Bowl, berry	85.00	Sauce, flat, 4½″ d	20.00
Butter Dish, cov	75.00	Spooner	50.00
Creamer, 4½″ h.	75.00	Sugar, cov	90.00
Goblet	90.00	Toothpick	85.00
Pitcher, water	200.00	Tumbler	75.00

VERMONT (Honeycomb with Flower Rim, Inverted Thumbprint with Daisy Band)

Non-flint made by U. S. Glass Co., Pittsburgh, PA, 1899–1903. Also made in custard (usually decorated), chocolate, caramel, and novelty slag, milk glass, and blue. Toothpick holders have been reproduced by Crystal Art Glass Co., and Mosser Glass Co., and Degenhart Glass (who marks its colored line).

	Clear w/ Gold	Green w/ Gold		Clear w/ Gold	Green w/ Gold
Basket, handle	30.00	45.00	Pickle	20.00	30.00
Bowl, berry	25.00	45.00	Pitcher, water	50.00	125.00
Butter, cov	40.00	75.00	Salt Shaker.	20.00	35.00
Card Tray	20.00	35.00	Sauce	15.00	20.00
Celery Tray	30.00	35.00	Spooner	25.00	75.00
Compote, hs			Sugar, cov	35.00	80.00
Cov.	55.00	125.00	*Toothpick	30.00	50.00
Open	35.00	65.00	Tumbler	20.00	40.00
Creamer, 4¼″	30.00	55.00	Vase	20.00	45.00
Goblet	40.00	50.00			

VICTORIA

Flint made by Bakewell, Pears and Co. in the early 1850s.

	Clear		Clear
Bowl, berry, master	25.00	Creamer	65.00
Butter, cov	100.00	Goblet	60.00
Cake Stand		Pitcher, water	150.00
9″	80.00	Spooner	55.00
15″	115.00	Sugar, cov	85.00
Celery Vase	60.00	Sweetmeat, cov, 6″	75.00
Compote			
Cov, hs, 8″	95.00		
Open, hs, 10″	75.00		

VIKING (Bearded Head, Bearded Prophet, Hobb's Centennial, Old Man of the Mountain)

Non-flint made by Hobbs, Brockunier, & Co., Wheeling, WV, in 1876 as its Centennial pattern. No tumbler or goblet originally made.

	Clear		Clear
Apothecary Jar, cov	55.00	Cup, ftd	35.00
Bowl		Egg Cup	40.00
Cov, 8", oval	55.00	Marmalade Jar	85.00
Cov, 9", oval	65.00	Mug, ah	50.00
Bread Plate	70.00	Pickle	20.00
Butter, cov	75.00	Pitcher, water	125.00
Celery Vase	45.00	Relish	20.00
Compote		Salt, master	40.00
Cov, hs, 9"	95.00	Sauce	15.00
Cov, ls, 8", oval	75.00	Spooner	35.00
Open, hs	60.00	Sugar, cov	65.00
Creamer, 2 types	50.00		

WAFFLE (Paneled Waffle)

Flint pattern attributed to Boston & Sandwich Glass Co., Sandwich, MA, c1850. Made in clear and rarely found in milk white or colors.

	Clear		Clear
Bowl, 8" oval	35.00	Pitcher, water	165.00
Butter Dish, cov	90.00	Sauce, flat, 4" d	20.00
Celery Vase	65.00	Spillholder	75.00
Compote, cov, hs, 6" d	90.00	Spooner	65.00
Creamer, ah	125.00	Sugar, cov	95.00
Goblet	60.00	Tumbler	65.00

WAFFLE AND THUMBPRINT (Bull's Eye and Waffle, Palace, Triple Bull's Eye)

First made by the New England Glass Co., East Cambridge, MA, c1868 and by Curling, Robertson & Co., Pittsburgh, PA, c1856. Shards have been found at the Boston and Sandwich Glass Co., Sandwich, MA.

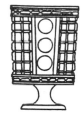

	Clear		Clear
Bottle, ftd	100.00	Lamp	
Bowl, 5 x 7"	30.00	9½"	115.00
Butter, cov	95.00	11", whale oil	175.00
Celery Vase	105.00	Pitcher, water	400.00
Champagne	90.00	Salt, master	45.00
Claret	110.00	Spooner	45.00
Compote, cov, hs	150.00	Sugar, cov	125.00
Cordial	100.00	Sweetmeat, cov, hs, 6"	150.00
Creamer	125.00	Tumbler	
Decanter, os		Flip Glass	125.00
Pint	100.00	Water, ftd	75.00
Quart	145.00	Whiskey	75.00
Egg Cup	45.00	Wine	70.00
Goblet, knob stem	65.00		

WASHINGTON

Made by U. S. Glass Co., Pittsburgh, PA, as part of its States series. Made in clear, frosted with colored floral decoration (add 25%), and ruby stained (add 40%). Rare in custard and milk glass. A very rare covered sugar is known in emerald green, $100.

	Clear		Clear
Bowl, flat		6" d	25.00
Oblong		7" d	25.00
6"	25.00	8" d	30.00
8"	35.00	Cordial	50.00
10"	50.00	Creamer	
Round		Individual	45.00
3"	15.00	Table	45.00
3½"	15.00	Tankard, pint	45.00
4"	20.00	Custard Cup	15.00
4½"	20.00	Fruit Bowl, hs	
5"	20.00	7½" d	40.00
6"	25.00	8½" d	45.00
7"	25.00	9½" d	50.00
8"	30.00	Goblet	
Butter, cov	60.00	Small	35.00
Cake Stand, 10"	50.00	Large	35.00
Celery Tray	35.00	Lemonade Cup	15.00
Celery Vase	45.00	Oil Bottle	50.00
Champagne	30.00	Pickle Dish, oval	30.00
Claret	30.00	Pitcher, milk, tankard	
Compote		Quart	65.00
Cov, hs		3 Pints	75.00
4½" d, jelly	55.00	½ Gal	75.00
5" d	55.00	Pitcher, water, tankard	
6" d	55.00	Quart	65.00
7" d	60.00	3 Pints	75.00
8" d	65.00	½ Gal	75.00
Cov, ls		Powdered Sugar, cov	95.00
5" d	45.00	Olive Dish, oval	30.00
6" d	50.00	Salt	
7" d	55.00	Individual	25.00
8" d	65.00	Master	25.00
Open, hs		Salt Shaker	45.00
4½" d, jelly	35.00	Spooner	45.00
5" d	35.00	Sugar	
6" d	35.00	Cov, table	60.00
7" d	40.00	Open, individual	35.00
8" d	45.00	Toothpick	35.00
Open, ls		Tumbler	35.00
3½" d	15.00	Wine	35.00
5" d	20.00		

WASHINGTON (Early Washington, Leafy Panel and Thumbprint)

Flint made by New England Glass Co., East Cambridge, MA, c1869.

	Clear		Clear
Ale Glass	125.00	Goblet	110.00
Bottle, bitters	85.00	Honey Dish, 3½"	30.00
Bowl, 6 x 9", oval	45.00	Lamp	150.00
Butter, cov	175.00	Lemonade Glass	85.00
Celery Vase	95.00	Mug	85.00
Champagne	125.00	Pitcher, water	375.00
Claret	110.00	Plate, 6"	60.00
Compote		Salt, individual	20.00
Cov, hs, 6"	125.00	Sauce, 5"	25.00
Cov, hs, 10"	175.00	Spooner	75.00
Cordial	150.00	Sugar, cov	125.00
Creamer	200.00	Tumbler	85.00
Decanter, os	150.00	Wine	125.00
Egg Cup	75.00		

WASHINGTON CENTENNIAL (Chain with Diamonds)

Non-flint made by Gillinder & Co., Philadelphia, PA, c1876 for the Centennial celebration. Shards have been found at Burlington Glass Works, Hamilton, Ontario, Canada.

Bowl	Clear		Clear
7", oval	25.00	Egg Cup	45.00
8", round	25.00	Goblet	45.00
9", round	25.00	Pickle, fish shape	25.00
Bread Plate		Pitcher, ah	
"Carpenter's Hall"	100.00	Milk, 1 qt	110.00
"George Washington"	100.00	Water, ½ gal	120.00
"Independence Hall"	100.00	Relish, claw handle, dated	50.00
Butter, cov	80.00	Salt	
Cake Stand		Ind, 2" d	20.00
8½"	45.00	Master	35.00
10"	60.00	Salt Shaker, orig top	65.00
Celery Vase	40.00	Sauce, flat	12.00
Champagne	65.00	Spooner	35.00
Compote		Sugar, cov	70.00
Cov, hs, 9"	75.00	Syrup, metal lid	150.00
Open, hs, 8"	45.00	Tumbler	40.00
Creamer, ah	80.00	Wine	50.00

WATER LILY AND CATTAILS

Made by Fenton Glass Co., Williamstown, WV; Northwood Glass Co., Wheeling, WV, c1900; and Northwood-Diamond-Dugan Co. Also found in carnival glass.

	Amethyst Opal	Blue Opal	Clear Opal	Green Opal
Bonbon, tricorn	50.00	45.00	30.00	35.00
Bowl, berry, 8", ruffled	50.00	75.00	35.00	45.00
Butter, cov	100.00	90.00	65.00	80.00
Creamer	75.00	60.00	45.00	55.00
Pitcher, water	200.00	175.00	65.00	125.00
Plate	35.00	35.00	25.00	30.00
Relish, handle	40.00	35.00	30.00	35.00
Sauce	35.00	30.00	24.00	26.00
Spooner	40.00	40.00	35.00	40.00
Sugar, cov	65.00	60.00	45.00	50.00
Tumbler	40.00	40.00	30.00	35.00

WEDDING BELLS

Made by Fostoria Glass Co., Moundsville, WV, c1900. Reported in clear with gold trim, sometimes found with cranberry and rose-ruby blush.

	Clear	Clear w/ Blush		Clear	Clear w/ Blush
Bowl, berry, 10"	65.00	85.00	Punch Bowl, 2 pcs	125.00	—
Butter, cov	50.00	125.00	Punch Cup	12.00	20.00
Celery Vase	30.00	65.00	Salt Shaker, orig top	30.00	45.00
Compote, cov			Spooner	30.00	60.00
hs	55.00	—	Sugar, cov	40.00	70.00
ls	45.00	—	Syrup	60.00	—
Creamer, ah	45.00	65.00	Toothpick	30.00	45.00
Cruet, os	55.00	125.00	Tumbler	25.00	45.00
Custard Cup	12.00	20.00	Waste Bowl	30.00	40.00
Decanter, os	75.00	95.00	Whiskey	20.00	40.00
Finger Bowl	30.00	40.00	Wine	35.00	50.00
Pitcher, water					
Regular, 1 gal	75.00	125.00			
Tankard, ½ gal	85.00	135.00			

WEDDING RING (Double Wedding Ring)

Flint, c1860; non-flint, c1870s. Toothpick, frequently seen in muddy purple, not originally made. Reproduced in various colors. Dalzell/Viking Glass Co., c1989, has issued several flat pieces in colors and clear that were not produced earlier, including a sherbet and tall toothpick.

	Flint		Flint
Butter, cov	100.00	Pitcher, water	185.00
Celery Vase	80.00	Relish	60.00
Champagne	95.00	Sauce	30.00
Cordial	85.00	Spooner	80.00
Creamer	85.00	* Sugar, cov	100.00
Decanter, os	125.00	Tumbler	85.00
Goblet	65.00	Wine	90.00
Lamp, oil, 5"	85.00		

WESTMORELAND (Spector Block)

Non-flint patented by Thomas W. Mellor, Gillinder and Sons, Philadelphia, PA, 1889. Made as late as 1907 by U. S. Glass Co.

	Clear		Clear
Butter, cov	45.00	Plate, 7" d	25.00
Celery Tray	20.00	Sauce	10.00
Cologne Bottle, os	30.00	Spooner	20.00
Compote, cov	60.00	Sugar, cov	40.00
Creamer	25.00	Syrup	60.00
Cruet	35.00	Tumbler	30.00
Goblet	40.00	Wine	30.00
Pitcher, water	60.00		

WESTWARD HO! (Pioneer, Tippecanoe)

Non-flint, usually frosted, made by Gillinder and Sons, Philadelphia, PA, c1879. Molds made by Jacobus who also made Classic. Has been reproduced since the 1930s by L. G. Wright Glass Co., Westmoreland Glass Co., and several others. This pattern was originally made in milk glass (rare) and clear with acid finish as part of the design. Reproductions can be found in several colors and clear.

	Clear		Clear
Bowl, 5", ftd	125.00	* Goblet	90.00
Bread Plate	175.00	Marmalade Jar, cov	200.00
* Butter, cov	185.00	Mug	
* Celery Vase	125.00	2"	225.00
* Compote		3½"	175.00
Cov, hs, 5"	225.00	* Pitcher, water	250.00
Cov, hs, 9"	275.00	* Sauce, ftd, 4½"	35.00
Cov, ls, 5"	150.00	* Spooner	85.00
Open, hs, 8"	125.00	* Sugar, cov	185.00
* Creamer	95.00	* Wine	200.00

WHEAT AND BARLEY (Duquesne, Hops and Barley, Oats and Barley)

Non-flint made by Bryce Bros., Pittsburgh, PA, c1880. Later made by U. S. Glass Co., Pittsburgh PA, after 1891.

	Amber	Blue	Clear	Vaseline
Bowl, 8", cov	35.00	40.00	25.00	35.00
Butter, cov	45.00	60.00	35.00	55.00
Cake Stand				
8"	30.00	45.00	20.00	30.00
10"	40.00	50.00	30.00	40.00
Compote				
Cov, hs, 7"	45.00	55.00	40.00	45.00
Cov, hs, 8"	50.00	55.00	45.00	50.00
Open, hs, jelly	32.50	40.00	30.00	35.00
* Creamer	30.00	40.00	28.00	35.00
* Goblet	35.00	47.50	25.00	40.00
Mug	30.00	40.00	20.00	35.00
Pitcher				
Milk	70.00	85.00	40.00	95.00
Water	85.00	95.00	45.00	100.00

	Amber	Blue	Clear	Vaseline
Plate				
7"	20.00	30.00	15.00	25.00
9", closed handles	25.00	35.00	20.00	40.00
Relish.	20.00	30.00	15.00	25.00
Salt Shaker.	25.00	30.00	20.00	22.00
Sauce				
Flat, handle	12.00	15.00	10.00	15.00
Footed	15.00	15.00	10.00	15.00
Spooner	30.00	40.00	24.00	30.00
Sugar, cov	40.00	50.00	35.00	40.00
Syrup	175.00	195.00	85.00	—
Tumbler	30.00	35.00	18.00	30.00

WILD BOUQUET

Made by Harry Northwood Glass Co., Wheeling, WV, c1900–05 and other companies.

	White Opal	Green Opal	Blue Opal
Bowl, Berry	50.00	80.00	—
Butter, cov	90.00	190.00	—
Creamer	40.00	50.00	—
Cruet	175.00	195.00	195.00
Cruet Set on Tray . .	300.00	300.00	300.00
Pitcher, water	180.00	245.00	245.00
Salt & Pepper Shakers, pr	100.00	100.00	100.00
Sauce	25.00	25.00	30.00
Spooner	80.00	90.00	90.00
Sugar, cov	120.00	125.00	130.00
Toothpick	100.00	120.00	125.00
Tumbler	40.00	40.00	50.00

WILDFLOWER

Non-flint made by Adams & Co., Pittsburgh, PA, c1885 and by U. S. Glass Co., c1891. This pattern has been heavily reproduced. Reproductions date as early as 1936. L. G. Wright Glass Co. and Crystal Art Glass Co. have issued items from new molds and in additional colors.

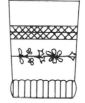

	Amber	Apple Green	Blue	Clear	Vaseline
Bowl, 8", sq	25.00	35.00	35.00	18.00	20.00
Butter, cov					
Collared base . . .	40.00	50.00	50.00	35.00	45.00
Flat	35.00	45.00	45.00	30.00	40.00
Cake Stand, 10½" . .	50.00	80.00	75.00	45.00	50.00
* Champagne	40.00	55.00	50.00	25.00	45.00
Celery Vase	55.00	60.00	55.00	35.00	55.00
* Compote					
Cov, hs, 8"	80.00	85.00	85.00	50.00	75.00
Cov, ls, 7"	—	—	70.00	—	—
Open, hs	80.00	—	—	—	—
* Creamer	35.00	50.00	45.00	40.00	48.00
* Goblet	30.00	40.00	40.00	25.00	40.00
Pitcher, water	55.00	95.00	65.00	40.00	70.00
* Plate, 10", sq	30.00	30.00	45.00	25.00	30.00
Platter					
10", oblong	40.00	45.00	40.00	30.00	30.00
11 x 8", deep scalloped edges . . .	—	—	45.00	—	—
Relish	20.00	22.00	20.00	18.00	20.00
* Salt, turtle	45.00	50.00	50.00	30.00	40.00
Salt Shaker	35.00	55.00	40.00	20.00	45.00
* Sauce, ftd, 4", round	17.50	18.00	18.00	12.00	17.50
Spooner	30.00	35.00	30.00	20.00	40.00

	Amber	Apple Green	Blue	Clear	Vaseline
* Sugar, cov	45.00	45.00	50.00	30.00	45.00
Syrup	125.00	150.00	140.00	65.00	150.00
Tray, water, oval . . .	50.00	60.00	60.00	40.00	55.00
* Tumbler	40.00	35.00	35.00	25.00	35.00
* Wine	45.00	45.00	45.00	25.00	45.00

WILLOW OAK (Acorn, Acorn and Oak Leaf, Bryce's Wreath, Stippled Daisy, Thistle and Sunflower)

Non-flint made by Bryce Bros. Pittsburgh, PA, c1885 and by U. S. Glass Company in 1891.

	Amber	Blue	Canary	Clear
Bowl, 8"	25.00	40.00	48.00	20.00
Butter, cov	55.00	65.00	80.00	40.00
Cake Stand, 8½" . . .	55.00	65.00	70.00	45.00
Celery Vase	45.00	60.00	75.00	35.00
Compote				
Cov, hs, 7½"	50.00	65.00	80.00	40.00
Open, 7"	30.00	40.00	48.00	25.00
Creamer	40.00	50.00	60.00	30.00
Goblet	40.00	50.00	60.00	30.00
Mug	35.00	45.00	54.00	30.00
Pitcher				
Milk	50.00	60.00	72.00	45.00
Water	55.00	60.00	72.00	50.00
Plate				
7"	35.00	45.00	50.00	25.00
9"	32.50	35.00	40.00	25.00
Salt Shaker	25.00	40.00	55.00	20.00
Sauce				
Flat, handle, sq . .	15.00	20.00	24.00	10.00
Footed, 4"	20.00	25.00	30.00	15.00
Spooner	35.00	40.00	48.00	30.00
Sugar, cov	68.50	70.00	75.00	40.00
Tray, water, 10½" . .	35.00	50.00	60.00	30.00
Tumbler	30.00	35.00	45.00	25.00
Waste Bowl	35.00	40.00	40.00	30.00

WINDFLOWER

Non-flint made by McKee & Bros. Glass Co. in the late 1870s.

	Clear		Clear
Bowl, 8", oval	30.00	Pitcher, water, ah	65.00
Butter, cov	50.00	Salt, master, ftd	25.00
Celery Vase	40.00	Sauce	15.00
Compote		Spooner	30.00
Cov, hs	65.00	Sugar	
Cov, ls, 8"	75.00	Cov	60.00
Open, ls, 7"	35.00	Open	35.00
Creamer, ah	40.00	Tumbler	40.00
Egg Cup	35.00	Wine	45.00
Goblet	38.00		

WISCONSIN (Beaded Dewdrop)

Non-flint made by U. S. Glass Co. in Gas City, IN, in 1903. One of the States patterns. Toothpick reproduced in colors.

	Clear		Clear
Banana Stand	75.00	6", oval, handled, cov	40.00
Bowl		7", round	42.00
4½ x 6½"	20.00	8", oblong, preserve	42.00

	Clear			Clear
Butter, flat flange	75.00	Cruet, os		80.00
Cake Stand		Cup and Saucer		50.00
8½"	45.00	Goblet		65.00
9½"	55.00	Marmalade Jar, straight		
Celery Tray	40.00	sides, glass lid		125.00
Celery Vase	45.00	Mug		35.00
Compote		Pitcher		
Cov, hs, 5"	45.00	Milk		55.00
Cov, hs, 6"	50.00	Water		70.00
Cov, hs, 7"	60.00	Plate, 6¾"		25.00
Cov, hs, 8"	75.00	Punch Cup		12.00
Open, hs, 5"	30.00	Relish		25.00
Open, hs, 6"	35.00	Salt Shaker		30.00
Open, hs, 7"	40.00	Spooner		30.00
Open, hs, 8"	50.00	Sugar, cov		55.00
Open, hs, 9"	60.00	Sugar Shaker		90.00
Open, hs, 10"	75.00	Sweetmeat, 5", ftd, cov		40.00
Condiment Set, salt & pep-		Syrup		110.00
per, mustard, horse radish,		*Toothpick, kettle		55.00
tray	110.00	Tumbler		40.00
Creamer	50.00	Wine		75.00

WYOMING (Enigma)

Made by U. S. Glass Co., Gas City, IN, in the States pattern series in 1903.

	Clear			Clear
Bowl		Creamer		
4"	15.00	Cov		50.00
8"	45.00	Open		35.00
Butter, cov	50.00	Goblet		65.00
Cake Plate	55.00	Mug		45.00
Cake Stand, 9", 10", 11"	70.00	Pitcher, water		75.00
Compote		Relish		15.00
Cov, hs, 6"	60.00	Salt & Pepper Shakers, pr		45.00
Cov, hs, 7"	75.00	Spooner		30.00
Cov, hs, 8"	85.00	Sugar, cov		45.00
Open, hs, 8"	60.00	Syrup, small, glass cov		65.00
Open, hs, 9"	65.00	Tumbler		55.00
Open, hs, 10"	75.00	Wine		85.00

X-RAY

Non-flint made by Riverside Glass Works, Wellsburgh, WV, 1896–98. Prices are for pieces with gold trim. A toothpick holder is known in amethyst ($125.00). Also a toothpick holder with marigold iridescence is known ($35.00).

	Clear	Emerald Green		Clear	Emerald Green
Bowl, berry, 8",			Goblet	20.00	35.00
beaded rim	25.00	45.00	Pitcher, water	40.00	75.00
Bread Plate	30.00	50.00	Salt Shaker	10.00	15.00
Butter, cov	40.00	75.00	Sauce, flat, 4½" d	8.00	10.00
Celery Vase	—	50.00	Spooner	25.00	40.00
Compote			Sugar		
Cov, hs	40.00	65.00	Individual, open	20.00	32.50
Jelly	—	40.00	Regular, cov	35.00	45.00
Creamer			Syrup	—	265.00
Individual	15.00	30.00	Toothpick	25.00	50.00
Regular	30.00	60.00	Tumbler	12.00	25.00
Cruet Set, 4 leaf clo-					
ver tray	125.00	350.00			

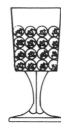

YALE (Crow-foot, Turkey Track)

Non-flint made by McKee & Bros. Glass Co., Jeannette, PA, patented in 1887.

	Clear		Clear
Bowl, berry, 10½"	20.00	Pitcher, water	65.00
Butter, cov	45.00	Relish, oval.	10.00
Cake Stand	55.00	Salt Shaker.	30.00
Celery Vase	35.00	Sauce, flat	10.00
Compote		Spooner.	20.00
Cov, hs	50.00	Sugar, cov	35.00
Open, scalloped rim	25.00	Syrup.	65.00
Creamer.	30.00	Tumbler	20.00
Goblet	30.00		

ZIPPER (Cobb)

Non-flint made by Richards & Hartley, Tarentum, PA, c1888.

	Clear		Clear
Bowl, 7" d.	15.00	Pitcher water, ½ gal	40.00
Butter, cov	40.00	Relish, 10" l	15.00
Celery Vase	25.00	Salt Dip	5.00
Cheese, cov	55.00	Sauce	
Compote, cov, ls, 8" d	40.00	Flat.	7.50
Creamer.	35.00	Footed	12.00
Cruet, os	45.00	Spooner	25.00
Goblet	20.00	Sugar, cov	35.00
Marmalade Jar, cov.	40.00	Tumbler	20.00

ZIPPERED BLOCK (Cryptic, Nova Scotia Ribbon and Star, Duncan #90)

Non-flint made by George A. Duncan & Sons, Pittsburgh, PA, c1887 and later by U. S. Glass Co., Pittsburgh, PA. Shards have been found at Trenton Glass Works, Trenton-New Glasgow, Nova Scotia as well as the Nova Scotia Glass Co. Comes frosted and frosted with cut stars. Add 20% for frosting.

	Clear	Ruby Stained		Clear	Ruby Stained
Bowl			Finger Bowl	75.00	145.00
6", shallow.	25.00	40.00	Goblet	40.00	60.00
7", deep	25.00	40.00	Lamp	85.00	—
7½", shallow, oval	15.00	30.00	Pickle, oblong	25.00	35.00
8", collared base .	55.00	75.00	Pitcher, water	125.00	175.00
9", flat, round. . . .	25.00	40.00	Salt Shaker.	50.00	80.00
Bread Plate	25.00	45.00	Sauce, 4", ftd	15.00	25.00
Butter, cov	75.00	150.00	Spooner	30.00	60.00
Celery Vase	40.00	—	Sugar, cov	60.00	100.00
Compote, cov, hs . .	125.00	—	Tumbler	30.00	45.00
Creamer.	45.00	100.00	Waste Bowl.	75.00	145.00

Lesser-Known
and Rare Patterns

Several minor patterns were made with an animal theme. Often the number of pieces was limited to goblets and pitchers in these patterns. Some patterns have etched or frosted animals while others have the animals actually molded as part of the pattern. Color in any of these patterns would be rare. The listing represents a sampling of the types of objects to be found with an animal theme. Many other animal patterns are included in the alphabetical listings, such as Deer and Dog, Deer and Pine Tree, Frosted Lion, Polar Bear, etc.

	Clear		Clear
Bird and Roses, goblet, etched.	35.00	Pitcher, water.	125.00
Bird in Swamp, goblet	65.00	Salt, individual	25.00
Birds at Fountain, cake		Spooner, two handles. . . .	40.00
stand	75.00	Sugar, cov, two handles . .	150.00
Bringing Home the Cows,		Giraffe, goblet, etched	75.00
pitcher.	350.00	Heron, pitcher.	150.00
Climbing Bear, goblet,		Ibex, goblet, etched.	65.00
etched.	95.00	Lion and Baboon	
Dancing Goat, ale glass,		Butter Dish, cov	125.00
frosted	55.00	Celery Vase.	75.00
Dog, Findlay, plate	75.00	Creamer	65.00
Dog and Hat, toothpick	80.00	Pitcher, water.	175.00
Dog (with rabbit in mouth)		Spooner	55.00
goblet, etched	115.00	Sugar, cov.	110.00
Dolphin, berry set, high stan-		Lion and Cable (Tiny Lion)	
dard open shell, six		Butter Dish, cov	50.00
sauces	190.00	Celery Vase.	40.00
Flying Stork, see illustration		Compote, cov, hs, 9" d . . .	85.00
Bowl	30.00	Creamer	35.00
Butter Dish, cov	50.00	Goblet.	45.00
Creamer	30.00	Pitcher, water.	65.00
Goblet.	65.00	Sauce	15.00
Marmalade Jar, cov	50.00	Spooner	35.00
Pitcher, water.	55.00	Sugar, cov.	45.00
Spooner	30.00	Lion with Scallops	
Sugar, cov.	45.00	Butter Dish, cov, crown	
Fox and Crow, pitcher	150.00	finial	45.00
Frog and Spider, goblet	125.00	Compote, cov, hs, 8¼" d .	65.00
Frosted Chicken		Creamer	35.00
Bowl, cov, ls	150.00	Pitcher, water.	65.00
Butter Dish, cov	125.00	Spooner	25.00
Celery Vase, two handles .	50.00	Sugar, cov, reclining lion	
Compote, cov, hs	175.00	finial	45.00
Creamer	45.00	Ostrich (looking at the moon)	
Goblet.	45.00	goblet	80.00
Salt Shaker, two handles .	30.00	Owl and Possum, goblet . . .	80.00
Spooner, two handles	35.00	Pigs in Corn, goblet.	300.00
Sugar, cov, two handles . .	150.00	Squirrel	
Frosted Eagle		Butter Dish, cov	225.00
Bowl, cov, collared base,		Creamer	150.00
6¼" d.	175.00	Goblet.	500.00
Butter Dish, cov, two		Pitcher, water.	225.00
handles	225.00	Sauce	25.00
Celery Vase.	75.00	Spooner	90.00
Compote, cov, hs	225.00	Sugar, cov.	200.00
Creamer, 6" h	45.00	Stork and Flowers, goblet,	
		etched.	50.00

Several patterns are found only in novelty pieces. There are also many patterns that were made in only a few items. The list illustrates some of the types of limited patterns and novelty pieces currently available in the marketplace.

	Clear		Clear
Aquarium		Spooner	35.00
Pitcher, water	100.00	Sugar, cov	70.00
Tumbler	45.00	Tumbler	55.00
Art Novo, miniature lamp	35.00	Icicle (Single Icicle), see illus-	
Assassination, mug, 2¼" h.	65.00	tration	
Balloon		Butter Dish, cov, ftd	85.00
Creamer	175.00	Compote, cov, hs, 6" d	75.00
Goblet	65.00	Creamer, ftd, ah	85.00
Sugar, cov	190.00	Goblet	60.00
Banner, butter dish, cov	65.00	Pitcher, water	200.00
Bicycle Girl		Sauce, flat, 4" d	15.00
Pitcher, water	285.00	Spooner, ftd	35.00
Tumbler	100.00	Sugar, cov	80.00
Block and Circle, miniature		Iron Kettle, creamer	40.00
lamp	40.00	Lightning, compote	45.00
Capitol Building, goblet	45.00	Little River, pickle castor	185.00
Ceres		Long Maple Leaf	
Candy Dish, cov	50.00	Celery Vase	20.00
Creamer	40.00	Creamer	25.00
Mug	25.00	Goblet	25.00
Spooner	30.00	Mug	20.00
Sugar, cov	45.00	Sugar, cov	35.00
Chestnut Oak		Mephistopheles	
Butter Dish, cov	50.00	Ale Glass	65.00
Egg Cup	40.00	Goblet	75.00
Goblet	45.00	Mug	60.00
Coolidge Drape, oil lamp	75.00	Odd Fellow	
Cornucopia		Cake Stand	50.00
Celery	25.00	Creamer	35.00
Creamer	35.00	Goblet	35.00
Sugar, cov	40.00	Sugar, cov	45.00
Double Donut, creamer	40.00	Pendelton	
Drum		Celery Vase	20.00
Butter Dish, cov	75.00	Creamer	35.00
Creamer	60.00	Sugar, cov	40.00
Mustard Jar	65.00	Tumbler	20.00
Spooner	50.00	Quihote	
Sugar, cov	70.00	Butter Dish, cov	45.00
Falling Leaves		Goblet	40.00
Bowl, berry	15.00	Snakeskin and Dot, creamer	35.00
Creamer	25.00	Tape Measure	
Sugar, cov	35.00	Butter Dish, cov	60.00
Flickering Flame		Creamer	30.00
Creamer, cov	40.00	Goblet	30.00
Sugar, cov	40.00	Sauce	10.00
Frosted Magnolia, cake		Tong (Excelsior Variant)	
stand	60.00	Butter Dish, cov	70.00
Horseshoe Stem		Celery Vase	100.00
Cake Stand, hs, 8" d	65.00	Creamer	65.00
Celery Vase	40.00	Goblet	60.00
Compote, cov, ls	90.00	Spooner	45.00
Creamer	65.00	Sugar, cov	50.00
Goblet	75.00	Tumbler	40.00
Pitcher, water	110.00	Wash Tub, soap dish	45.00
Sauce, ftd	15.00		

INDEX